GLOBAL AIDS:
MYTHS AND FACTS

D0167068

GLOBAL AIDS: MYTHS AND FACTS

Tools for Fighting the AIDS Pandemic

Alexander Irwin, Joyce Millen, and Dorothy Fallows

South End Press
Cambridge, MA

Cover design by Ellen P. Shapiro.
Cover photo of Treatment Action Campaign (TAC) demonstration
in South Africa courtesy of Gideon Mendel/Network Photographers;
back cover photo of protest in Thailand courtesy of Associated Press.
All chapter photos courtesy of Associated Press or Partners in Health.
Graphs courtesy of UNAIDS.

Library of Congress Cataloging-in-Publication Data
Irwin, Alexander. 1960–
Global AIDS: myths and facts: tools for fighting the AIDS
pandemic/Alexander Irwin, Joyce Millen, and Dorothy Fallows.
    p.cm.
Includes index.
ISBN 0-89608-674-7 (alk. paper)—ISBN 0-89608-673-9 (pbk. : alk.
paper)
    1. AIDS (Disease)—Prevention. 2. AIDS (Disease)—Social
aspects. 3. World health. 4. AIDS activists. I. Millen, Joyce (Joyce
V.), 1962– II. Fallows, Dorothy, 1956–III. Title.

RA643.8.I79 2003
616.97'9205—dc 21   2002042666

South End Press, 7 Brookline Street, #1, Cambridge, MA 02139
    06 05 04 03   1 2 3 4

Printed in Canada

TABLE OF CONTENTS

The following people contributed substantially to this project:

Siripanth Nippita
Heidi Fischbach
Paul Farmer
Karem Harth
Joia Mukherjee
Sylvia Aparicio
Sayres Rudy
Jennifer Lewey
Scott Lee
McGregor Crowley
Chris Vanderwarker
Mary Kay Smith-Fawzi
Jim Yong Kim
Cathryn Christensen
Ophelia Dahl

Acknowledgments

The Institute for Health and Social Justice (IHSJ) is the research, education, and advocacy arm of the international health organization Partners In Health. One of the IHSJ's chief missions is to inform people in the US and other affluent countries about the vulnerability and health threats facing those who live in poverty. We pursue this goal through our writing, teaching, and organizing. We believe commitments to fight injustice arise when people grasp the magnitude and devastation of global health inequalities. This book aims to promote such awareness and to foster active solidarity in response to AIDS.

AIDS is not only a deadly disease; it is the greatest scientific, political, and moral challenge of our era. In this time of abundant resources and increased global connectivity, we have the means and the knowledge to control the pandemic. Yet to do so will require unparalleled global cooperation and a shared recognition that AIDS threatens not only individuals, but entire societies and the very notion of a global order based on respect for human dignity and rights. When privileged people and the leaders of wealthy countries disregard the AIDS disaster in the developing world, the entire foundation on which such a humane order might rest is threatened.

The decision to base this primer for AIDS activism on myths about the pandemic underlines our debt to an earlier work, *World*

Hunger: Ten Myths, by Frances Moore Lappé and Joseph Collins. Originally published in 1979, *World Hunger: Ten Myths* targeted a set of issues quite different from those we address. Yet Lappé's and Collins's work laid down a valuable blueprint. The situation today with respect to broad-based struggle against AIDS corresponds in important respects to the context in which Lappé and Collins wrote about global hunger: above all, in that certain mistaken assumptions must be dismantled before we can see how positive action is possible, and how ordinary people can take a role in confronting a global threat. Like Lappé and Collins, we adopt the principle that "learning has to begin with unlearning." Yet, like theirs, our book aims to go beyond debunking and critique to respond to the decisive question: "What can we do?"

In writing *Global AIDS: Myths and Facts,* we have drawn inspiration from friends and allies in the AIDS activist movement, including the members of ACT UP New York, ACT UP Philadelphia, the Health GAP Coalition, the Student Global AIDS Campaign, and the Treatment Action Campaign. We have learned much from health and justice organizations, such as Physicians for Human Rights and Doctors without Borders, whose members combine praxis with analysis and advocacy, moving between their clinics and the corridors of power in Geneva, Brussels, and Washington. Above all, we acknowledge and honor the healers and people living with HIV/AIDS in resource-poor settings, who face a daily struggle against deprivation, sickness, and despair. May our collective efforts support these colleagues and comrades in their fight for life with dignity.

We are indebted to the scores of people who devoted time and intellectual talents to this project. First and foremost, we gratefully acknowledge the contributions of Jill Petty, our editor at South End Press, without whose determination and professionalism this book would not exist. Jill worked closely with us from the original conception of the book through each idea, picture, and page. Her demands—for intellectual rigor, lucid prose, and timeliness—were delivered with infinite patience and grace. To Jill, along with her colleagues in the South End Press collective, we offer our deepest thanks.

Many colleagues and IHSJ interns and associates offered assistance at various stages. We extend our most sincere thanks to all those listed on the opening page, especially Siripanth Nippita, Karem Harth, Paul Farmer, Joia Mukherjee, Heidi Fischbach, Jennifer Lewey, Sayres Rudy, and Cathryn Christensen. We also appreciate the contributions of Faiz Ahmad, Heidi Behforouz and the entire Prevention and Access to Care and Treatment (PACT) team, Arachu Castro, Jennifer Chen, Meredith Fort, Jennifer Furin, Nicole Gastineau, Melissa Gillooly, Yusuf Karacaoglu, Rachel Lockman, Kedar Mate, Molly McNairy, Joan Paluzzi, Rich Pegler, Tom Ribaudo, Michael Rich, Cynthia Rose, Aaron Shakow, Mary Kay Smith-Fawzi, Erich Strom, Laura Tarter, Chris Vanderwarker, Loune Viaud, Michele Welshhans, and Amy Wisehart.

For housing us and permitting us to break from tradition, we thank our mentors and colleagues in the Department of Social Medicine at Harvard Medical School.

We were also blessed throughout this project with the support of our loved ones. Despite their extremely busy schedules, Evan Lyon and Dave Harrison provided guidance and encouragement. Laurie Wen gave generously of her time, tolerated repeated visits from Juan Carlos and Fernanda, and maintained the mail station in impeccable order. Thanks also to Judy Fallows and Adrian Gropper for providing a home and help over many months.

Lastly, we would like to commend you, the readers. Simply by picking up this book, you signal your interest in the fight against the global AIDS pandemic. We hope you find a cautious optimism here that will encourage you either to join, or continue, in the struggle to end the suffering, devastation, and death wrought by AIDS.

Preface
by Zackie Achmat

More than 28 million people on the African continent are infected with HIV, including some five million people in South Africa alone. Without treatment, most of these people will die over the next decade. This constitutes a crime against humanity. Governments, multilateral institutions, the private sector, and civil society both in and outside Africa must act without delay to stop a holocaust against the poor. This book is a call to join the struggle and build a movement of international solidarity against AIDS.

To fight back against the tide of death by promoting access to effective treatment for all HIV-positive South Africans is the mission of the Treatment Action Campaign. TAC was launched on December 10, 1998, International Human Rights Day. Its objectives are: to ensure access to affordable, high-quality treatment for all people with HIV/AIDS; to prevent new HIV infections; and to improve health-care access for all South Africans. TAC was founded by a handful of activists; today, its members and supporters number in the tens of thousands.

Our movement has achieved many successes and met many challenges over the last few years. From 1999 to 2001, TAC led the international campaign that forced the withdrawal of pharmaceutical companies' lawsuit against the South African government that put profits before people's lives by challenging the legal framework that could provide inexpensive generic AIDS medications to poor South Africans. Later, TAC's pressure in the courts, the media, and the streets forced the South African government to accept responsibility for providing all HIV-positive pregnant women with access to therapies shown to dramatically reduce mother-to-child transmission of the AIDS virus. In August 2002, we joined with representatives from 20 other African countries to launch a Pan-African HIV/AIDS Treatment Access Movement dedicated to mobilizing our communities and our continent to ensure access to HIV/AIDS treatment for all our people who need it.

The past years have seen victories, but also the loss of too many friends and comrades, struck down by AIDS in the midst of their productive years, or even before they could reach adulthood. The greatest challenge lies ahead: the challenge of saving millions of lives by expanding access to AIDS treatment to all those who need it, while simultaneously fighting the social and economic forces that have accelerated the spread of HIV/AIDS.

Alleviating the effects of the AIDS epidemic will demand political leadership and greater accountability from national governments, international organizations, the private sector, especially the pharmaceutical industry, and wealthy countries—particularly the US and the countries of the European Union. We confront enormous barriers: national governments do not prioritize HIV/AIDS treatment; donor countries refuse to fulfill commitments to mobilize necessary resources; pharmaceutical companies deny access to essential medicines and diagnostics by charging exorbitant prices; and debt owed by poor nations to rich countries and international financial institutions hampers financing of vital social services, including health care. Community mobilization and civil society action are essential for forcing change and ensuring greater accountability from all these institutions.

When the XIIIth International Conference on AIDS met in Durban, South Africa, in 2000, TAC and other AIDS treatment activists had hope and ethical arguments for HIV treatment. Today we have facts. In Khayelitsha, outside Cape Town, a pilot treatment program run by Médecins Sans Frontières (MSF) has demonstrated that people with HIV/AIDS, a majority with severely damaged immune systems, can recover life, health, and dignity when treated using advanced antiretroviral medications (ARVs). This follows on the success of Paul Farmer, Partners In Health, and the people of Haiti. So today when we speak to you of AIDS treatment access in poor countries, we speak not only with ethical arguments, not only with hopes, not only with desperation, but with facts and the lives of the people themselves.

From a pure public health perspective, it is shortsighted not to treat AIDS, to say that we must focus on HIV prevention and exclude treatment. On the other hand it is unconscionable, because we are speaking not about cold statistics, but our lives. Our lives matter. The five million people in South Africa with HIV matter, and the millions of people throughout the world already infected with HIV matter. So it is not simply a question of cold statistics we are putting to you, but a question of valuing every person's life equally. Just because we are poor, just because we are black, just because we live in environments and continents that are far from you does not mean that our lives should be valued any less.

In the words of the labor movement, "an injury to one is an injury to all." *Global AIDS: Myths and Facts* challenges complacency and clarifies the tasks that lie ahead for those who want to make international solidarity a reality in the age of AIDS. Such solidarity must be built from the ground up. Over the last few years it has been the power of ordinary people that has begun to hold drug companies and governments accountable, and to awaken the global community to its responsibility. Bayard Rustin (whom historians will know as a black gay man and chief organizer of the march on Washington led by Dr. Martin Luther King Jr.) said protest confers dignity on a people whose dignity is denied. TAC believes that it is an individual's responsibility to study ethics, science, law, politics and economics, medicine and history. This is the duty of every HIV/AIDS activist, whether HIV-positive or -negative, literate or illiterate, and it is the key to stopping the epidemic. Our education takes place on picket lines, on marches, and in workshops. We use handwritten posters, printed propaganda, the Internet, phones, songs, pen and paper, and faxes. To the public in South Africa and other countries, and to the readers of this book, we say: Correct us when we make mistakes. Or better yet: Join the struggle, make mistakes—and make history—with us!

Introduction
by Paul Farmer

Medical science alone cannot overcome AIDS. Tools to contain the spread of HIV and prolong life for people with AIDS exist. Yet in 2002 an estimated five million new HIV infections occurred, and three million men, women, and children died of AIDS.[1] One reason for this failure is that prevention efforts are underfunded and rely, in the absence of a vaccine, on barrier methods requiring male assent. Another reason HIV has become the world's leading infectious cause of adult deaths is that most of the 42 million people now infected live in the developing world and cannot afford the drugs that might extend their lives. Health professionals seeking to serve these patients stand by helplessly, absent the financial resources and political will required to deliver prevention, care, and treatment within the poor communities that have borne the brunt of AIDS.

To fight the plague on a global scale, we need a massive international campaign able to pressure political and economic power holders to take AIDS seriously and to sustain such commitment until the pandemic is brought under control. The medical and public health communities cannot hope to lead such a campaign alone. Nor is it reasonable to expect those already gravely ill with complications of HIV infection to go it alone. Over the past 15 years, a vibrant international AIDS activist movement has emerged. The movement, which has brought together people living with HIV and many who seek to make common cause with them, has scored dramatic victories. The Pharmaceutical Manufacturers Association lawsuit against the South African government, withdrawn in April 2001 largely because of a mobilization spearheaded by the Treatment Action Campaign (TAC) and other civil society groups committed to equity of access to care, stands as an important case in point.[2] Yet the international fight against AIDS will fail, in the long run, without intensified grassroots activism in countries like the US, where a disproportionate share of global wealth and political power is concentrated.

Among the greatest obstacles to a broad mobilization against HIV/AIDS is misinformation about the pandemic. To act effectively, people must have sound knowledge. Ignorance breeds passivity, pessimism, resignation, or a sense that AIDS is someone else's problem. Accurate knowledge may awaken a sense of urgency about global AIDS and enable effective action. To disseminate such activist-oriented knowledge and to combat ignorance about AIDS are the goals of this book.

It is important to be clear about whose ignorance we are referring to. Perhaps more than any other recent health crisis, AIDS has spawned intellectual confusion and unsubstantiated theories—here termed "AIDS myths." By myths we do not refer to beliefs about AIDS in so-called traditional societies, whose ignorance of Western science has sometimes been decried by health experts as a reason for the failure of AIDS control efforts. We mean instead the myths that often dominate discussions among the experts themselves, as well as among political leaders and ordinary citizens in wealthy countries. Myths such as the belief that the HIV/AIDS pandemic is driven primarily by promiscuity; that endemic corruption in poor countries dooms AIDS control efforts to failure; that developing countries must view AIDS prevention and treatment as mutually exclusive options;

or that AIDS treatment with antiretroviral medications is not feasible in resource-poor settings. And there are other, more subtle distortions. What does it mean, for example, to consider AIDS prevention primarily in terms of individual psychology or suspect "cultural practices"? Does such an analysis reflect genuine cultural competence, or does it in fact distort facts, amplify prejudice, and erase important considerations of poverty and inequality? Is it true, as certain high-ranking US officials have argued recently, that antiretroviral agents cannot be used on the world's most HIV-affected continent because Africans "have a different concept of time"?[3] Or is this claim an example of yet another AIDS myth, one expedient to those who wish to hide the real reasons that these life-saving medications are not more readily available?

This book examines and refutes 10 such prominent misconceptions about HIV/AIDS. Taken together, these beliefs constitute a stock of conventional wisdom about the disease drawn upon by many political and health officials and ordinary citizens in wealthy countries. To debunk each myth, the book combines lessons from medicine, public heath, epidemiology, and the social sciences relevant to these disciplines. We also draw upon our own experiences as AIDS activists and as providers of integrated prevention and care services in settings of great poverty. Our goal is to expose what is wrong with received wisdom and to replace it with accurate information that can foster a more robust response to the pandemic. We hope readers of *Global AIDS: Myths and Facts* will become protagonists of that response—educators and advocates in their turn. We hope that readers will use these lessons and rectifications to refute mistaken claims about AIDS when they encounter them in publications, policy debates, classrooms, or daily conversations.

AIDS myths are only part of the problem. Another is that debates about HIV have become overly fragmented. Some discussions of HIV focus only on the clinical aspects of the disease. Others, especially those heard in resource-poor settings, focus only on prevention. Others raise questions regarding the feasibility of integrated HIV prevention and care as a means of stopping rather than starting a conversation.

Today, it is no longer tolerable to evade such questions as they relate to the politics both of HIV prevention and AIDS treatment. We will argue here that entrenched poverty, economic inequality, racial discrimination, the subordination of women, and other forms of structural injustice contribute overwhelmingly to the spread of HIV infection and render current prevention efforts less effective than they are in other settings. At the same time, we will challenge the willingness of many power holders to deny lifesaving AIDS treatment to poor people.

Since 1996, combination antiretroviral therapies, the so-called AIDS "drug cocktails," have dramatically increased life span and life quality for patients who can afford them.[4] Yet today these expensive therapies remain beyond the reach of the vast majority of people living with AIDS. Many international health officials, particularly from the US and Europe, have argued that state-of-the-art AIDS treatment is too complicated for people in the developing world and not "cost-effective" enough to be implemented in resource-poor settings. Such claims lead some policymakers and ordinary citizens to conclude that tens of millions of people are in essence "too poor to treat."[5] This book seeks to refute these positions with analyses based on clinical experience, on public health arguments, and on moral principles.

Those who contributed to this book argue that it is unwise in a mature epidemic to focus exclusively on preventing new infections. The hour is late. The devastation of HIV/AIDS can best be countered, we conclude, through a combination of (1) vigorous preventive measures to protect the uninfected; (2) treatment, including antiretroviral therapy and prophylaxis and treatment of opportunistic infections, for those with advanced HIV disease; and (3) a sustained attack on the poverty and inequality that have fueled the pandemic from the beginning. To speak of radically expanded AIDS treatment for the poor and of a united global fight against the disease will appear utopian to some. Yet what can be more pragmatic than to expand access to tools that could reduce the number of new infections, relieve suffering, and prevent premature deaths? As we confront a scourge that has claimed millions of human lives and now menaces tens of millions more, it seems no exaggeration to say that history will judge us by our response to a crisis that not only challenges our scientific capabilities, but reveals the scope—and the limits—of our moral vision.

Global AIDS: Myths and Facts emerges from a collaborative effort involving contributors from many different professional backgrounds. Our team includes physicians, medical anthropologists, microbiologists, epidemiologists, and specialists in religion and ethics. Some members have for many years provided medical care to patients suffering with HIV/AIDS and other infectious diseases in Haiti, Peru, Russia, and elsewhere. Other contributors have worked on AIDS prevention campaigns or have conducted anthropological research on HIV transmission in African countries. Some are involved locally in the work of activist organizations like ACT UP. Many of us are teachers.

We are connected through the organization Partners In Health (PIH) and its research arm, the Institute for Health and Social Justice. PIH was founded in 1987 to provide high-quality medical treatment to undersereved areas in some developing countries and in poor neighborhoods of North American cities. At the core of PIH's philosophy is the commitment to a "preferential option for the poor" in health care, a concept adapted from Latin American liberation theology. In cooperation with sister organizations such as

Zanmi Lasante (Haiti) and Socios En Salud (Peru), PIH links the resources of wealthy medical and academic institutions with the experience and aspirations of people living in poverty. The goal is to overcome health problems conventional wisdom currently deems "insoluble." PIH's major projects include treating multidrug-resistant tuberculosis in squatter settlements in Haiti and Peru and delivering HIV care, including antiretroviral drugs, to patients in a destitute region of Haiti's Central Plateau.

At PIH, experience has repeatedly shown us that when the courage and determination of poor communities are brought together with the resources of people and medical institutions from the global North, the limits of "what is possible" in the health field can be retraced. *Global AIDS: Myths and Facts* is written in this spirit.

No single book can dismantle all the myths and mystifications that surround HIV/AIDS, and this becomes increasingly true as AIDS myths change over time.[6] There are two main areas of AIDS mythology we do not explore here. The first is the question of the origin of HIV (including beliefs that the virus was intentionally unleashed by organizations like the CIA). The second is the territory of HIV and AIDS "denialism," claims either that the AIDS epidemic is a hoax and the disease doesn't really exist or that AIDS is not caused by the virus known as HIV. Readers can consult the large body of literature on these topics.[7]

Denialist positions and conspiracy theories about the origin of AIDS have sparked debate in a variety of settings. In South Africa, a few government officials until recently showed undisguised sympathy for certain denialist views, and combating denialist claims has been an important task for some AIDS advocacy organizations. Yet conspiracy and denialist myths are not the ones that have been most influential in shaping mainstream opinions about HIV/AIDS in high-income countries. In this book, we focus on myths with wide credence today among the general public in the US and other affluent countries. These are the misconceptions US—and Europe–based activists must seek to expose and refute as we work to build support for the international AIDS struggle in our communities and among political officeholders.

As we make choices about fighting AIDS, we are doing more than deciding how to confront the most devastating infectious disease of modern times. We are shaping the moral character of the world we and our children will inhabit. The choice before us is stark. We can accept a world of radical polarization between haves and have-nots, in which the calculus of cost-effectiveness determines that poor people must die of diseases for which the affluent are successfully treated as a matter of course. Or we can work for a world of solidarity, in which people from different backgrounds cooperate to mobilize resources and build the foundations of a dignified life for all, prioritizing the needs of the most vulnerable. The global AIDS struggle moves us toward this horizon of pragmatic solidarity.

HIV/AIDS Basics

What is HIV?

Human immunodeficiency virus (HIV) is the virus that causes AIDS. Once introduced into the bloodstream, HIV attacks certain cells of the immune system called the "helper T-cells," or CD4 cells, which are responsible for helping the body to fight off infections. HIV invades CD4 cells, reproducing within the infected cells, and then bursting out into the bloodstream. The immune system responds by producing antibodies to fight the virus and making more CD4 cells to replenish those killed. But this immune response is ultimately ineffective. In the late stages of infection, HIV destroys increasing numbers of CD4 cells until the body's capacity to fight other viruses and bacteria gradually begins to decline. Eventually, the immune system stops functioning, leaving the body defenseless against other infectious agents.

What is AIDS?

Acquired Immunodeficiency Syndrome (AIDS) is the medical designation for a set of symptoms, opportunistic infections, and laboratory markers indicating that a person is in an advanced stage of HIV infection, with an impaired immune system. Although some people may develop AIDS much sooner, it takes an average of 10 years from the time one is infected with HIV to develop clinical AIDS. As immune functions begin to decline, the body becomes prone to certain opportunistic infections, so called because they are able to cause illness as a result of a weakened immune system. The characteristic spectrum of opportunistic infections that a person is likely to get will vary in different regions of the world, depending upon the locally predominant infectious agents. For example, although tuberculosis (TB) is not frequently encountered in North America or Europe, it is a common opportunistic infection in many developing countries.

What does it mean to be HIV-positive?

An HIV serologic test looks for the presence of antibodies against HIV in the blood. A person who is HIV-positive (or seropositive) has been infected but does not necessarily have AIDS. Because of the long delay between the time of infection and onset of disease, the number of HIV-positive people in a population is always much greater than the number of people with AIDS. In the absence of treatment, however, nearly everyone who is HIV-positive today will develop AIDS within the next decade.

How is HIV transmitted?

HIV is spread through having unprotected sex with an infected partner, sharing needles or other drug injection equipment previously used by an infected person, or receiving a transfusion of blood or blood products contaminated with HIV. The virus can also be passed from a mother to her infant before or during birth or through breast-feeding. The fact that HIV-positive people can remain free of symptoms (asymptomatic) for years greatly increases the chances that they may unwittingly pass the virus to others through sexual contact, needle sharing, or breast-feeding.

How can infection be prevented?

Risk of contracting HIV through sex can be sharply reduced by the use of barrier methods such as male or female condoms. Transmission among intravenous drug users can be blocked by eliminating the sharing of needles and other injection equipment. Administering a short course of antiretroviral medications to an HIV-positive mother at the time of delivery dramatically reduces transmission of HIV from mother to child. Proper monitoring of blood supplies virtually eliminates the risk of contracting HIV through transfusions. Unfortunately, while methods for preventing new HIV infections are clear in theory, social and economic constraints complicate the practical application of all these strategies.

What is the current medical management of AIDS?

The drugs used to treat HIV/AIDS are called antiretrovirals (ARVs); they work by stopping HIV from replicating. The most effective treatments are combinations of these drugs, referred to as highly active antiretroviral therapy (HAART). Treatment with HAART usually reduces the amount of virus in a patient's bloodstream, allows the CD4 cells to be replenished, and restores immune function. However, HAART is not a cure. Patients must remain on lifelong treatment, and ARV drug regimens can produce debilitating and, rarely, dangerous side effects. Over time, most patients develop resistance to at least some of the medications. Despite such shortcomings, antiretroviral therapy has slashed AIDS death rates in wealthy countries and has dramatically enhanced life quality for many of those able to obtain treatment.

What is the difference between risk and vulnerability?

Risk of HIV infection is defined as the probability that a person could become infected. Epidemiologists often look for "risk factors," or characteristics that correlate with an increased risk of infection. Behaviors associated with the transmission of HIV, such as having multiple unprotected sexual contacts or using intravenous drugs, are some of the risk factors for HIV infection. But looking at individual risk factors alone provides only a limited understanding of how to control the spread of HIV. Underlying socioeconomic factors—including poverty, discrimination, and gender inequality—continue to drive the pandemic. It is these socioeconomic determinants that often lead people to adopt "risky behaviors" and render them vulnerable to HIV infection. Rather than focusing narrowly on efforts to change individual risk-taking behaviors, prevention programs must be directed towards reducing vulnerability.

What is prevalence and how does it differ from incidence?

Prevalence is the percentage of people in a population with a specific disease or condition at a given moment in time. When we talk about the prevalence of HIV infection in a community or country, we mean the percentage of the total population that is HIV-positive. Prevalence is useful for describing the overall burden of disease, but a low prevalence of HIV/AIDS can be falsely reassuring for two reasons. First, because prevalence is an average value, a low prevalence of HIV/AIDS in a population with widely varying risks of HIV infection can mask small high-risk groups with high prevalence of HIV/AIDS. Secondly, countries with a low prevalence of HIV/AIDS but a very large population can have more total cases of HIV/AIDS than countries with a high prevalence but much smaller populations. Moreover, prevalence does not provide information about the trends of an epidemic over time. If we would like to know about the dynamics of an HIV/AIDS epidemic—if it is declining, stable, or growing—we would need to look at the rates at which new infections are occurring. This number, called the incidence, is usually expressed as the number of new HIV infections per year. By comparing the annual rates of new HIV infections, we can learn how an epidemic is proceeding.[1]

Marchers wear masks to remain anonymous during
World AIDS Day events in Lima, Peru.

MYTH ONE:
AIDS and Africa

Myth: AIDS is primarily an African problem. The disease exists in many places but is unlikely to affect other regions as it has Africa. In wealthy countries like the US, AIDS has been brought under control and no longer poses a major threat.

Response: Sub-Saharan Africa currently suffers by far the most devastating effects of the AIDS pandemic. Of the estimated 42 million people worldwide living with HIV or AIDS, more than 29 million, some 70 percent, live (and die) in sub-Saharan Africa. Approximately 2.4 million Africans died of AIDS in 2002, and 3.5 million new infections occurred in the region. In 16 African countries, at least 10 percent of people aged 15 to 49 are infected with HIV. The list includes seven countries where infection rates exceed 20 percent of the adult population.[1]

Despite such statistics, however, the automatic association of AIDS with Africa is problematic for two main reasons. First, while the effects of AIDS in sub-Saharan Africa have been brutal, AIDS is not an "African problem," if this means a "problem" for which Africans alone bear responsibility. AIDS in Africa is best viewed as a "transnational" problem. The long history of violence and injustice inflicted on the African continent by colonialism and neoliberal economic and trade policies shaped the socioeconomic context in which HIV proliferates. Second, while so far AIDS has struck hardest in Africa, today the disease is advancing in many other regions, moving along fault lines of poverty, inequality, and conflict between and within countries.[2] AIDS is not solely an African problem but a global medical and moral crisis that demands a global response. In the following pages, we look first at the historical background of AIDS in Africa. Then we survey the epidemic's spread through every region of the world, paying attention to the increased concentration of HIV/AIDS among poor and marginalized communities within wealthy countries, particularly the US.

Colonialism and AIDS in Africa

HIV/AIDS emerged as a major health crisis for Africa less than 20 years ago, yet the stage was set for its explosive dissemination long before. The economic and social roots of the disease date back over 500 years to the European conquest and, later, colonization of the African continent. An examination of the history and political economy of modern Africa shows that, for Europeans and North Americans, the African AIDS crisis is also our crisis, because the policies carried out by our governments, armies, businesses, and, more recently, by the international financial institutions we dominate, helped create many of the conditions that have enabled the rapid spread of HIV infection.

The AIDS epidemic is only one recent chapter in a longer history of health catastrophes that started with the arrival of Europeans in Africa. From the fifteenth century onward, slave-trafficking, military conquest, colonial rule, and sustained economic exploitation undermined Africans' health directly and indirectly. Even after the cessation of more than four hundred years of the transatlantic slave trade, the colonial powers continued to brutalize Africans who resisted their authority. European colonialists imposed forced labor, uprooted families and communities through involuntary displacements and labor migration, undermined traditional African political and legal systems, and broke down indigenous agriculture, plunging millions into destitution.[3] The socioeconomic and political disarray intensified the susceptibility of African populations to a host of old and new health scourges, including malnutrition, maternal and childhood illnesses, and infectious diseases.

In some parts of Africa, entire peoples were wiped out during the colonial conquest by direct military violence, sickness, or starvation.[4] Contact with Europeans and population displacements during the colonial period unleashed repeated epidemics in local African populations unprotected by immunity. In 1918–19, hundreds of thousands perished on the continent from influenza brought back by Africans forcibly conscripted by Europeans to fight in World War I. As African men were forced into labor in European-owned industries such as mining, indigenous food production declined, leading to recurrent famines.

Hunger further heightened African people's vulnerability to outbreaks of infectious sickness, creating a persistent cycle of deprivation and disease. When the colonial powers established health care systems in their African dependencies, these systems focused first on the needs of Europeans, then on caring for those Africans who were directly useful to the colonial regime, such as soldiers and overseers. Most Africans had no access to this European medical care.[5]

African colonies began to achieve independence in the early 1960s, and several newly independent countries realized impressive health gains in their early years. Yet the political dislocations and social injustices inherited from the colonial period left new African states with daunting challenges. The poverty, weak institutions, and epidemic disease created during colonialism, reinforced each other and undermined progress. As the post-independence era unfolded, many poor African countries remained economically dependent on their former colonial powers and the international financial institutions those powers controlled. Under this arrangement, often termed "neocolonialism," the new African states were promised economic growth and "development" as rewards for cooperating with Western Cold War political strategies and commercial interests.

Throughout the 1960s and 1970s, many African governments—in some cases oppressive, corrupt regimes—borrowed heavily from foreign sources. European and American banks enticed developing countries with low-interest loans. By the early 1980s, many African countries confronted high foreign debt burdens compounded by falling international prices for key African commodities such as copper, coffee, and cocoa. The countries' leaders appealed for help to institutions such as the World Bank and the International Monetary Fund (IMF), whose response came in the form of Structural Adjustment Programs (SAP's). Indebted countries were obliged to accept these far-reaching economic reform packages in order to qualify for loan rescheduling and continued international assistance.[6]

SAP's mandated a reorganization of poor countries' economic and social policy structures in line with the emergent ideology of economic neoliberalism. The role of the state was to be minimized, the private sector deregulated, and market forces freed. Fundamental features of SAP's included privatization of many government assets, sharp public sector budget cuts (especially on health and education), scaling back of labor protections, the elimination of price controls and subsidies on food, and the imposition of "user fees" for health services and education. In theory, SAP's were intended to stimulate growth and help reduce the burden of debt; in practice, the austerity measures often exacerbated poverty.[7]

The World Bank report laying the groundwork for the SAP strategy in Africa appeared in 1981, the same year American health officials published the first reports of AIDS.[8] The coincidence of these two events meant that SAP-mandated cuts in government spending undermined the viability of health services in many parts of Africa at the moment when AIDS was poised to explode. Massive public-sector layoffs, subsidy cuts, and sharp reductions in nonexport agricultural spending raised unemployment and deepened poverty, while the introduction of user fees often led to sharp declines in the use of health services. Meanwhile, the promised reward of greater economic growth failed to materialize in most cases.

The exact degree of damage inflicted on African health systems by SAP's is debated. Yet many African and Africanist scholars concur that the consequences of these programs for the health of poor Africans have been severe. SAP's have exacerbated the impact of AIDS directly and indirectly, through health sector budget cuts and user fees that barred access to health services for the poor, and by deepening poverty and social instability, key drivers of the crisis.[9]

Despite two decades of SAP austerity measures, many poor countries' foreign debt continues to grow. A recent Oxfam briefing paper draws the connections between unsustainable debt and the HIV/AIDS pandemic. It points out that one-third of all people living with AIDS live in countries classified by the World Bank and IMF as heavily indebted. Over half of the countries currently receiving debt relief spend more on servicing their debt than on their total health budgets. With one of the highest HIV/AIDS prevalence rates in the world, Zambia spends 30 percent more on its annual debt payment than it does on health care. Malawi's debt service equals its health spending. In Cameroon, debt repayments are the equivalent of three and one-half times the health budget; while Mali channels $1.60 toward its debt for every $1 that it spends on health.[10]

The SAP policies were designed in Washington boardrooms, just as for centuries Africa's economic despoilment had been supervised from Western capitals. Through these ties of past and current political and economic history, people living today in the wealthiest countries are intimately connected to the pandemic unfolding on African soil.

A Global Killer

To think of AIDS as an exclusively African problem is wrong historically and morally; it is also epidemiologically inaccurate. If Africa's history left the continent particularly vulnerable to the initial onslaught of HIV/AIDS, socioeconomic conditions in many other regions now endanger their populations in turn. Current data show that HIV/AIDS is spreading fast in the Caribbean, Asia, and Eastern Europe, as well as in poor urban neighborhoods in the US.

Some factors influencing HIV transmission patterns, such as the prevalence of injection drug use, vary considerably from region

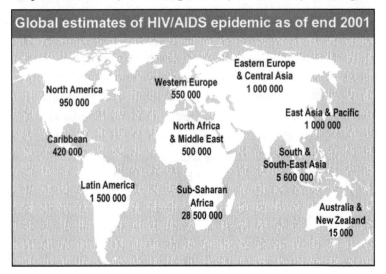

Global estimates of HIV/AIDS epidemic as of end 2001

North America
950 000

Western Europe
550 000

Eastern Europe
& Central Asia
1 000 000

East Asia & Pacific
1 000 000

Caribbean
420 000

North Africa
& Middle East
500 000

South &
South-East Asia
5 600 000

Latin America
1 500 000

Sub-Saharan
Africa
28 500 000

Australia &
New Zealand
15 000

to region, and from one community to another. Yet the most critical factors heightening vulnerability—poverty, inequality, armed conflict, and the disempowerment of women—pervade many parts of the world. Globalization and increased mobility within and between countries have also hastened the spread of the pandemic. In the following pages, we present epidemiological data to show the worldwide reach of AIDS and highlight the need for a global offensive against the disease.

Eastern Europe and Central Asia

Eastern Europe and Central Asia are now witnessing the fastest growing epidemic in the world.[11] UNAIDS estimates that 250,000 people were newly infected in the region in 2002, bringing the total number of people living with HIV/AIDS there to 1.2 million.[12]

Already at the end of 2002, the adult HIV prevalence in Ukraine stood at one percent.[13] In the Russian Federation, newly reported HIV diagnoses have almost doubled annually since 1998 with actual infections probably far outnumbering official figures. According to US National Intelligence Council estimates, without a greatly expanded response to the epidemic, between five and eight million Russians may be HIV-infected by 2010.[14]

In the Russian Federation and other parts of the former Soviet Union, most reported HIV infections are related to injection drug use, which has become alarmingly widespread among young people during the past decade. One study of Moscow secondary-school students found that four percent had injected drugs. In some countries of the ex-USSR, an estimated one percent of the population is injecting drugs.[15] In Ukraine, while injection drug use is currently responsible for three-quarters of HIV infections, the proportion of sexually transmitted HIV infections is growing, suggesting that the epidemic is moving into the wider population.[16]

Intravenous drug use is widespread among the huge prison population in Russia, where HIV/AIDS overlaps with a tuberculosis epidemic. In the absence of effective prevention and treatment programs, prisoners returning home risk infecting their families and spreading HIV and TB.[17]

The former Soviet Union's transition to a market economy has been accompanied by mass unemployment, heightened economic insecurity, and a sense of exclusion and hopelessness among many young people. These factors appear to spur rising drug use, fueling the spread of HIV.[18] A shortage of available job opportunities and the growing numbers of young people failing to complete secondary school increase the likelihood that many in the next generation will join the ranks of vulnerable groups such as intravenous drug users, prisoners, and sex workers.[19] Moreover, since the breakup of the Soviet Union, Russia and several other newly independent states have implemented harsh austerity measures to meet the demands of international financial institutions and Western governments providing loans and aid during the transition from socialism to capitalism. As a result of budget cuts, public health services have deteriorated in many areas, leaving the newly independent states ill-equipped to scale up HIV prevention and treatment.[20]

Asia and the Pacific

Asia and the Pacific are home to more people living with HIV/AIDS than any other region except Africa.[21] While prevalence rates are lower in Asia than in Africa, such aggregate figures can be misleading. Low overall prevalence rates mask localized concentrations of infection which may spark generalized epidemics.[22] Moreover, low prevalence across very large populations still means massive numbers of people living with HIV/AIDS.

In China, the number of people living with HIV/AIDS was estimated at one million by mid-2002, and projections indicate that the number could rise as high as 10–15 million by 2010.[23] China faces, in certain regions, high rates of injection drug use, poorly monitored blood supplies, high population mobility, and a burgeoning sex industry. Yet despite signs of an epidemic on the brink of eruption, the country's AIDS prevention programs are years behind those of many African nations. The marked lack of AIDS education has allowed widespread ignorance about the disease to persist.[24] One journalist visiting China found:

> With only scattershot education programs, even those at very high risk of getting AIDS often do not know how to protect themselves; many have never even heard of HIV. In a country where patients generally receive no counseling after testing positive for HIV, known carriers often have only a vague idea of how [the virus] is transmitted, and they inadvertently infect others.[25]

HIV levels in specific population groups like injection drug users are rising in several Chinese provinces, with prevalence rates as high as 70 percent reported among drug users in some areas.[26] A devastating epidemic is occurring in central China's Henan province, where hundreds of thousands of poor rural farmers have been infected by the unsafe blood collection procedures commercial blood processing companies used in the early 1990s.[27]

Many researchers foresee an explosion of HIV/AIDS in India. Projections from the US National Intelligence Council panel indicate that 20–25 million Indians may be infected by 2010.[28] Local epidemics, initially concentrated in highly vulnerable groups (e.g., sex workers, truck drivers, injection drug users), are beginning to cross over into the broader population. India's adult (defined as 15–49 years) HIV prevalence is currently less than one percent. Yet, given the country's vast population, this means more than 3.8 million

Indian adults were living with HIV/AIDS at the end of 2001—more HIV-positive men and women than in any other country except South Africa.[29] Prevention efforts have been hampered by widespread poverty, illiteracy, and inequalities based on caste and gender.[30]

In Indonesia, the world's fourth most populous country, HIV/AIDS prevalence rates among injection drug users were not even measured until 1999–2000. When measurements finally began, a staggering 38 percent of injection drug users were found to be HIV-positive in the capital city of Jakarta.[31] Screening blood donations is one way to monitor levels of HIV/AIDS in the general population. Between 1999 and 2000, a surge in HIV infection among blood donors was observed, indicating that the disease may no longer be confined to the most vulnerable groups, such as female sex workers and injection drug users.[32]

The Caribbean and Latin America

While the Caribbean epidemic has not yet reached the devastating proportions seen in Africa, current trends show an accelerating spread of infection. AIDS is now the leading cause of death among men aged 15–44 in the English-speaking Caribbean.[33] More cases of HIV were reported in the Caribbean between 1995 and 1998 than had been identified in the whole period from the early 1980s up to 1995.[34] Although there is some transmission among injection drug users and among men who have sex with men, (MSM), HIV in the Caribbean is spread mainly through heterosexual sex.

At 6.1 percent, national HIV prevalence in Haiti is the highest in the Western hemisphere and the highest of any country outside sub-Saharan Africa.[35] Together, Haiti and the Dominican Republic account for 85 percent of HIV/AIDS cases in the region.[36] Not coincidentally, Haiti is also the Western hemisphere's poorest country. As in the case of Africa, studies of Haitian history show how the military, political, and economic agendas of foreign powers (in the 20th century, primarily the US) have fostered immiseration, extreme economic inequality, political turmoil, and recurrent violence: all factors that facilitate transmission of HIV.[37]

The contrast between Haiti and Cuba is instructive. Cuba is also a relatively poor country, but one whose government has prioritized equitable access to education and high-quality health care. Adult HIV prevalence in Cuba stands at only 0.03 percent.[38] When HIV was first detected on the island, Cuban health officials moved to place AIDS patients in specialized sanitoria, drawing international criticism. In large part because the first cases of HIV infection were diagnosed among soldiers and aid workers returning from Africa, the problem was managed initially by the Ministry of Defense. After the management of the centers passed to the Ministry of Health, however, restrictions on patients' movements were relaxed. The Cuban government's multidimensional response to the AIDS threat has included HIV education and testing for wide segments of the population, substantial government-funded AIDS research, and advanced medical care (including certain antiretrovirals, or ARVs) supplied free of charge to HIV-positive people.[39]

Elsewhere in Latin America, an estimated 1.5 million people are living with HIV/AIDS. Mexico's epidemic has been concentrated mainly among MSM; in some studies, just over 14 percent have tested positive for HIV.[40] Prevalence is lower among commercial sex workers and those being treated for sexually transmitted infections. Among countries in Central America, Nicaragua and Costa Rica have observed infection patterns similar to that of Mexico. However, Honduras, Guatemala, and Belize (significantly poorer countries than Mexico and Costa Rica) are experiencing rapid increases in heterosexual transmission.[41]

Brazil, Latin America's most populous country, is also home to the largest number of people living with HIV/AIDS in the region.[42] Yet the number of Brazilians infected would be far higher if political leaders, health officials, and civil society groups had not joined forces to respond energetically to the epidemic. Brazil's policy of providing free antiretroviral medicines has propelled the country to the forefront of international debates on AIDS treatment equity.[43] Cooperation between health officials and grassroots groups has also strengthened prevention. For example, prevention programs among injection drug users have led to a substantial decline in HIV prevalence among drug users in Brazil's large urban centers.[44]

Resurgence of HIV/AIDS in High-Income Countries

Often entwined with the perception of AIDS as an African problem is the belief that AIDS is no longer a significant threat in the US. In part, this assumption reflects the real gains made in the

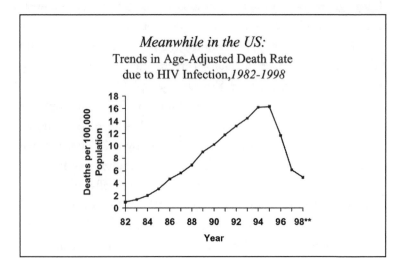

Meanwhile in the US:
Trends in Age-Adjusted Death Rate
due to HIV Infection,*1982-1998*

fight during the 1990s. In that period, aggressive HIV education and prevention campaigns significantly cut infection rates in the US and other high-income countries. Then, beginning in 1996, combination antiretroviral therapies turned AIDS from a death sentence into a manageable chronic disease for many North Americans and Europeans. In 1994, an estimated 48,000 Americans died of AIDS. Four years later, US AIDS mortality had been reduced to 16,000, a two-thirds drop, largely as a result of the wide availability of ARVs.[45]

Unfortunately, rapid gains proved short-lived. According to recent analyses from the Centers for Disease Control and Prevention (CDC), both AIDS mortality and rates of new HIV infections in the US have not decreased since mid-1998.[46] In fact, the US and other rich countries have since seen disturbing upward trends in risk behaviors and infection levels in certain key subgroups, suggesting the danger of what Dr. Helene Gayle terms a "newly expanding epidemic."[47]

Some of the most alarming patterns have been reported among gay men. The CDC reports that, in a 12-city study, "19 percent of HIV-positive MSM engaged in unprotected anal sex between 1996 and 1998, compared to 13 percent between 1995 and 1996."[48] A study in Seattle echoed this result, finding a "sharp increase in the number of HIV-positive gay men reporting unprotected anal sex, from 10 percent in 1998 to 20 percent in 2000."[49] While younger gay men may never have developed rigorous safer sex habits, some older men who once did so are now experiencing an "AIDS burnout" effect that leads them to give up safer behaviors.[50] The result has been a dramatic surge in HIV infections among MSM. The CDC's recent Young Men's Survey found a 4.4 percent infection rate among 23- to 29-year-old MSM. This rate is significantly higher than in any other recent US incidence study and is comparable to levels seen among

MSM in the mid-1980s, when AIDS exploded to epidemic proportions in gay communities.[51]

While the abandonment of safer sex practices and the increased spread of sexually transmitted infections have been particularly notable among MSM, these patterns are not limited to any single group. Estimated incidence of HIV/AIDS transmitted through heterosexual sex has also risen in recent years.[52] In 2001, for every AIDS case diagnosed among gay or bisexual men in the US, two were diagnosed among heterosexual men or women.[53]

The demographics of HIV/AIDS are changing in the US. AIDS is now a disease patterned by race and income level. African-Americans, for example, make up only 12 percent of the US population but in 2000 accounted for 50 percent of new AIDS cases and 57 percent of new HIV diagnoses.[54] The CDC's Young Men's Survey found that 15 percent of Latino MSM are HIV-positive before age 30. Among African-American MSM, the rates are even more devastating, with nearly one in three African-American MSM infected before reaching the age of 30.[55] Women of color also suffer disproportionate rates of HIV infection. In the northeastern US in 1999, HIV incidence among women stood at three cases per 100,000 for whites, 57 cases per 100,000 for Hispanics, and 104 cases per 100,000 for African-American women.[56]

Similar differentials are seen in treatment outcomes. From 1987 to 1995, before the advent of effective ARV therapy, African-American women saw the greatest increase in age-adjusted HIV death (425 percent), while the increase was smallest among white males (133 percent).[57] Today, effective treatment options exist, but HIV-positive Americans do not enjoy equal access to their benefits. African-Americans, Latinos, and the rural and urban poor have low rates of health insurance coverage and limited access to medical care. As a result, they are more likely to go undiagnosed and untreated during the early stages of HIV infection and to develop full-blown AIDS more rapidly.[58]

The Need for Global Mobilization

The AIDS crisis has struck sub-Saharan Africa with exceptional force. Yet Africa's struggle with AIDS, like many of the continent's battles, shows not Africa's uniqueness and isolation but rather the extent to which Africa's history and destiny are intertwined with those of other regions, above all the wealthy former colonial powers of Europe and the US. There is nothing intrinsically African about the key factors driving the spread of HIV/AIDS—above all poverty, socioeconomic inequality, instability and armed conflict, and the disempowerment of marginalized groups. These phenomena are widespread in the contemporary world. Thus, AIDS is advancing rapidly today in many regions.

The AIDS disaster unfolding in sub-Saharan Africa can happen elsewhere. Indeed, we can say with grim confidence that it *will* happen elsewhere—unless we take action. As Louise Fréchette, UN deputy secretary-general, observes, "Globalization, travel, and migration add to the risk of increased spread to what we might think of as 'safe' countries. The reality is that in our globalized world, there are no 'safe' countries."[59] It is said that, compared to countries in sub-Saharan Africa, other countries and regions are "low prevalence" when it comes to HIV. But low-prevalence statistics may mask great suffering for large numbers of people. And with the history of the epidemic in mind, low prevalence is not a timeless condition. All countries, including South Africa, Zimbabwe, and Botswana, were once low-prevalence countries.[60] If energetic action is not taken to combat the spread of HIV, low-prevalence areas—in particular those characterized by poverty and deep socioeconomic inequalities—will inexorably turn into high-prevalence areas.

For over 20 years, Africans have borne the greatest burden of the AIDS pandemic—not only because the disease has so far claimed the majority of its victims on African soil, but also because people in other parts of the world have stigmatized and blamed Africans for the origin and spread of AIDS. But AIDS is not and never was an African problem. No group, whether Africans or Americans, singlehandedly created the conditions which allow this disease to flourish. And no group will singlehandedly end the pandemic. This crisis crosses geographical and political boundaries, while highlighting the polarization between "haves" and "have-nots" worldwide. Defeating the pandemic will demand an unprecedented international effort, offering people in affluent countries, like the US, an opportunity to recognize our interdependence with people in low-income countries, and to work cooperatively for global health equity.

Former sex workers at the Maiti Nepal Center for HIV-positive girls and women sold into prostitution in Kakarvitta, Nepal.

MYTH TWO:
Dangerous Behavior

Myth: How HIV spreads is not a mystery. To stop it, people simply need to give up promiscuous sex, drug use, and other dangerous behaviors. HIV continues to proliferate in poor regions of the world because people from these areas refuse to alter their traditions and lifestyles in response to the crisis.

Response: The drive to assign guilt or blame in relation to AIDS has been a persistent feature of the epidemic. From the beginning, discussions of AIDS—including those among political leaders and health officials—have tended to fuse the language of scientific explanation with the vocabulary of moral censure.[1] Early commentators did not hesitate to explain AIDS as the result of a decadent "gay lifestyle."[2] In the early 1980s, North American journalists and also some scientists blamed Haitians for AIDS and indulged in lurid fantasies about transmission of the virus through ritual sex and blood-drinking at voodoo ceremonies.[3] In more recent years, with the globalization of the epidemic, "promiscuity" in Africa and other parts of the developing world has become a favored theme.[4] Confronting steadily rising HIV infection rates in many regions, health experts have criticized people's apparent unwillingness to use condoms; to stop engaging in commercial sex; to reduce their number of sexual partners; and, in the case of drug users, to give up needle sharing and other dangerous practices.

experts' frustration is understandable. Multiple sex ... failure to use condoms are unquestionably correlated with heightened HIV risk. HIV prevalence among sex workers and injection drug users is often extremely high. However, we maintain that to frame discussions in terms of "promiscuity" or "lifestyle choices" is misleading when we seek to explain the rapid spread of HIV. To support this argument, we look at a series of factors that constrain many people's ability to make free choices regarding behaviors that place them at risk. These factors include economic insecurity, gender and racial inequalities, labor migration, and armed conflict. The reality behind the HIV/AIDS epidemic in poor communities has more to do with socioeconomic constraints than with individual proclivities or cultural attitudes. Stopping HIV/AIDS will require exposing socioeconomic structures that often curtail people's options for avoiding exposure to the virus and using education, empowerment, and social change to loosen these constraints.

Impact of Poverty and Economic Insecurity

The myth that people contract AIDS because they refuse to make "lifestyle changes" is based on a belief that everyone can select from the same menu of options. The daily lives of affluent, educated people in wealthy countries do provide numerous opportunities to make choices—from trivial consumer selections to far-reaching decisions about education, career paths, marriage, and family.[5] Yet while this model of personal choice may offer an appropriate lens for understanding middle-class behavior in a consumer society, it distorts our view when projected into contexts of poverty, like those on the front lines of the AIDS crisis. The language of sexual or lifestyle choice exaggerates the degree of agency that many people (especially poor people and women) are able to exercise. It obscures the extent to which people may be constrained by factors they cannot effectively control. And it brings with it an implicit tendency to see people living with HIV/AIDS as the authors of their own misery—individuals who have acted hedonistically or recklessly and are now suffering the consequences. Often, the most powerful factor restricting people's abilities to make sound choices about sexual practices and substance use is poverty. In combination with other social factors—above all inequality in the distribution of wealth and social power—poverty limits people's options for protecting themselves and forces them into situations of heightened risk.[6]

When AIDS prevention campaigns, for instance, tell economically disadvantaged young women to avoid "sugar daddies" or older women to stick to one partner, they may be admonishing women to discard their only survival option—and in many cases the only source of support for their families.[7] Similarly, knowledge that barrier methods like condoms can prevent transmission of HIV is of little value if people cannot afford to buy condoms, or if a woman's situation of economic dependence leaves her unable to negotiate with her sexual partners.

The situation of Rhaki, a 19-year-old woman from an agricultural area of Rajasthan, India, typifies a pattern faced by poor rural women in many areas of the world. When she was 13 years old, Rhaki was arranged to be married to a man 10 years her senior. Although she had never been far from her family, she was forced to travel 350 miles from her home to join her husband and her new in-laws. For the first two years of marriage, before she began to menstruate and was considered sexually mature, Rhaki was treated in the household like one of her husband's sisters. At age 15, Rhaki had her first sexual encounter with her husband, who had returned home for one month during the high holidays. Long before their marriage, he had migrated to Mumbai, where he worked in the jewelry-making trade, earning money to support his impoverished rural family, which was suffering the effects of a 10-year drought.

Under the watchful eyes of her husband's family and neighbors, Rhaki worked in the fields, helped take care of her in-laws, and awaited her husband 11 months of every year. She never engaged in extramarital sexual relations, did not use IV drugs, and had never received a blood transfusion. To her knowledge, her husband had remained faithful to her while working in the city—though he admitted in confidence to AIDS researchers that he had other sexual partners in Mumbai, including two commercial sex workers.

When Rhaki learned that her husband, her two-year-old son, and she were all HIV-positive, she was at a loss to explain what had happened. She had learned of AIDS from the local health post and had followed preventive measures to the best of her ability. Because her husband lied to her and to his family about his extramarital sexual liaisons in the city, Rhaki was blamed by her in-laws for "contaminating" the family. She feared being thrown out on the street upon her husband's death and not having the money to return to her own family.[8]

Rhaki's only HIV "risk factor" was having sexual relations with her husband. One might suppose she could have asked her husband to use condoms. But this ignores the enormous power differential characterizing relations between genders and generations in most of rural India. Rhaki's lower status constrained her ability to negotiate with her husband. His will was the way, and he chose to forgo condom use.

Around the world, many married women, particularly those whose husbands migrate for labor or serve in the military, share Rhaki's fate. For other women, HIV risk comes through exchanging sex for money, goods, or services. But denunciations of prostitution or promiscuity contribute little to our capacity to improve AIDS prevention. A structural economic analysis is more to the point, as the factors prompting women's involvement with multiple sexual partners or participation in commercial sex are most often economic in nature. They concern the need to survive, and in many cases to support children or other dependents, in a context of destitution and economic exclusion that offers few other options for earning money.[9]

Evidence from all regions of the world shows that the primary motive driving women to engage in sex work, whether commercial or occasional, is economic hardship.[10] In a study among 130 Baganda women (50 percent of whom were HIV-positive) in Uganda, for example, destitution was the primary reason for women to engage in risky sexual behavior.[11] Such studies confirm what many of us intuitively feel: that, for the majority of women, commercial sex work is not a "lifestyle choice," but a last-ditch survival strategy in a situation where other possible escape routes have been shut down. Indeed, the term "survival sex" is far more accurate than commercial sex work.

A study of the sexual histories of 25 HIV-positive and 25 uninfected women in rural Haiti revealed an insignificant difference in the average number of lifetime sexual partners between the two groups (an average of 2.7 partners for the patients with HIV disease, 2.4 for the uninfected control group). The decisive risk factor for these women was not the number of sexual partners, but the professions of the partners. The HIV-positive women were much more likely to have had relationships with truck drivers or soldiers, two categories of men whose job mobility placed them in increased danger of contracting and transmitting the virus (see the discussion of labor migration below). Researchers found that poor rural women's motivation for seeking relationships with soldiers and truck drivers was largely economic. Amid the crushing poverty of Haiti's rural Central Plateau, soldiers and truck drivers are conspicuous because they receive a regular salary. Peasant women often pursue relationships with these men as part of a desperate "quest for some measure of economic security."[12] To understand the AIDS epidemic now affecting rural Haiti, we must grasp the significance of financial insecurity and destitution as compared with supposed promiscuity.

When researchers and health care providers assume that risk for HIV infection is based solely on intractable cultural habits and unwise personal choices, their efforts to control the spread of the disease will focus myopically on individual behavior. While culturally sensitive approaches to HIV prevention are essential, they often fall short by neglecting wider socioeconomic constraints imposed on people's day-to-day lives. Too frequently, the "prescription for HIV prevention" presented by social scientists and public health authorities involves calling "for the 'cultural transformation' of gay men, poor women, and injection drug users—but not for the structural transformation of a society that distributes risks so unevenly."[13]

Rural women from poor countries are not the only people to face economic insecurity that heightens risk for HIV infection. Men, urban dwellers, and people living in wealthy countries are also vulnerable to the health risks associated with poverty. Social scientists have shown how the disintegration and immiseration of urban neighborhoods in places like New York City accelerate the spread of HIV, heightening vulnerability among poor communities, in particular communities of color. In city neighborhoods caught in a process of "urban desertification," the economic base erodes, populations fluctuate, social networks are disrupted, public services atrophy, and rates of substance abuse and HIV infection climb.[14]

In some cases in the US, the destabilization of urban communities has been the result of deliberate policies of neglect and service withdrawal designed to force outward migration and produce "planned population shrinkage" in neighborhoods judged as overcrowded. In large American cities, as in developing regions in the grip of civil conflict, such population movements encourage the spread of infectious disease, including HIV. New York's South

Bronx was the target of a "planned shrinkage" program in the 1980s. In successive waves, populations from burned-out areas were displaced to adjacent zones, which themselves became overcrowded and destabilized—ripe for another wave of targeted service reduction and subsequent burnout and migration. At the height of this pattern in the late 1980s, a hospital in the south-central Bronx found that 25 percent of patients admitted to its emergency room tested positive for HIV.[15]

In socioeconomically marginalized communities, chronic unemployment and the limitation of job options to low-skill, low-wage positions frustrate and humiliate men still taught to see themselves as economic providers. Combined with the effects of racism, endemic poverty breeds fatalism and deep-seated anger that may encourage both personal risk-taking and indifference to others' welfare.[16] Thus, for some men, protecting themselves and their partners during sex may be a low priority. Anthropologist Philippe Bourgois has traced the roots of much dangerous or violent behavior among young men in blighted urban neighborhoods to the combination of institutionalized ethnic discrimination with a "rigidly segmented labor market, and all the hidden injuries to human dignity that this entails."[17] For Bourgois, the anger felt by disenfranchised men is not a matter of deviant individual psychology, but instead a reflection of the "objective, structural desperation of a population without a viable economy," facing the "barriers of systematic discrimination and marginalization." Such frustration is often "channeled into self-destructive cultural practices."[18] Bourgois's ethnographic studies of urban America's "mean streets" show how, "in the day-to-day experience of the street-bound inner-city resident, unemployment and personal anxiety over the impossibility of providing a minimal standard of living for one's family translate into intracommunity crime, intracommunity drug abuse, intracommunity violence," entwined social patterns that create an enabling environment for the spread of HIV.[19]

Discrimination and lack of access to education are barriers that can severely limit poor people's employment opportunities, in some cases forcing them into forms of work that involve increased risk of contracting HIV. We see this pattern in low-income countries throughout the world where long-distance truck drivers, soldiers, and migrant laborers are found to have unusually high infection rates. A similar pattern exists in wealthy countries, where undereducated people in poor urban neighborhoods often find involvement in the illicit drug trade one of their few economic options.[20] The story of Carlos, 48, a Puerto Rican now living in the US, shows how poverty, exclusion, drug use, and disease can entrap those at the bottom of a steeply graded socioeconomic hierarchy.

Carlos was born into an impoverished family in rural Puerto Rico. From an early age, his parents pressured him to work to help support his large extended family. As a boy, Carlos worked in fields owned by transnational fruit companies. Frustrated by the low wages and his inability to help his younger siblings, Carlos grew disillusioned. As an adolescent, he learned from a neighbor that he could easily quadruple his earnings by selling marijuana. Within weeks, Carlos's involvement in the drug market had become more lucrative than his manual labor jobs, which he subsequently abandoned. For the first time, Carlos was praised by his parents for contributing "like a man" to the family income.

From marijuana, Carlos soon shifted to dealing harder, more expensive drugs, in response to his customers' demand. As his circle of friends became his most consistent clients, business and pleasure mixed, and Carlos became addicted to the drugs he sold. When his drug dependency first developed, he had no knowledge about AIDS.

By the time he and his family moved to Massachusetts in 1990, Carlos was supporting a heroin habit, injecting three to four times a day. Although Carlos now knew abstractly that AIDS was a deadly disease that could be transmitted by sharing needles, he did not accurately assess his own level of risk. To acknowledge those risks would have threatened his livelihood. As Carlos later explained, he believed cleaning needles or refusing to share needles would reveal an anxiety he could not afford to show the friends and customers upon whose business he relied for his own and his family's survival. Moreover, as Carlos put it, "I knew then that I was sharing with friends who already had AIDS. But they were my friends. They didn't look sick, and who am I to think that I deserve any better than them?"

Carlos was diagnosed with HIV in August 1996. Since that time, he has suffered multiple lengthy hospitalizations and, for over five years, the hazards and indignity of homelessness. Asked in 2002 when he had contracted the virus, he could only guess. Carlos now speaks with sadness about his past and regrets having entered the drug trade. "Had my parents been able to support our family, I could have gone to school and become an electrician."[21]

Carlos's story shows how poverty, social pressures, and the denial of education and economic opportunity can combine to place people on a path whose end point is a fatal infection. Many of Carlos's key life decisions were made for him by the economic vulnerability that afflicted his family and community. Within the constricted space created by poverty and discrimination, Carlos, like many participants in the illicit drug trade, displayed determination and what, in the mainstream economy, would be admired as entrepreneurial spirit; unfortunately, he operated within a perverse economic system that turned these qualities into risk factors for contracting a deadly illness.[22]

As poverty and inequality beget AIDS, so AIDS drives an intergenerational dynamic of deprivation. When AIDS-infected parents die, they leave orphans who in many settings must fend for themselves. Without guidance or financial assistance, orphans are forced to leave school. Without schooling they are relegated to work in the informal sector: begging, selling trinkets or candy on the streets, cleaning car windows, serving as domestic workers, becoming commercial sex workers, or selling drugs. Such children are themselves destined to increased vulnerability to HIV.[23] Nowhere is this cycle more pronounced than in the southern African countries hardest hit by the HIV/AIDS pandemic. But the cycle is not unique to Africa. In China's rural heartland, AIDS is ravaging poor farming communities and producing a generation of destitute orphans.

In the early 1990s, tens of thousands of poor farmers in China's Henan Province routinely sold their blood at collection centers run by commercial blood processing firms. After pooling blood from several donors, the centers centrifuged the blood to skim off plasma for sale to companies manufacturing medicines. Remaining red cells were then transfused back into the donors. Selling blood provided many poor farmers with an opportunity to buy food, pay off debts, repair a roof, or send children to school. In some localities, most adults sold blood on an occasional basis and many sold it every week. Because HIV infection often produces no distinctive symptoms for long periods of time, years elapsed before problems were detected. But it soon became clear that the blood collection and retransfusion process created a ruthlessly efficient mechanism for transmitting blood-borne diseases, including hepatitis and HIV/AIDS. In some villages in the early 1990s, most of the entire adult population was simultaneously infected with HIV.[24]

Whereas in other areas of the world extended families are able to care for the sick and take in orphans, in Henan, sick people's relatives are often infected themselves. Moreover, with China's strict population control policies limiting families to one or two children, young orphans rarely have older siblings to serve as surrogate parents. Children whose parents are living with AIDS are routinely forced out of school because their families can no longer afford to send them and school administrators and other students fear contagion.

With so many adults simultaneously disabled, entire communities have sunk into dire poverty. Families are forced to sell *off their possessions to meet basic food and health care needs. They borrow money to purchase medicines for their loved ones, but the remedies they can afford are ineffective against AIDS. Those still able to farm cannot sell their grains, fruits, and vegetables in nearby cities, whose residents are afraid the infection might somehow be passed through these products. "It really brings you to tears," said a medical worker who recently visited the province. "You see these pretty decent houses, built with the money from selling blood, but inside there is nothing. They've sold the farm tools, the animals, even the furniture. People who are dying are lying on the floor."*[25]

Here once again, the language of "lifestyle choice" offers no insights. The relevant issues are economic vulnerability and the exploitation of the poor by unprincipled companies—with deadly effect. In many villages, the synergy of material deprivation and AIDS has destroyed one generation and placed the next at risk. Many children in Henan watch helplessly as their parents die of AIDS. The orphans then face a bleak future—burdened with the stigma of their parents' disease and in many cases denied social support and educational opportunities.

Like Rhaki and Carlos, the Henan farmers found a strategy for escaping poverty that became, in the presence of HIV, a path to infection and death. Their very efforts to behave responsibly—by practicing marital fidelity in Rhaki's case, by seeking a better livelihood for their families in Carlos's and the farmers'—exposed them to the virus. Today, HIV transmission patterns are increasingly well understood, and more-effective prevention messages are beginning to reach even the remotest areas. But with almost half the world's population living on less than the equivalent of two dollars a day and struggling to obtain adequate food, water, and shelter, the fundamental economic and social mechanisms that ensnared Rhaki, Carlos, and the Henan farmers continue to grip vast numbers of people, exposing them to similar risks.

AIDS and Structural Racism

Economic vulnerability is often exacerbated and perpetuated by racism and other patterns of social exclusion—producing, in the words of Philippe Bourgois, a dynamic of "conjugated oppression" that is "more than the sum of its parts."[26] The effects of racism significantly increase HIV risk for people of color living in the US. As the AIDS pandemic enters its third decade, racial and ethnic minorities continue to suffer disproportionately and now account for the majority both of new infections and of people living with HIV/AIDS. African-Americans and Latinos represent 12 percent and 13 percent of the US population, respectively. However, by the end of the 1990s they accounted for 47 percent and 19 percent of newly reported AIDS cases. Among people 25–44 years old, AIDS is the second-leading cause of death for African-Americans and the fourth-leading cause of death for US Latinos, compared with the fifth-leading cause of death for whites.[27]

In June 2001, the National Black Leadership Commission on AIDS (BLCA), in conjunction with other groups including the Congressional Black Caucus, convened a Meeting of the Millennium in Atlanta to call for the declaration of an "HIV/AIDS state of emergency" in African-American communities. BLCA leaders argued that the ongoing devastation of AIDS in communities of color demands a "new chapter in the civil rights movement."[28] In August 2001, at a conference in Harlem, New York City, African-American and Latino citizens' groups confirmed the gravity of the AIDS crisis among the city's Blacks and Latinos and criticized proposals by state lawmakers to cut AIDS funding. National Black Leadership Commission president Debra Frazer-Howze emphasized that 83 percent of new AIDS cases in New York City occur among people of color.[29]

Gender Discrimination and Violence Against Women

Rhaki's story illustrates how women are often prevented from effectively controlling important dimensions of their own lives, including choices about when, with whom, and under what conditions to have sex. In fueling the spread of HIV and other sexually transmitted infections (STIs), systemic discrimination against women is among the deadliest forms of inequality.[30]

AIDS, domestic violence, and sexual violence against women are intertwined epidemics in some regions. For many women, economic dependency and social vulnerability lead to the daily terror of physical abuse at the hands of spouses or partners. In a study involving 1660 Ugandan women between 20 and 44 years old, 58 percent reported being beaten or physically harmed by a partner at some point in their lifetime.[31] In the US, one woman in five is subjected to physical abuse in her lifetime.[32] Surveys examining the incidence of domestic abuse over shorter time periods were conducted in Korea, the West Bank and Gaza Strip, and Nicaragua, where, respectively, 37 percent, 48 percent, and 27 percent of women surveyed had been physically abused by a partner within the past year.[33]

Physical battering often goes hand in hand with sexual violence. In a Namibian study, 95 percent of 1020 women surveyed reported that their first sexual encounter was forced.[34] Thirty-one percent of women surveyed in Sierra Leone and seven percent in the US reported similar experiences.[35] Under such circumstances, condom use is an unlikely option. Researchers in the US have found that women in abusive relationships are less likely than other women to have partners who use condoms and are more likely to encounter verbal abuse and threats of physical abuse when they discuss condom use.[36] In Zimbabwe, women report being raped and beaten following attempts to refuse their partner's sexual advances.[37]

Researchers, activists, and advocates have long stressed that women who are economically and socially dependent on men cannot effectively negotiate for condom use or other forms of safe-sex practice. This is true regardless of their awareness of the risks of HIV transmission through unprotected intercourse. The inability of women to insist on sexual fidelity, or on methods to prevent being infected with sexually-transmitted diseases, can have fatal consequences in societies where men have the implicit right to have extramarital sexual relationships.

In many cases, age differentials and intergenerational power dynamics introduce an additional level of risk for girls and young women. A 1996 survey of 10,868 adolescent females from the Midwestern US found that 10 percent had suffered sexual abuse by an adult or by someone older than themselves—nine percent in the past and one percent in an ongoing situation.[38] In areas with high HIV prevalence, such dynamics can be fatal.

Compounding the problem in some African regions is the tendency for men to seek "clean" adolescent or preadolescent extramarital sex partners. This practice may reflect both a male strategy for avoiding AIDS and the widespread myth that sexual intercourse with a virgin can reverse the disease's course. Many girls accept relationships with elder male partners, or "sugar daddies," to defray their school fees or pay for other basic expenses including food and rent. However, they rarely have any influence over the desires and demands of these older men.[39] Such practices may play a role in the soaring rates of HIV prevalence now seen among young women in many sub-Saharan African countries.[40] As the AIDS pandemic leaves more young girls without parents, this trend, and the unequal power dynamics associated with it, will likely continue.

The Effects of Labor Migration

A key factor placing many men and women in poor countries at increased risk for HIV infection is the phenomenon of labor migration. In many poor regions, people, especially male breadwinners, are obliged to travel long distances to find work or as part of the work itself (for example, in the case of truck drivers and military personnel). Due to heavy workloads, long distances, and the expense of travel, many are forced to live away from home for weeks, months, even years at a time. Such displacements are associated with increased vulnerability to HIV infection. Migration brings about long periods of separation from spouse and family life; increased opportunities to establish multiple sexual liaisons or to frequent prostitutes; and forms of escapism such as the binge use of alcohol and drugs during off-work downtime. Many migrant workers face loneliness and isolation, which increase the yearning for companionship. For men with little free time, displaced from ordinary social networks, casual sex may be an easy way to escape such loneliness.

When separated from their mothers and spouses, some men learn to fend for themselves in terms of cooking, cleaning, and laundry. Other men—especially those in societies with clear sexual divisions of labor, as in most of Africa—choose instead to pay women to perform these domestic tasks for them. In polygamous societies, it is not uncommon for men to dodge such expenses while residing in the city by marrying a second or third wife, who then prepares meals and attends to the laundry. Whether formal or informal, such multipartner arrangements pose heightened risks to all parties: the migrant laborer, the urban spouse, and the rural spouse or spouses.

South Africa provides a stark example of the AIDS effects of an institutionalized system of labor migration. In apartheid South

Africa, mines and other white-owned industries depended on the availability of cheap black labor. To keep these businesses productive, the government helped pressure large numbers of black men to leave their homes and become part of a rootless migrant labor force. This agenda was relentlessly pursued from the late 19th century through the 1980s.[41] The institutionalization of migrant labor was supported by an entire apparatus of laws, beginning with the Land Act of 1913, which abolished the remnants of traditional subsistence farming arrangements, forcing previously independent African farmers off the land and into the pool of laborers available to be exploited in South Africa's burgeoning gold and diamond mines. Denied the right to own land and simultaneously subjected to heavy taxes, black men had no choice but to seek wage labor to support their families.[42]

Under the post–World War II apartheid regime, the migrant labor system continued, along with the systematic uprooting and resettlement of black and colored communities.[43] Many black men were forced to live far from their families in men-only "hostels" close to mines and other industrial facilities. Such patterns of worker itinerancy have dramatically accelerated the spread of AIDS, at first among the migrant groups themselves, then in the wider population. In a study of 4,531 miners in a rural South African community in the early 1990s, migration was associated with an elevated risk of HIV infection.[44]

As in the Haitian case cited previously, regular, comparatively high pay makes male migrants especially desirable to women who are unable to meet basic survival needs unassisted. Such advantages in income and prestige make it easier for these men to multiply their sexual contacts. In general, migration dramatically increases opportunities for casual sex, and thus the number of situations in which self-control must be exercised—often in the face of pressure from peers or the male migrant's own sense of his masculine "needs" and prerogatives. The results can be grim for those with the mixed blessing of mobility. HIV prevalence rates among 5,553 Ugandan adults in a 1995 study were lowest among those who never moved, higher among those who moved to a different village within the study area, and highest among those who moved into the study area from outside.[45] Similar results were shown in Senegal.[46] These findings suggest mobility is an independent risk factor for acquiring HIV. Data from Ivory Coast support this view. Ivory Coast is the primary destination of migrants in West Africa. One-quarter of the country's 12 million inhabitants are migrants, and migrants represent 40 percent of the population of Abidjan, Ivory Coast's largest city and economic center. Not coincidentally, HIV prevalence rates in Ivory Coast are the highest in West Africa.[47]

Among the forces that have been fueling the AIDS epidemic in parts of Africa is the mobility afforded by transportation networks. By facilitating work migration, this infrastructure also eases the spread of the virus.[48] In a study conducted along the trans-African highway in southwest Uganda, HIV prevalence was 40 percent, with rates above 50 percent found in women aged 20–34 and men aged 35–44. The rates of infection among those in the study who reported having only one sexual partner was 17 percent, revealing once again a lack of association between monogamy and protection.[49]

Social Instability, Armed Conflict, and War

War almost completely removes the ability to exercise basic forms of personal freedom. In many parts of the world, the spread of AIDS has been propelled by war and by chronic patterns of civil strife and social instability. In countries including Rwanda, the Democratic Republic of the Congo, Sierra Leone, and Haiti, armed conflict and an increasing encroachment of armed groups into the space of civil society have been significant cofactors in the proliferation of the virus.

There are several ways militarization and armed conflict contribute to increased AIDS risks. Armed conflict often spawns large-scale population displacements, including movements of refugees as well as soldiers. Such displacements have been shown to be a significant factor in the spread of infectious diseases, including AIDS. During a war, concentrations of military men, often mobile and separated from family and loved ones, combined with high poverty levels among women, create a climate for prostitution and increased risks for HIV transmission.[50] HIV infection rates in African armed forces are among the highest in the world, in some cases exceeding 50 percent.[51]

Military conflict is also associated with a high incidence of rape, which is sometimes consciously employed as a weapon to intimidate and humiliate enemy populations. The recent conflicts in East Timor, Rwanda, the former Yugoslavia, Azerbaijan, and other areas have focused attention on the toll war takes on women.[52] During the three-year conflict in Bosnia-Herzegovina between 20,000 and 50,000 women were raped as part of a deliberate strategy to destroy social bonds.[53] In Uganda, a village health worker reported that soldiers had raped approximately 70 percent of the women in her community in the early 1980s. Some of these women were assaulted by as many as 10 soldiers in a single episode of gang rape.[54] Understandably, women who have survived such attacks often flee, joining refugee streams. Of a random sample of 20 Ethiopian refugees who had fled ethnic persecution and resettled in Somalia during 1986, 13 reported that a family member had been raped by Ethiopian militiamen.[55] Clearly, in addition to the other forms of emotional and physical damage these women suffer, their risk of HIV infection often increases dramatically.[56] During the Rwandan genocide of 1994, intentional HIV transmission through rape was inflicted by some Hutu men on Tutsi women and girls.[57]

War and other forms of conflict also contribute to the spread of HIV/AIDS through the deterioration of social and political order; the destruction of health, education, and communications infrastructure; and the killing, kidnaping, or flight of health care providers. Furthermore, when social services collapse, it prevents people from accessing medical care and learning about and safer sex practices.[58]

Structural Violence and Realistic Prevention Strategies

AIDS prevention efforts must acknowledge and address structural forces in culturally sensitive ways. Otherwise these efforts appear disingenuous and may alienate the populations they are meant to serve. When the simplest AIDS prevention messages—such as "avoid sugar daddies," "practice monogamy," or "insist on safe sex"—do not square with a social critique of poverty, inequality, racism, gender discrimination, and other structural factors, these simple slogans can fuel stigmatization and project blame on the victims of the disease. Infection becomes evidence of a moral failure.

Obviously it is simpler to blame the victims for the rapid spread of AIDS in poor countries than to analyze the socioeconomic and political structures that underlie, frame, and often predetermine such personal "choices." Yet if we really want to understand the dynamics of the AIDS pandemic, and take meaningful action to end it, we must move beyond moral judgment and accusation. Instead, we must grasp how the vastly unequal distribution of global wealth produces wide differentials in human freedom and capacity for informed, reasoned choice.

The implications of this perspective for the global AIDS

struggle are significant. The first and clearest consequence is that education and action against HIV/AIDS must go beyond insuring that people understand the physical mechanisms of HIV transmission and are given access to barrier devices like condoms (though these are indispensable first steps). Effective AIDS prevention must recognize the structural forces that constrain individual agency and must seek ways to overcome these constraints.

Promoting female-controlled prevention such as the female condom is one way of addressing gendered power differentials. While the female condom poses problems for some users, several studies from the US and developing countries have shown that women are generally willing to try the device, and that with practice it can function well.[59] Perhaps the most effective means of woman-controlled HIV prevention would be safe, effective microbicides—chemical agents that could be introduced into the vagina or rectum prior to sex and that would kill HIV or prevent it from entering the bloodstream.[60] Studies have confirmed a strong interest in microbicides among women, but efforts to develop such agents have lagged due to inadequate investment.[61] Microbicide research should be a top scientific priority, and activists should bring pressure to bear on political leaders, funders, research institutions, and drug companies to advance this agenda.

Across the board, the AIDS fight must involve a deepened commitment to poor women's empowerment and autonomy.[62] At the same time, AIDS education and counseling must reach out to men and seek ways to alter male attitudes, using the tools of political economy to understand how structural violence also limits men's autonomy and obstructs behavior change. While the wider availability of female-controlled protection tools is vital, it is clear that in the long run effective AIDS education and prevention must find ways to bring men on board as full participants in the fight against the disease. Use of the female condom, for example, still requires acceptance from a male partner. In studies undertaken in Thailand and South Africa, men's reluctance to accept the female condom was cited as the primary factor discouraging women from employing the device.[63]

In societies marked by ingrained patterns of gender inequality, outreach efforts must seek to enable changes in men's practices, even as activists work to bring about legal, institutional, and structural reforms that will guarantee women greater freedom. While enormous challenges remain, some HIV prevention efforts have successfully engaged men. A recent study in Rwanda explored the impact of a testing and counseling program specifically targeting men. The husbands and cohabiting partners of 684 Rwandan women were recruited. Following up with the couples after one year, researchers found dramatic increases in rates of condom use during sexual intercourse for the serodiscordant couples (couples with one HIV-positive and one HIV-negative partner). Women reported lower rates of coercive sex by their male partners after the men had completed the counseling program. The researchers conclude that this type of male-focused or couple-focused testing and counseling program appears to be effective in reducing risky sexual behaviors in heterosexual couples.[64]

The gains recorded in such studies are small on the scale of a global epidemic. They confirm the painstaking effort required to counter the effects of powerful structural pressures and social conditioning on individual behavior. Yet, these projects show that success is possible when individual agency is neither denied nor overestimated. Effective strategies acknowledge constraining social forces while using the margin of freedom these forces allow.

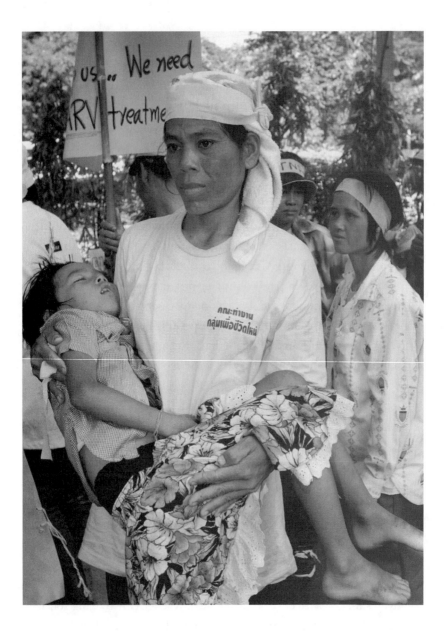

Woman carries her daughter during successful protest
for government-funded AIDS treatment program
in Bangkok, Thailand.

MYTH THREE:
Corruption

Myth: Developing countries are unable to fight AIDS effectively because they are corrupt and badly governed. Increased contributions to AIDS work in Africa and other underdeveloped regions serve little purpose, because most of the money goes into the pockets of dishonest officials, rather than to preventing new infections and treating the sick.

Response: Corruption afflicts both the developing world and high-income countries.[1] However, many Americans perceive corruption as being much more pervasive in poor regions and believe a large portion of US assistance for developing countries, including money for AIDS control, is siphoned off by corrupt officials.[2]

Cronyism, bribery, and embezzlement hamper the AIDS fight in many countries and communities. Yet three strong arguments support the view that the existence of corruption should not slow expanded support for global AIDS work from wealthy countries like the US. First, evidence shows that efforts to fight corruption and direct resources efficiently toward AIDS control are gathering momentum today, particularly in Africa. Second, international institutions such as the Global Fund to Fight AIDS, Tuberculosis and Malaria (GFATM) have incorporated strict new monitoring and accountability mechanisms to ensure proper use of resources as anti-AIDS efforts are scaled up. Third, some developing countries grappling with stubborn cultures of corruption have already managed to implement highly effective HIV/AIDS programs. Evidence from Thailand, Uganda, and Brazil shows that countries do not need to wait until systemic corruption has been eliminated before implementing large-scale programs against HIV/AIDS with success. Corruption and AIDS can be battled simultaneously.

International Efforts to Fight Corruption

Corruption is widespread in many countries and has obstructed the delivery of HIV/AIDS services, along with other humanitarian initiatives. Yet recent years have seen people around the world joining forces as never before to expose, document, and resist corrupt practices and to replace cultures of corruption with structures promoting openness and accountability.

While Western analysts' complaints about corruption often focus on African officials, patterns of bribery, diversion of public funds, kickbacks, and other abuses are frequently documented in wealthy countries as well. Recent corporate governance and financial scandals in the US highlight the extent of the problem. Meanwhile, businesses based in US, European, and Asian economic centers directly contribute to international corruption by bribing officials in developing countries.[3]

Addressing corruption is a global responsibility, not just a task for poor countries. This underscores the importance of new international mechanisms such as the Anti-Bribery Convention recently ratified by member countries of the Organization for Economic Cooperation and Development (OECD), including the US, major European powers, and Japan. The convention formally makes it a crime for citizens of signatory countries to bribe foreign public officials in order to obtain or retain international business.[4]

The convention is part of a growing international movement against corruption documented by the Berlin-based NGO Transparency International (TI) in its *Global Corruption Report*. According to TI, corruption is attracting greater public scrutiny in high-income countries and in the developing world than ever before. "The secretive web that once shrouded corruption is fast unraveling."[5] Examples of progress in 2000–01 include: Indian Internet reporters' filming of alleged payoffs on weapons contracts; Peruvian journalists' documentation of bribe taking by politicians; and popular anger against corruption in the Philippines, which sparked a mass movement forcing the resignation of President Joseph Estrada.[6]

The fight for greater openness has been assisted by new technologies, the increasing power of civil society in many regions, and the expansion of independent media. Technologies such as the Internet make it much easier for individuals and groups to share information about patterns of corruption and to focus local, national, and international attention on problems when they emerge. The same tools can be used to publicize and reward positive achievements and to present "best practice" models. Transparency International offers a vast array of anticorruption resources on its multilingual website. The site includes a searchable database of Best Practice Documentation and a Corruption Fighters' Toolkit providing guidance for civil society groups, policy makers, scholars, activists, and businesspeople seeking to promote anticorruption measures in their countries and communities.[7]

Increasingly, governments attempting to carry through anticorruption reforms are using Internet and new communications technologies to open their finances and other dealings to public monitoring. "E-government," including, for instance, Internet bidding for procurement contracts, has been adopted in countries from Chile to Estonia to South Korea. Increasingly, governments are making their financial records and other forms of documentation available online.[8] Of course, the wider and more instantaneous circulation of information does not eliminate all opportunities for corruption, but increased information does make it more difficult for public officials to conceal improper activities.

Civil society groups and the independent media are powerful factors in helping reduce corruption. In parts of Africa, for example, civil society organizations and an increasingly aggressive media play vital roles in the region's efforts for reform. Analysts argue that wasteful, corruption-driven development disasters such as Kenya's Turkwell Gorge dam project—completed in 1987 despite popular opposition and protests from Kenyan and international experts—would probably not be allowed to happen in today's climate "precisely because of the influence of civil society and the independent press."[9]

An example of the use of independent media to challenge governmental inertia on AIDS comes from China. There people living with HIV/AIDS, many of whom are silenced by the official state press, have sought out Western media sources to publicize victims' stories and shame the government over its failure to move resolutely against the expanding epidemic.[10]

Building Political Commitment for the AIDS Fight

While anticorruption efforts in all parts of the world are crucial, assessing progress against corruption in Africa is particularly important for those involved in the AIDS fight. This is not because African states are uniformly more corrupt than governments in other regions. Rather, the concern reflects two factors: (1) the severity of Africa's HIV/AIDS epidemic and the immediate need for vastly increased foreign assistance to AIDS programs on the continent; (2) the perception among many rich-country officials that public-sector dishonesty and waste are particularly rampant in Africa. Presenting a balanced picture of the state of reform efforts in Africa is important for AIDS advocates as they seek to win political support for increased spending on global AIDS by rich-country governments and donor institutions.

The deep roots and daunting scope of corruption in many African countries must be clearly acknowledged. Recent stories of misappropriated oil revenues in Angola and the long-running scandals associated with regimes such as Daniel Moi's administration in Kenya and Robert Mugabe's in Zimbabwe testify to the difficulty of maintaining sound governance in countries ravaged by decades or centuries of colonial exploitation, poverty, conflict, and authoritarian rule.[11] Corruption ranks high on the list of many African countries' significant political challenges.[12]

However, recent developments within African countries, as well as a number of regional initiatives, reflect genuine progress. In 1989, only five African countries were considered democracies. In the following 10 years, 20 countries acquired democratically elected governments, including Benin, Malawi, South Africa, and Zambia. Several other countries, such as Cameroon, Ghana, and Kenya, were in transitional stages.[13]

Of course, a transition to democracy does not guarantee a sweeping end to corruption; in fact, some government transitions have led to increases in political instability and new kinds of corruption fueled by previously impotent opposition parties. Even longstanding democracies such as the US are not immune to the corrupting influences of, for example, corporate financial interests, which in recent years have compromised all three branches of the US government. However, democratic institutions do tend to favor greater accountability, economic transparency, and civic participation in government, all of which help check corruption.

Local anticorruption agencies now exist in most countries in southern Africa.[14] Transparency International analysts have praised the legal design of institutions such as Tanzania's recently created Prevention of Corruption Bureau and Uganda's anticorruption inspectorate, while pointing out that the agencies' impact has been limited by lack of resources and skilled personnel.[15] Donors and international financial institutions such as the World Bank have incorporated corruption reduction stipulations into their funding agreements, intensifying pressure on African governments to measure and curb corruption, though also raising the risk of justified resentment when anticorruption agendas are seen as imposed on African countries from outside.[16] Where robust successes have been achieved, local civil society, NGOs, and independent media are often credited with leading the struggle.

In the fight against AIDS, top government officials of many African countries have embraced the need for dynamic political leadership and rigorous accountability. Meetings and speeches are not in themselves sufficient to stop the pandemic's spread, yet a series of recent high-level conferences, consultations, and declarations in Africa have given a new tone to political leaders' response to AIDS. The meeting of the African Development Forum 2000 adopted as its theme "AIDS: The Greatest Leadership Challenge." In 2001, the Organization of African Unity (OAU) brought together African heads of state and government in Abuja, Nigeria, to reflect on the challenges posed by AIDS and other infectious diseases and to develop plans for more vigorous action. In the "Abuja Declaration on HIV/AIDS, Tuberculosis, and Other Related Infectious Diseases," the leaders vowed to "place the fight against HIV/AIDS at the forefront and as the highest priority issue in our respective national development plans."

They expressed a shared commitment to multisector AIDS strategies linking governments, NGOs, and community-based organizations, notably including organizations of people living with HIV/AIDS and women's groups. The leaders engaged themselves to take personal responsibility for the African response to AIDS and to "lead from the front" in the ongoing struggle to control the infectious disease epidemics attacking the continent.[17]

Other new initiatives to tackle the African pandemic include the International African Association (IAA), a coalition bringing together African governments, the United Nations, donor organizations, NGOs and civil society groups, and the business sector. IAA aims to develop national-level coordinating mechanisms to overcome the fragmentation that has often characterized past efforts against HIV/AIDS. National strategic plans were to be reviewed, implemented, and financed in 20 African countries by the end of 2002. To date, no other region besides Africa has developed such a comprehensive political and economic framework for the AIDS fight.[18]

Overall, as stepped-up anticorruption efforts are underway in many parts of Africa, determination among Africa's political leaders to take action against AIDS has reached an all-time high.[19] And in some cases where governments have remained sluggish in their anti-AIDS efforts, grassroots citizens' groups have used public education campaigns, street protests, and lawsuits to challenge official positions and catalyze a more vigorous response. The most striking example to date is the successful 2001–02 legal effort by the Treatment Action Campaign (TAC), South Africa's groundbreaking AIDS activist organization, to require the South African government to expand programs against mother-to-child transmission of HIV using the antiretroviral drug nevirapine. Not an issue of corruption in the strict sense, the mother-to-child transmission dispute did target reckless policy choices among a leadership elite and showed how civil society pressure can compel changes in the behavior of public officials who have lost touch with the needs of citizens.[20]

Beginning in April 2002, largely as a result of pressure from TAC and other civil society groups, the South African government enacted a conspicuous about-face in its discourse on AIDS. South African leaders publicly distanced themselves from statements they had previously endorsed claiming that the causal link between HIV and AIDS is dubious and that antiretroviral medicines do more harm than good.[21] While the situation continues to evolve, the change in government rhetoric suggests that in this instance, grassroots groups like TAC have been able to educate the country's political leadership or at least convince top officials that the political costs of continued inaction were unacceptably high.

Civil society organizations in other countries are now borrowing TAC's strategy to spur their governments to more-determined action on AIDS. In June 2002, the Women and AIDS Support Network (WASN), a Zimbabwean NGO, announced that it would take the Zimbabwean government to court if the country's health officials did not develop a plan to provide mother–to–child transmission prevention with nevirapine in all state-run health centers by the end of the year. WASN's press statements specifically cited the South African precedent.[22] In August 2002, civil society representatives from 21 African countries met in Cape Town to launch a Pan-African HIV/AIDS Treatment Access Movement aiming to expand TAC's successes to the scale of the continent.[23] Supported by an international solidarity network, participating groups in a score of African countries will now be emboldened to hold pharmaceutical companies, donors, the international community, and their own governments accountable for rapid fulfillment of commitments on AIDS. With groups throughout the continent now seeking to replicate TAC's organizing, advocacy, and watchdog functions, issues of corruption, government inertia, and other obstacles to the rollout of effective AIDS prevention and treatment programs will prove easier to overcome.

The Role of New Global Institutions

Today, new international institutions and funding mechanisms are helping promote health interventions protected from corruption and waste. Minimizing corruption is a paramount concern among the architects of the new Global Fund to Fight AIDS, Tuberculosis and Malaria (GFATM), who have established stringent selection and monitoring mechanisms to ensure responsible management of money disbursed through the fund.

The GFATM application and funding process demands rigorous financial documentation and scrupulous accountability and oversight mechanisms for each successful proposal. Success targets must be met, or the countries or institutions granted support will see funding quickly cut. Outcomes are subject to independent monitoring and will be evaluated with special reference to the results achieved among vulnerable communities.[24] To guarantee effective stewardship of resources, the GFATM encourages the involvement and active participation of multiple stakeholders, including not only government authorities but also NGOs, civil society groups, and the private sector. Private auditing firms will be used to strengthen financial oversight and speed the flow of funds to the communities that need them, tightening program effectiveness.[25]

The ultimate impact of the GFATM on the pandemic remains to be seen. To date, donor countries have slowed progress by dragging their feet in delivering money pledged to support the new institution.[26] However, if adequately funded, the GFATM will contribute significantly to guaranteeing more efficient use of resources in the AIDS struggle. Activists working to increase global AIDS spending by the US government and other key donors can point to the GFATM as a management mechanism crafted to ensure that monies flowing to its carefully screened projects will bring results on the ground.

Other new global initiatives will also help hold both developing-country governments and donor governments accountable for their progress toward meeting commitments on HIV/AIDS, such as those agreed to at the United Nations General Assembly Special Session on HIV/AIDS (UNGASS) in June 2001. At the XIV International AIDS Conference in Barcelona held in July 2002, scientists and policy experts from UNAIDS and other agencies unveiled a new set of multidimensional statistical indicators which will be used to track countries' performance in HIV/AIDS policy and programming. The new indicators, to be incorporated into reports and publications for international dissemination, provide tools for measuring national decision makers' success in designing and implementing effective AIDS policies. These indicators will immediately make it easier to hold leaders to account. The tools will help overcome donors' lingering doubts about whether HIV/AIDS control programs really work and whether donated funds are producing tangible results.[27]

Gains Against AIDS, Despite Corruption

Several concrete examples show that a significant level of corruption in a country's public life does not preclude effective action against HIV/AIDS when a strong national mobilization against the epidemic takes place. Thailand, Uganda, and Brazil all have deep-rooted problems with corruption. Yet all three have been able to mount successful national HIV/AIDS programs. The lesson is that corruption and AIDS can be fought simultaneously. We do not have to wait for developing countries to fully uproot corruption before moving to assist them with the implementation of large-scale, well-funded AIDS control programs.

Transparency International's annual Corruption Perceptions Index (CPI) ranks 102 countries according to the level of corruption businesspeople and country experts find in politics, administration, and business life. The lower the rank, the more corrupt the country is seen to be. The CPI is by definition not a strictly objective measure, but it provides a useful general reflection of how some stakeholders assess the quality of governance. The 2002 CPI placed Thailand far down in the ratings, 64th out of 102, reflecting the stubborn patterns of graft and influence buying that mark the country's political and economic sectors.[28] Yet despite its governance problems, a combination of sound public health policy, NGO vigilance, and commitment from the top political ranks has enabled Thailand to mount a widely admired national response to HIV/AIDS that now serves as a model for other countries.

In the late 1980s, Thailand was the first country in Asia to publicly acknowledge and document an HIV/AIDS epidemic among intravenous drug users and female sex workers. After a brief period of confusion and denial, the Thai government moved vigorously to fight the epidemic. A multisector National AIDS Prevention and Control Committee chaired by the prime minister initiated a series of well-organized and robustly financed prevention measures.[29] Members of every segment of Thai government, from the royal family to health outreach workers on the streets, became involved in disseminating information about the HIV/AIDS threat and promoting prevention. Princess Soamsawali led a national effort to reduce mother-to-child transmission of HIV, serving as official patron and first major donor to a campaign for bulk purchase and free distribution of the drug zidovudine (AZT). The drug was used to block mother-to-child transmission during pregnancy and delivery.[30] Grassroots civil society organizations, including peer education groups among prostitutes, also played a significant role in prevention initiatives.[31]

Having identified commercial sex as a key nexus of HIV transmission, Thai authorities instituted sweeping national HIV/AIDS education and condom use campaigns targeted at female sex workers and their male clients. The well-known "100 percent condom program" supplied approximately 60 million free condoms annually.[32] In addition, in the late 1980s, the government invested in an effective national HIV surveillance system, which has enabled public health officials to closely monitor patterns in HIV transmission in all 76 Thai provinces. The results of this strong response have been dramatic. Following the government's HIV education and condom distribution campaigns, the percentage of Thai men visiting female sex workers fell from 25 percent to 10 percent, and condom use in commercial sex encounters became the norm.[33] Levels of HIV infection among female sex workers and their clients declined significantly.[34] By the late 1990s, the annual number of new HIV infections in Thailand had fallen by about 80 percent from its peak early in the decade. Public health experts estimate that the government's measures have prevented approximately 200,000 new HIV infections in the past 10 years.[35]

Today, Thai AIDS activists, led by the Thai Network of People Living with HIV/AIDS (TNP+), are on the forefront of global efforts to lower the price of AIDS treatment and enable production of low-cost generic versions of patented AIDS medicines in countries battered by the pandemic. In October 2002, TNP+ and its allies won a favorable ruling from Thailand's Central Intellectual Property and International Trade Court in a suit against the international pharmaceutical giant Bristol-Myers Squibb. The suit challenged the legality of the company's patent registration in Thailand of its antiretroviral drug ddI, an important first-line medicine in many AIDS treatment regimens. The court's decision in favor of the activists could pave the way for generic production of ddI in Thailand, reducing drug costs and expanding treatment possibilities for the nearly one million Thai people living with HIV/AIDS.[36]

Like Thailand, Uganda consistently scores poorly on the CPI; in 2002 it was listed as one of the 10 most corrupt countries in the world, with a transparency score of 2.2 out of a possible 10.[37] Nonetheless, despite stubborn corruption, poverty, and the affliction of an extended civil war, Uganda has registered remarkable successes in AIDS control.

Uganda's political leadership responded boldly to the AIDS challenge as early as 1986. President Yoweri Museveni took a prominent leadership role, declaring the AIDS struggle a national priority early in the epidemic. The government encouraged the participation of traditional religious and community leaders to promote AIDS education throughout the country. These efforts fostered an environment of relative societal openness, allowing reliable information about the disease to reach those at risk.[38] Using a multisector approach that bridged governmental and nongovernmental agencies and organizations, political leaders and health officials created a network of 12 AIDS control programs and an AIDS policy integrating active community participation with the media, popular culture, the arts, and the school system. AIDS prevention efforts successfully emphasized delaying sexual relations and changing sexual behavior among students. The programs catalyzed what one journalist called a quiet revolution in sexual behavior patterns among Uganda's youth.[39] HIV infection rates among 15- to 19-year-old prenatal clinic attendees fell dramatically.[40] The government also introduced counseling and support to people and families living with AIDS.[41]

Leaders in the Ugandan government and national AIDS program have sought innovative ways of partnering with civil society groups and the private sector. Local groups such as The AIDS Support Organization (TASO) have helped ease some of the pressure on the country's hospitals by establishing community-based health facilities that integrate governmental and NGO services and funding.[42] The Ugandan government has also shown leadership in pursuing options for antiretroviral (ARV) treatment through a UNAIDS pilot drug access initiative launched in 1997 with the participation of major pharmaceutical companies. In another important initiative, in May 2000, the Ugandan Ministry of Health joined with the International AIDS Vaccine Initiative (IAVI) to organize the first-ever AIDS vaccine trial in an African country.[43]

The Ugandan government's effective leadership against HIV/AIDS has paid off in terms of heightened public awareness, changed behaviors, and lower infection rates. While adult HIV infection levels rose sharply in many other African countries between 1997 and 2000—from about 13 percent to nearly 20 percent in South Africa and from about 25 to over 35 percent in Botswana—the rate decreased in Uganda, falling from 9.5 to 8.3 percent during the same period.[44]

In Brazil, widespread symptoms of governance problems, including the impeachment of a president on corruption charges, have not stopped the country from developing an AIDS program many international health officials consider exemplary. The Brazilian Ministry of Health deployed effective prevention and treatment efforts amid the turmoil surrounding President Fernando Collor de Mello's expulsion from office in 1991. Today, ranked an unimpressive 45th out of 102 countries in TI's Corruption Index,

Brazil remains a widely acclaimed success story in the global fight against HIV/AIDS.[45]

From the early 1990s, the Ministry of Health set the goal of providing access for all Brazilians to the best AIDS medications available. In 1996, soon after studies revealed the efficacy of antiretroviral "triple therapy," this commitment to universal access was enshrined in Brazilian law. Over the past decade, Brazil's national AIDS program has grown from a relatively modest effort to distribute AZT and medications for opportunistic infections into an intricate network involving inpatient and outpatient care centers, sophisticated laboratories, a computerized record-keeping system for drug dispensaries, and domestic pharmaceutical manufacturing.[46] Providing antiretroviral therapy to patients has nearly halved AIDS-related mortality rates.[47] In the large urban centers of São Paulo and Rio de Janeiro, where nearly one-third of all HIV and AIDS cases are concentrated, deaths due to AIDS have decreased by 54 and 73 percent, respectively.[48] The growth of outpatient care options—day hospitals, specialized care services, and therapeutic home care—has reduced the number of hospitalizations by 75 percent.[49]

Brazil's policy on procuring and producing antiretroviral drugs has provoked widespread international debate.[50] By investing in state-run pharmaceutical research labs, the Ministry of Health has been able to produce local generic versions of medications used in triple-therapy cocktails. Brazil's proven capacity for domestic generic drug production in turn furnishes leverage in price negotiations with multinational pharmaceutical companies, bringing down the prices of branded drugs.[51]

Undoubtedly, Brazil's economic power as a middle-income country made the creation of its ambitious AIDS program feasible.[52] But relative national wealth alone would not have been enough. The active participation of NGOs and other civil society organizations, the gay community, and dedicated health workers contributed decisively to building the political commitment needed to sustain the program. The inclusion of grassroots groups alongside international development agencies in discussions of goal setting, program management, and evaluation insured that planned measures would respond to the communities' real needs and capabilities.[53] And again, the lesson should not be lost that this strong response to HIV/AIDS was carried through despite persistent corruption problems and social turmoil.

Coalition Building and Political Will

That Thailand, Uganda, and Brazil have been able to establish relatively effective HIV/AIDS programs despite persistent corruption does not mean that, in general, corruption is not a significant barrier to progress against AIDS. These three countries are exceptions. Most high-prevalence countries with high corruption levels have so far been unable to generate similar results. But the examples of Thailand, Uganda, and Brazil show that corruption is not an insuperable obstacle. The claim that corruption is a prohibitive factor, dooming AIDS work in developing countries, is incorrect. There is no need to wait until corruption has been purged before moving to scale up assistance to developing countries for the fight against HIV/AIDS.

Each of these three successful countries has employed a multisectoral approach to AIDS involving prominent roles for national and international health NGOs, grassroots citizens' groups, and the private sector, in addition to state authorities. National-level, comprehensive AIDS care and treatment programs cannot be implemented by NGOs alone. They require the political power, leadership, and resources of states—ultimately the only actors able to secure the health of whole populations over time. Yet NGOs and participatory civil society groups can take a key role in combating health sector corruption and ensuring that funds allocated for HIV prevention and AIDS treatment actually reach intended targets.

On the one hand, national civil society organizations such as South Africa's TAC and global groups like Transparency International can monitor governments' AIDS policies and their use of resources, pressing for greater accountability and publicizing abuses. On the other hand, in partnership with government health authorities or, if necessary, as a temporary alternative to them, health NGOs can deliver AIDS services in poor countries—many are already doing so.[54] By providing support to the public sector, health NGOs, and local civil society groups in the developing world, donors can empower people to resist corruption and fight AIDS at the same time. This balanced support, guided by careful consultation with local community-based groups, is the right approach for rich-country governments and donors. Withholding support from a developing country government for lifesaving health initiatives, under the pretext that corruption must be eliminated before any large scale AIDS programs would be effective, is the wrong approach.

"Political will" has become a cliché of development discourse. But the reality is political actors can have great impact in the fight against AIDS, as Thailand, Uganda, and Brazil show. Many international health and development experts agree that the political commitment for the fight against AIDS, and other diseases primarily afflicting the poor, is at the highest level in history.[55] Where the will to confront HIV/AIDS is gaining strength among political officeholders, as in many developing countries today, rich-country governments and international donors must act immediately to ensure that financial and technical resources are available to assist poor countries in translating political resolve into effective action on the ground.

Homeless people, living in a city park because they are
HIV- positive, receive medicine from a community health
worker in Phnom Penh, Cambodia.

MYTH FOUR:
Prevention vs. Treatment?

Myth: The best way to control AIDS in the developing world is by putting all available resources into stronger prevention programs. In developing countries, costly treatment for people already infected with HIV should wait until prevention programs have been fully funded and deployed.

Response: Until the mid-1990s, the public health battle against AIDS in both rich and poor countries focused almost entirely on efforts to prevent new HIV infections, because no effective treatment for AIDS existed. Prevention during the first 15 years of the epidemic gradually grew more sophisticated: from behavioral education and condom promotion, HIV counseling and testing, to the treatment of sexually transmitted diseases (STDs) that can facilitate HIV transmission, and the blocking of mother-to-child transmission of HIV with drugs such as AZT.[1]

Advances in knowledge have strengthened the response to AIDS, yet, with each increment in technology, the gap between rich and poor has widened. In 1996, when highly active antiretroviral therapy (HAART) was introduced at the XI International Conference on AIDS in Vancouver, the gap became a chasm. In North America and Europe, HAART dropped AIDS mortality rates dramatically and improved life quality for people with AIDS.[2] At a cost of more than $10,000 per patient per year, HAART became and remains the standard of care for AIDS in wealthy countries.

In developing countries, where the world's HIV/AIDS burden is concentrated, a different standard applies. Though the cost of antiretrovirals (ARVs) has decreased sharply, more than 90 percent of people with HIV/AIDS remain without access to these lifesaving drugs. The worldwide struggle against AIDS has become a two-tiered system. While people in high-income regions (along with developing-world elites) enjoy access to effective antiretroviral treatment, public health authorities in low-income countries are advised to concentrate exclusively on prevention, and avoid the technical challenges and expense of treatment programs.[3]

This two-tiered strategy on HIV/AIDS has powerful defenders among academics, public health experts, and leaders of some of the world's most influential international health and development organizations.[4] Writing in the pages of scholarly and medical journals, many experts insist that for the foreseeable future, a choice between prevention and treatment will be unavoidable for poor countries because of the inadequacy of global AIDS funding and the weakness of many developing countries' health care systems.[5]

While respecting many of the scholars and health experts who defend this view, we disagree with their claims. We join the growing number of voices—represented by groups of people living with HIV/AIDS, various NGOs, and health care providers—who are challenging the prevention vs. treatment dichotomy.[6] Prevention of HIV and treatment of those suffering from the disease should not be seen as mutually exclusive, but as mutually reinforcing, complementary arms of a comprehensive global AIDS strategy. The following considerations argue for the immediate scaling up of prevention *and* treatment: (1) moral and social implications of denying treatment to millions of people already infected; (2) the structural limits to the efficacy of prevention programs when no treatment is available;

(3) the evidence of synergy between HIV prevention and treatment, and (4) treatment's role in providing political leverage for AIDS control, including stronger prevention efforts.

Moral and Social Crises

By recent UNAIDS estimates, more than 42 million men, women, and children are living with HIV and AIDS worldwide. At current rates, each day more than 15,000 people are newly infected with the virus and 8,000 die. The vast majority of people with HIV/AIDS live in the developing world and currently have no access to medical treatment for HIV disease itself or for the opportunistic infections associated with AIDS.[7] A strategy that emphasizes prevention to the exclusion of treatment offers no hope to these tens of millions of human beings. In fact, it passes a death sentence on them. One international official, speaking anonymously to the *Washington Post*, put it bluntly: "We may have to sit by and just see these millions of people die."[8] Such a position may be seen as public health realism. Yet realism of this type contradicts the basic principles of equity and human rights and acquiesces to what has been called a system of "global medical apartheid."[9]

The apartheid analogy has been drawn by people who fully measure its resonances. Among them are leaders of South Africa's Treatment Action Campaign (TAC), many of them antiapartheid veterans, and South African Supreme Court judge Edwin Cameron, an HIV-positive man who also struggled publicly against apartheid and now stands in the front ranks of the AIDS fight. Cameron argues that "the moral choices of the 1980s," which pitted people of conscience against South Africa's apartheid government, are "replicating themselves in a different form in the 2000s" in the battle for equal access to AIDS treatment.[10]

A first step toward altering the existing injustice is for the voices of poor people with AIDS to be heard. Increasingly today, activists living with HIV/AIDS from the developing world are speaking out, claiming a role in shaping international AIDS policy. They demand that decisions about such issues as the apportioning of funds for prevention and treatment no longer be made without consulting the people most directly concerned: people living with the virus, the vast majority of whom are poor. People living with HIV/AIDS "are 40 million strong and growing, and they are not telling us to concentrate all of our AIDS activities on prevention...They are not arguing that costly therapeutic interventions are not 'sustainable' in poor settings, not 'appropriate technology' for low-tech areas of the globe."[11]

Matthew Damane, a 25-year-old South African man from the township of Khayelitsha, outside Cape Town, receives ARV medications through a pilot program run by Médecins Sans Frontières (MSF) and the Treatment Action Campaign (TAC). Damane has drawn national and international attention as a spokesperson arguing from his own experience that AIDS treatment can be effectively implemented in resource-poor settings, and that poor Africans can indeed learn to comply with complex drug regimens:

> Because I have been helped so much by this medication, I wish I could share it with all the others in South Africa who face the same problem. Recently I went with a delegation of people from MSF and TAC to Brazil. We imported some generic antiretroviral medicine in defiance of the drug company patents....In Brazil, I saw a country that is not rich, but everybody there has access to antiretrovirals. That has the effect of reducing the stigma and bringing down the rate of infection. South Africa could do the same....The MSF programme, which is a trial providing antiretrovirals to people in Khayelitsha, is working very well. It

shows that people living in poor squatter communities can take the drugs properly and benefit from them. There are just millions more people waiting in the queue.[12]

Another resident of Khayelitsha receiving HAART through the MSF program echoed these sentiments: "People must know that a poor person like me living in a shack can take these drugs properly. They are my chance to live."[13]

Advocates of a prevention-only approach to HIV/AIDS in low-income countries argue that providing ARV treatment is not cost-effective in poor regions. A year of productive life can be gained in sub-Saharan Africa at a cost of about US$1, using HIV prevention strategies such as condom distribution and blood product screening in hospitals.[14] To gain a year of life with adult antiretroviral therapy will cost hundreds of times more.[15] Yet cost-effectiveness is only one factor to be examined in weighing clinical strategies.[16] Ethical and humanitarian aspects also demand consideration.

Moreover, as a physician who administers HAART to patients in the MSF pilot program has argued: "Narrow cost-effectiveness analyses of AIDS treatment in developing countries promote a medical ethic that would never be considered in the developed world." Rich countries apply cost-effectiveness analyses only very selectively in evaluating health care options. For the privileged to advise those in less-developed countries to adopt cost-effectiveness as their exclusive criterion in HIV/AIDS control is iniquitous.[17]

In addition to the moral problems raised, a prevention-only strategy fails to take seriously the overwhelming social and economic costs for countries with high HIV prevalence. Many of these infected people will die of AIDS in the midst of their most productive years of work and parenting, generating enormous losses not only for individuals and families, but for society as a whole.[18] Plummeting numbers of teachers, medical staff, and farmers have been already documented in the hardest-hit countries.[19] The generation of orphans to AIDS is growing exponentially, and four decades of gains in infant mortality and life expectancy have been lost to HIV in many African countries.[20] (For further discussion, see Myth 8.) Providing treatment to infected people, enabling them to continue fulfilling their parental responsibilities and contributing to society through work, will bring important social and economic payoffs. As Dr. Peter Piot, head of UNAIDS, has argued, prevention efforts will help save people from falling prey to infection in the future. But people, societies, economies, and whole countries are in urgent danger *now*, because of the threat of millions of premature deaths, and "only treatment can change that trajectory." The quality of the future that awaits numerous high-burden countries depends heavily on the quality of life they are able to provide to their HIV-infected citizens in the present.[21]

The Limits of Prevention

The prevention of new HIV infections must be the cornerstone of a comprehensive global AIDS strategy. Yet there are limits to what prevention efforts can achieve. Notably, though AIDS education and prevention have been underway in many countries since the 1980s, the spread of HIV has not been halted, and indeed has worsened steadily in many areas. While numerous moderately effective prevention initiatives and some dramatic successes can be cited, such victories are exceptional.

Inadequate support for prevention programs explains a substantial part of this failure. In 2001, a prevention leadership forum sponsored by several major foundations pointed out that "less than $1 billion is spent each year on HIV prevention programs in low- and middle-income countries," despite UNAIDS estimates that between $4 and $5 billion annually would be needed to sustain an effective global HIV prevention campaign.[22] Constrained budgets have meant that effective but relatively costly prevention measures— e.g., voluntary testing and counseling, treatment for STDs, and prevention of mother-to-child transmission of HIV using maternal antiretroviral therapy—have scarcely penetrated the poorest and most heavily burdened areas.[23] Yet, even where relatively vigorous prevention programs operate, structural obstacles often limit their effectiveness.

Early programs focusing on individual behavior change (for example, condom use) proved largely ineffectual in many settings. In recent years, some public health practitioners and scholars have shifted their attention to structural and environmental factors influencing people's ability to implement prevention messages. Important gains in knowledge have been achieved, and a growing "structural-factors literature" has emerged.[24] Yet this effort is relatively new, and numerous gaps in the research remain. Moreover, understanding how social and economic factors determine individuals' vulnerability to infection does not necessarily mean public health officials will be able to alter these patterns. As discussed in Myth 2, prevention strategies continue to clash with relentless social and economic pressures, including the effects of poverty, class disparities, structural racism, and gendered power differentials.

On matters such as condom use, carefully crafted, culturally appropriate programs are needed both to empower women and to change attitudes among men. Yet even the best planned initiatives—informed by social science research and relying on peer educators—often meet with frustration.[25] Individual risk behaviors are framed by a predisposing social context whose mechanisms escape the control of at-risk individuals and AIDS educators alike. Social obstacles and economic constraints must be negotiated before ordinary people can translate prevention theory into practice.

In areas where the epidemic has already gained a powerful hold, with adult prevalence rates reaching five percent or higher, conventional prevention strategies, even good ones, bring limited success. Once the epidemic has moved out from relatively focused high-risk groups into the general population, fully containing the spread of infections becomes virtually impossible. This is the current situation in many high-prevalence countries. Most HIV-positive people remain asymptomatic for years, so they can unwittingly transmit the virus to numerous others before learning they are infected. Under such conditions, traditional education and prevention campaigns can bring new infection rates down, but will not reduce them to zero. Even where prevention scores victories, as in Uganda, the epidemic continues, and the question of treatment for infected people demands to be addressed.[26]

Treatment/Prevention Synergy

HIV prevention and treatment for people with HIV and AIDS are not mutually exclusive options. On the contrary, a growing body of evidence suggests that the availability of treatment actually advances prevention goals. Prevention and treatment support each other.[27]

This synergy is clearest in the area of voluntary counseling and testing. Widespread HIV testing that gives people knowledge of their status is a cornerstone of effective prevention programs. When HIV-positive people are aware they are infected and receive appropriate counseling, they are better able to cope with the disease and to take action to protect their partners from infection. Similarly, people who know they are HIV-negative, especially in a high-prevalence area, find encouragement to reduce risk behaviors and maintain their health. Thus, voluntary counseling and testing programs have been shown to be one of the most effective prevention tools.[28]

Voluntary counseling and testing has been a pillar of Uganda's widely admired AIDS control program, as a means of fostering a collective response to the epidemic and bringing both seropositive and seronegative people into the system for counseling and support.[29] The role of voluntary counseling and testing is expanding in the US through the CDC's new campaign: a Serostatus Approach to Fighting the Epidemic (SAFE).[30] Its efficacy and cost-effectiveness in promoting risk-reducing behaviors has been demonstrated in randomized control trials.[31] For example, testing women of reproductive age is a critical part of programs to prevent mother-to-child transmission.[32]

However, broad-based community participation in voluntary counseling and testing is often difficult to achieve. Discrimination against HIV-infected people discourages many from seeking testing and counseling services.[33] Fears of stigmatization and the possibilities of domestic violence and desertion by husbands and family are strong barriers to women.[34] Hopelessness and fear of dying also discourage participation. In a study in Zambia, many people who did not want testing said they were probably infected anyway, and since there was no medical help for them, it was better not to know.[35] Where a significant number of people in the community already have AIDS, fatalistic attitudes are easy to understand. Without access to medical treatment, people may have much to lose by knowing their status and very little to gain. The psychological stresses are high not only on people undergoing the test but also on counselors.[36] Emotional difficulties such as anxiety and depression have been reported among health care workers in AIDS-endemic regions where no therapy is available to offer patients.[37] In such contexts, both counselors and prospective HIV test subjects may feel that an HIV-positive diagnosis amounts to a death sentence.

New approaches are desperately needed to encourage acceptance of voluntary counseling and testing. Linking it with access to life-saving treatment offers real hope and provides a clear incentive for testing, greatly strengthening AIDS control programs. When ARVs are offered, people have something important to gain from voluntary counseling and testing, whatever their test results.

Research has also shown that access to AIDS treatment can help reduce the stigma associated with HIV infection.[38] Over time, the availability of effective treatment modifies the social perception of the disease. This effect has been observed not only in the US and Europe, but also in rural Haiti. In the years before effective treatment, the uniformly fatal infection often inspired reactions of terror; people's fears of the virus spread to include individuals infected with it. In recent years, the availability of therapy has changed the situation by bringing about what has been called a "normalization" of HIV disease. Stigmatization and discrimination have been reduced, so HIV/AIDS can now be dealt with as a more straightforward, "normal," medical problem.[39] In wealthy countries, AIDS is now thought of by many as a chronic disease rather than as a death sentence. The greatly increased numbers of people seeking voluntary counseling and testing in low-income settings where treatment has been made available have confirmed the synergy between prevention and treatment. This effect has been observed in Brazil and in a pilot HAART programs in rural Haiti and in South Africa. At the Haitian clinic, use of free HIV counseling and testing services increased by more than 300 percent after the introduction of antiretroviral treatment for qualifying patients. An MSF program in South Africa saw a rise of over 1100 percent in the number of people voluntarily seeking testing after ARV therapy was introduced.[40]

Another public health consideration for expanding access to AIDS treatment is that ARV therapy may reduce the level of infectiousness. The evidence is mainly indirect, but convincing. Antiretrovirals act to suppress active replication of the virus and have been shown to reduce viral load in blood and semen.[41] Decreased viral load has been associated with lower risk for transmission of HIV infection.[42]

Unfortunately, easy access to ARVs in the absence of strong prevention programs can introduce new dangers, both for individuals and populations. While viral loads in patients undergoing treatment may fall below "detectable" levels, it does not necessarily fall to zero.[43] The risk of infection through sex with a person undergoing antiretroviral therapy treatment is reduced but *not* eliminated. This may not be fully appreciated by the wider population; alarming new trends in parts of the US and Europe show a decrease in the level of safer sex practiced among people living with HIV/AIDS and people at high risk for contracting the virus.[44] Studies among traditional high-risk groups suggest the availability of treatment may be reducing perceptions of risk. In the US, while many people living with HIV/AIDS are reaping the lifesaving benefits of improved treatment, prevention efforts remain inadequate and should be stepped up. Prevention and treatment must be strengthened together, in balance. A one-sided focus on either component reduces the efficacy of the overall program and hampers health authorities' capacity to control the pandemic.

Treatment Programs Create Political Leverage

Health experts have noted that treatment for current victims of a disease is easier to "sell" politically than prevention programs whose beneficiaries are not identifiable men, women, and children but rather an abstract, faceless statistical population. "Politicians would usually prefer to point to living individuals whose lives they can claim to have saved, than to point to a line on a graph representing future deaths averted because of their support for prevention." This may be because those who benefit from prevention "cannot be sure that they in fact benefitted as individuals and are therefore less likely to be grateful (and to show their gratitude at the ballot box)."[45]

We should hear the warning that emotional appeals may introduce confusion into rational debates on AIDS control. However, supporters of strengthened prevention efforts are mistaken to view the political appeal of AIDS treatment as necessarily harmful to the cause of effective HIV prevention work. On the contrary, the rising political force of AIDS treatment activism is the best hope for mobilizing greater worldwide support for all aspects of the AIDS struggle, including prevention.

These debates would not be happening at all—and they would not be generating the current level of international attention and concern—if it were not for the emotional and moral intensity of campaigns led by treatment activists. Through the pathos of individual faces and stories, a decisive human truth emerges: the lives of people with HIV/AIDS matter. When policymakers and ordinary people respond to this truth and allow it to influence their decision-making, it is a sign that political and economic rationality can be informed by solidarity and compassion.[46]

The demand for treatment creates a degree of political leverage that prevention alone is unlikely to generate.[47] By forming a strategic alliance with the treatment community, HIV prevention advocates can add moral and political force to the analytic strength of their call for dramatically increased international investment in prevention. Just as prevention and treatment reinforce each other in AIDS control efforts, so they should join forces in the political arena to demand increased resources for balanced, multisectoral AIDS control programs.

HIV/AIDS and Health Care in an Unequal World

At the dawn of the ARV era, observers like Dr. Jonathan Mann had discerned an evolving economic caste system within the global AIDS struggle. The 1996 Vancouver AIDS conference at which HAART was introduced bore the title "One World, One Hope." Mann noted the title's unintended irony: "Today, there is not 'one world' against AIDS, and this reality of separatism...threatens progress against AIDS and is the central reason why real leadership and coherent global action against [the pandemic] have become virtually impossible." Unfortunately, Mann's concern with "separatism" has lost little of its relevance in the years since he issued his warning.[48]

Fundamental considerations of equity demand that we organize to transform a system that assigns people with identical clinical conditions to life or death, based only on their ability or inability to pay. Of course, the determination of health outcomes by economic status is in no way unique to HIV/AIDS. Yet this fact increases, rather than reduces, the importance of confronting egregious injustices in the availability of AIDS treatment. AIDS crystallizes the biological and structural violence of a whole global system in which poverty kills by direct and indirect means. But breaking this cycle for AIDS would be a powerful step toward justice in health care and the sign of a renewed determination to foster solidarity in a deeply divided world. Thanks to the work of treatment activists, AIDS focuses public attention and concern; other deadly diseases that disproportionately affect poor people have not created similar constituencies. The charged character of HIV/AIDS debates should be used politically to maximum effect. AIDS can become the "wedge issue" that enables a new level of awareness, debate, and action to attack the full range of global health inequalities.

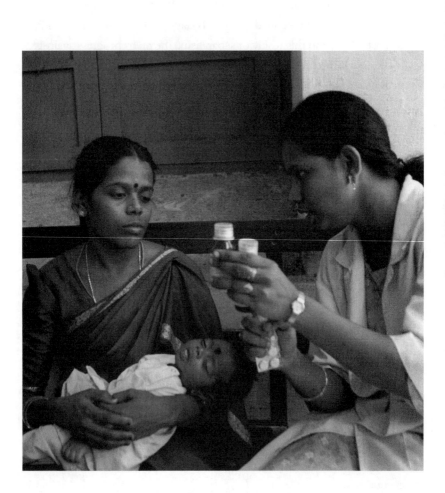

New mother gets medicine and advice from nurse at
government-run hospital in Madras, India.

MYTH FIVE:
Obstacles to AIDS Treatment in Poor Countries

Myth: AIDS treatment for the poor makes sense morally, but it is not feasible technically. The antiretroviral drugs (ARVs) used to treat AIDS are so expensive that it is not economically realistic to provide them to the tens of millions of HIV-infected people in the developing world. Moreover, the successful delivery of ARVs requires networks of sophisticated health facilities, fully equipped clinical laboratories, and trained physicians. Very few poor countries have adequate facilities and services, and trying to deliver ARVs without sufficient infrastructure will lead to widespread mishandling of the medicines, unleashing drug-resistant strains of HIV and causing a public health disaster.

Response: Since 1996, highly active antiretroviral therapy (HAART) has been the standard of care for people with AIDS living in high-income countries. In sub-Saharan Africa, by contrast, less than one percent of those patients who need treatment are able to obtain it.[1] The moral iniquity of this situation is obvious. Yet some specialists maintain that, while the ethical arguments may be compelling, delivering ARV treatment on a large scale in developing countries is impossible in practice. In this chapter, we will examine critically the three chief objections emphasized by health experts and political officials when they question the technical feasibility of AIDS treatment in the developing world: (1) excessive costs; (2) inadequate infrastructure; and (3) the risk of spreading drug-resistant strains of the virus.

The High Cost of Treatment

A yawning gap separates the yearly per-patient cost of HAART from the average per capita income in the countries with the highest HIV/AIDS burden. This fact should not end the debate about HAART in resource-poor settings but begin it. Three points need to be considered with the claim that AIDS treatment for the poor is prohibitively expensive: (1) the sharp downward trend in ARV prices; (2) the new institutions and partnerships working to make HAART affordable in poor communities; and (3) the heavy costs of not treating the millions of people living with HIV/AIDS, coupled with the positive economic returns of investing in health.

In the late 1990s, the annual costs of combination therapy in wealthy countries could exceed $20,000 per patient when laboratory tests and provider fees were factored in.[2] In 2001, drug costs alone for most HAART regimens in high-income countries still ran more than $10,000 per patient per year.[3] However, by 2002, the cost of ARVs for many poor countries had been pushed precipitously downward by a combination of activist pressure on the pharmaceutical industry, price concessions from research-based drug manufacturers, and the dissemination of generic ARVs. (See Myth 7.)

Throughout the late 1990s and into the present decade, activist organizations including ACT UP, the Health GAP Coalition, and South Africa's Treatment Action Campaign (TAC) have carried on sustained campaigns targeting large multinational pharmaceutical firms' prices on AIDS medications. Activists' direct-action tactics were complemented by the policy and advocacy work of international medical organizations like Médecins Sans Frontières (MSF), whose "Access to Essential Medications" campaign was launched in 1998.[4] By bringing international public attention to bear on the research-based pharmaceutical companies' pricing policies, activists and progressive health organizations pressured the firms to institute systems of differential pricing that would open the possibility for government health services and NGOs in developing countries to purchase ARVs at discounted rates.

The entry of generic drug manufacturers into the international HIV/AIDS drug market transformed the context of AIDS treatment debates. In February 2001, Cipla Ltd., an Indian generic drug firm, offered to make generic versions of three leading ARV medications available in Africa for a total of less than $1 a day per patient ($350 a year) through MSF, or for $600 a year if the drugs were purchased by governments.[5] Subsequent cuts have reduced the price of generic ARVs still further, with the Indian firm Aurobindo offering one three-drug combination for $209 a year in mid-2002.[6] Responding to the pressure of public opinion and market competition from the generics industry, major research-based pharmaceutical companies announced initiatives to lower their own prices on AIDS medications in poorer regions, especially sub-Saharan Africa.[7]

If the annual cost of treating an AIDS patient using ARVs can be brought down from $10,000 to near $200, then assumptions about the economic impossibility of providing HAART in the developing world must be revised. Of course, the cost of AIDS treatment involves more than the price of drugs. Transportation and storage of medicines, personnel, monitoring, and the clinical management of side effects must all be factored into the final price tag. Two hundred dollars per patient per year, plus these additional expenses, is still too heavy a burden for very poor countries.

However, the parameters of the debate have shifted irrevocably. With adequate international assistance for poor countries on the front lines of the crisis, purely financial arguments against the provision of ARVs crumble.

Moreover, new institutions and partnerships are working to further lower the costs of expanded AIDS treatment in poor countries. The most prominent of these new initiatives is the Global Fund to Fight AIDS, Tuberculosis, and Malaria (GFATM), inaugurated in 2001 by UN secretary general Kofi Annan.[8] In October 2002, in a dramatic and widely discussed move, the GFATM leadership announced that it would encourage programs receiving money from the fund to purchase generic medicines in cases of equal qaulity, rather than more expensive, branded products. This announcement from GFATM executive director Dr. Richard Feachem was welcomed by treatment activists as a significant step toward making HAART globally affordable.[9]

If we are going to discuss the high cost of ARVs, we must also ask what the price will be if people with HIV/AIDS in poor countries are not treated. The enormous social and macroeconomic costs inflicted on countries hit by soaring AIDS morbidity and mortality are discussed in Myths 4 and 8. Here we focus on specific costs and cost savings in the health sector. A growing body of evidence suggests that treating patients with ARVs can actually save health systems money. While the initial drug procurement outlays are considerable, ARVs in the US, Europe, Canada, and Brazil have brought demonstrable savings by reducing the need for other forms of medical interventions, such as costly hospitalizations and treatment for opportunistic infections. The example of Brazil, a country with a GNP far lower than the US and Western European countries, is most instructive. The Brazilian Ministry of Health estimated that over a quarter of a million AIDS-related hospital admissions were prevented during the period 1997–2000 by the government's universal-access ARV treatment policy. The averted hospitalizations saved the Brazilian Unified Health System US$677 million, suggesting that the price of ARV therapy is substantially counterbalanced by associated cost reductions.[10]

In calculating the costs of delivering HAART to poor countries and communities, we should also remember that the 42 million HIV-positive people in the world will not all require ARV therapy immediately. While all people living with HIV/AIDS will eventually need treatment, HIV disease progresses very slowly in some cases, and HAART coverage can be extended step by step, with priority given to the most seriously ill. WHO estimates that approximately six million people in developing regions were in immediate need of ARV treatment as of the end of 2002.[11]

"Inadequate Infrastructure"

A second objection to providing HAART is that the lack of infrastructure and trained health professionals makes distribution unfeasible. Indeed, elements of the health infrastructure that people from affluent countries generally take for granted are inadequate or absent in large areas of the developing world, and many low-income countries face serious shortages of qualified health workers. Yet these deficiencies should not halt efforts to deliver treatment to people living with HIV/AIDS in poor regions. Rather, where infrastructure is lacking, the new challenges of providing AIDS treatment bring opportunities to expand and improve previously suboptimal health services.

The "inadequate infrastructure" argument is untenable for four distinct reasons. First, all poor countries are not alike. Relevant infrastructure in many regions is more robust than most health experts from wealthy countries have acknowledged. Second, specialists are finding ways to streamline and simplify the delivery of ARVs in resource-poor settings. Third, where infrastructure or health personnel are lacking, new local, national, and international partnerships and alliances can be forged to strengthen capacity. Fourth, although poor regions by definition lack material resources and tools, their social resources can be mobilized to strengthen health care delivery, including the provision of ARVs, even as their clinical infrastructure is being built up.

Unexpected Strengths

Health infrastructure in developing countries varies widely, and even very poor regions are not uniformly deprived. In Africa, for example, as dozens of countries gained independence from colonial rule in the 1960s, many realized significant health improvements. Newly independent states expanded health services, built large modern hospitals, established research institutes, initiated community dispensaries, and strengthened disease control programs. Access to sanitation and clean water improved dramatically.[12]

Despite setbacks caused by the debt crisis and the implementation of structural adjustment programs in the 1980s (see Myth 1), fruits of these early infrastructural investments survive.[13] In some countries, such as South Africa, Zimbabwe, and Kenya, health infrastructure is considerable. An analysis of the 14 sub-Saharan African nations most heavily impacted by HIV/AIDS reveals that 72 percent of children in these countries are vaccinated against measles every year, and over 80 percent of pregnant women receive some form of prenatal care.[14] Even the poorest nations have well-established networks of rural primary-care and district-level secondary care facilities, and virtually every country in the world has some health service mechanisms in place to expand childhood immunization coverage and to control tuberculosis, leprosy, and other communicable diseases. Where the public sector is lacking in many of the world's poorest countries, NGOs and private mission hospitals often fill the gap by providing health services in both rural and urban settings.[15] This important infrastructure should not be overlooked simply because it does not always match rich-country standards. In the short term, HAART may be impracticable in many localities, but it does not mean that it is impracticable for an entire country, much less the whole "developing world."

Streamlining and Simplifying ARV Delivery

Though we have just stressed the need to avoid sweeping generalizations, it is safe to say that most people in poor countries have little regular contact with health care facilities run by fully trained physicians. Rather, most generally receive medical care from small local primary care clinics staffed by nurses or village health workers. Most of these clinics have no rudimentary laboratory capability. Unquestionably, providing safe, effective ARV therapy under such conditions is a major clinical and administrative challenge.

Good AIDS treatment is not just a matter of handing out fistfuls of ARVs but of providing the medications within a rational framework. Decisions about when to begin therapy and what drug regimens to use are based on a continuously evolving body of medical knowledge. Health workers need special training to administer ARVs and manage side effects. Since ARVs can have both short- and long-term side effects that range from transient discomfort to life-threatening toxicities, health workers must learn to recognize and respond rapidly to symptoms of drug complications. Reliable drug distribution systems and mechanisms for assessing treatment adherence and monitoring clinical effectiveness must be in place. Yet pilot ARV treatment programs in resource-poor settings around the world have begun to show that these daunting challenges are not insurmountable.

In 2002, based on evidence from these pilot programs and experience with ARVs in wealthier countries, WHO released a set of guidelines for initiating and monitoring ARV therapy in settings with limited resources and clinical infrastructure.[16] Recommendations for management of side effects are included, as well as specific requirements for certain subgroups of patients, such as children, pregnant women, and people with hepatitis or TB co-infections. The guidelines are directed towards health policy makers in resource-poor countries to serve as a practical framework for implementing AIDS treatment programs. Instead of producing a single set of protocols, the document provides information for designing treatment manuals appropriate to local contexts. Standardized drug combinations are recommended, rather than individually tailored regimens, to facilitate decision making for health workers issuing prescriptions and to streamline the procurement and management of drug supplies.

The tests used in affluent hospital settings for monitoring a patient's response to ARV therapy, such as viral load and CD4 cell counts, are costly and depend upon sophisticated equipment and expertise. Where such technology is unavailable, the guidelines recommend using algorithms, based on observable physical symptoms, and simple laboratory tests to monitor the progress of treatment. At the same time, there is a need to develop reliable, yet inexpensive, tests that require only basic lab skills and no specialized equipment. A November 2001 meeting entitled "Monitoring and Diagnostic Tools for the Management of Antiretroviral Therapy in Resource-Poor Settings," sponsored by Gay Men's Health Crisis and Project Inform, brought together researchers and field workers from around the world, along with representatives of equipment manufacturers and pharmaceutical companies to discuss how to develop viable alternatives.[17] Several new technologies were advanced and discussed. Support for more initiatives of this kind is needed.

Building Infrastructure Through Partnerships

Bringing together health workers from countries with considerable experience in treating HIV/AIDS, and from countries just beginning to expand access, offers an excellent means to strengthen medical infrastructure in resource-poor settings. One such initiative, unveiled at the United Nations General Assembly Special Session on HIV/AIDS (UNGASS) in June 2001, involves hospitals in a number of European countries (including France, Italy, Luxembourg, Portugal, and Spain) that have established direct ties with partner hospitals and clinics in Africa. Such partnerships enable staff exchanges and skill sharing between European and African health facilities, as well as direct transfers of money, equipment, and medical supplies. Similar programs exist among some US health facilities and partner institutions in developing countries, and efforts are under way to multiply these connections. Partners In Health and Physicians for Human Rights have developed materials to assist people in the US interested in creating or supporting links with medical institutions and care providers in low-income countries.[18]

Another promising partnership is the Academic Alliance for AIDS Care and Prevention in Africa, initiated by 13 leading experts in HIV/AIDS from Africa and North America. The alliance involves local and international NGOs and participating pharmaceutical companies, as well as the Infectious Disease Society of America (IDSA). At the Makerere University Medical School in Kampala, Uganda, the alliance is creating the first large-scale medical training center in Africa dedicated to training health workers in HIV/AIDS treatment. The program, slated to open in

2003, will expand access and improve care for people living with HIV/AIDS throughout the continent.[19] A contribution of $11.7 million from the Pfizer Foundation has paid for the building, equipment for the facility, and initial operating costs. The program aims to bring patients the highest standards of care, including the latest ARV therapies. According to Dr. Nelson Sewankambo, dean of the Makerere Medical School and member of the alliance:

> Our goal is to strengthen medical infrastructure, replicate it across Africa and bring the latest medicines to bear on treating this disease so that African doctors and nurses can offer modern AIDS care to their patients. We expect to train at least 80 clinicians per year in the latest AIDS treatment techniques, and as they return to their posts in Uganda and other African countries they will, in turn, train many more doctors and other medical personnel. Once the facility is fully operational, we also expect to treat up to 50,000 HIV/AIDS patients with the kind of care that is available in the developed world but not yet widely used in Africa.[20]

Linkages between academic institutions also provide a way to improve infrastructure, transfer technology, and train health personnel. Public health experts, medical doctors, and researchers from dozens of universities throughout the US and elsewhere are actively working on HIV/AIDS-related research projects in collaboration with their counterparts from poor countries. In the process, they are bringing resources to areas in need and helping build health infrastructure. Many university-based ventures have recently expanded their activities to include the provision of ARVs. Although most are currently modest in scope, such programs provide an additional potential for scaling up AIDS treatment in disadvantaged settings.[21]

Community-Based AIDS Treatment in Haiti

Where local health infrastructure is initially inadequate, linking outside technical support to the mobilization of a community's own social resources can enable the successful deployment of ARV treatment. Dedicated community health workers without advanced medical training can take on numerous responsibilities vital to the functioning of an effective treatment program. Meanwhile, treatment projects will prove most effective when they integrate the provision of ARVs with support for patients' social and economic well-being. These principles are demonstrated by a growing number of pilot HAART programs in resource-poor settings.

One example comes from Haiti's rural Central Plateau, one of the most deprived regions of the Western Hemisphere's poorest country. It is the site of Clinique Bon Sauveur, operated cooperatively by the Boston-based medical NGO Partners In Health (PIH) and its Haitian NGO partner Zanmi Lasante (ZL). These organizations have worked together to combat HIV/AIDS in the Central Plateau region since the late 1980s. Efforts focused initially on community-based prevention. In 1995–96, however the clinic's prenatal unit began providing AZT to HIV-positive pregnant women to prevent mother-to-child transmission of the virus.

Amid political conflict, deepening poverty, and dangerous migration patterns driven by economic desperation, central Haiti's AIDS crisis worsened during the 1990s.[22] In late 1998, PIH and ZL launched the HIV Equity Initiative, offering ARV combination therapy free of charge to patients with advanced HIV disease who were judged to be in imminent danger of death. Infrastructure to support the treatment program was minimal, by wealthy-country standards, and the high cost of medicines raised questions about sustainability. However, the decision was made to prioritize poor patients' urgent need for lifesaving treatment over deliberations about the appropriateness of introducing "first-world" therapies in a "third-world" setting.[23] When the program began, laboratory tests for CD4 cell counts and viral load were unavailable in Haiti. Instead, to identify patients in greatest need and to monitor the progress of therapy, medical staff relied on clinical assessment, including the nature and frequency of opportunistic infections, patients' weight and neurological status, and very basic laboratory studies.

The treatment model used to deliver HAART at Clinique Bon Sauveur reflects previous experience with Directly Observed Treatment (DOT) for tuberculosis: hence the combined acronym DOT-HAART.[24] In the DOT-HAART approach, community health workers, known as *accompagnateurs*, visit patients daily and supervise their pill-taking. *Accompagnateurs* come from the local community and have no formal medical training beyond what they receive through the clinic staff. The staff is also responsible for general social support—including assistance with children's school fees and the organization of monthly meetings in which patients can discuss their illness and other problems. The program also supplies limited nutritional supplements.

When strategies like DOT-HAART are used, much more can be achieved in resource-poor settings than AIDS treatment skeptics suggest. Of course, even in the most favorable contexts, patients may struggle with adherence to daily medication regimens that must be continued for life and that can produce disturbing side effects. Yet patient compliance and good treatment outcomes depend less on cutting-edge medical technology than on a commitment to equity, individualized care, and concern for the full range of patients' needs, including social and financial support.[25] Such challenges can be effectively addressed in a community clinic setting characterized by close personal attention from staff, strong relationships between health workers and the surrounding community, and the mobilization of local social capital in support of health goals. This does not mean that advanced medical technologies are unimportant or "inappropriate" for resource-poor regions. It does mean, even as we work to bring the best available technologies to areas that lack them, that we can begin the progressive rollout of HAART, working with tools that currently exist and integrating new ones as they become available.

The results of the HIV Equity Initiative demonstrate compellingly that ARV therapy can be delivered successfully in a setting of extreme material poverty. The majority of patients have shown striking health improvements, characterized by weight gain and abatement of AIDS-related symptoms.[26] These positive changes are reflected in patients' subjective reports about their quality of life and sense of agency and hope. Today the HIV Equity Initiative provides treatment to over 350 patients (about 12 percent of all HIV patients followed by the PIH team in Haiti) using the DOT-HAART strategy.[27] Many have returned from extreme debilitation to lead healthy and productive lives. (See photos on next page.)

Though modest in size, the Haitian DOT-HAART program is set to expand in coming years if support from international donors is forthcoming.[28] The lessons learned are already significant. The HIV Equity Initiative and other pilot projects have developed clinical tools for the specific challenges of ARV therapy in resource-poor settings. They have confirmed the efficacy of community-based approaches in providing psychosocial support for patients, promoting treatment adherence, and reducing stigma. The Haitian program has linked prevention and care tightly. Perhaps most important, such initiatives have underscored the human resources that already exist in many disadvantaged communities. Observes Paul Farmer, medical director of the

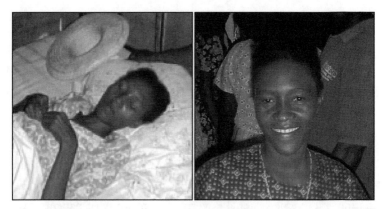

Adeline, a single mother of two boys, was diagnosed with HIV infection when she was in her early twenties. For almost ten years, she was treated for opportunistic infections. By October 1999, Adeline, overcome with a life-threatening diarrheal infection, weighed only 79 pounds. In late November, she began ARV therapy. After five weeks, she had gained 26 pounds. In 2003, she remains asymptomatic, is able to care for her family, and is an HIV-outreach worker at the Clinique Bon Sauveur. "What the medicines have done for me is amazing," she said.

Clinique Bon Sauveur, "Within every community beset by poverty and HIV are scores of willing individuals who wish to be trained to serve as community health workers."[29] Only by drawing fully on these local capacities will health organizations be able to expand pilot projects to meet the demand for HAART.

"Scaling Up" from Pilot Treatment Programs

A growing number of programs in other regions confirms the feasibility of ARV treatment in resource-poor settings. Médecins Sans Frontières (MSF) has led some of the most successful efforts. In 2001, the organization began AIDS treatment projects in Cambodia, Cameroon, Guatemala, Honduras, Kenya, Malawi, South Africa, Thailand, Uganda, and Ukraine, enrolling nearly 2,200 patients by the following year.[30] By the end of 2003, MSF aims to double the number of people on ARVs in its existing projects and to open new projects in Burkina Faso, Burma, Ethiopia, Indonesia, Laos, Mozambique, Peru, Rwanda, Zambia, and Zimbabwe.[31]

Ultimately, scaling up to move beyond the level of pilot projects will require integration of ARV treatment into comprehensive national AIDS control programs. Treatment must be coordinated with prevention efforts and ongoing patient care and provided within a context of reliable patient monitoring and psychosocial support. WHO guidelines on ARV therapy in resource-poor settings are part of a broader strategy to facilitate a global scale-up of AIDS treatment. The organization's goal is to see, in such settings, three million people on treatment by the year 2005. In the developing world, this would represent an enormous increase in the number of patients currently on ARVs.[32] Achieving this ambitious target will extend millions of lives, gain millions of years of productive work for struggling economies, and keep millions of threatened families intact. The missing element is the financial backing needed to make the goal a reality.

To complete the discussion of infrastructure, it is important to point out that systematic implementation of AIDS treatment with ARVs can be a way to create and strengthen infrastructure in places where it is currently inadequate. Since HAART was introduced in wealthy countries, doctors have been learning as they go how best to care for patients on therapy. Because of the urgent need to assist very ill patients, research and the refinement of treatment protocols have necessarily gone hand in hand with the delivery of treatment. During this time, no one suggested waiting until the research was complete to treat ill and dying patients.

With proper levels of international funding and technical support, medical personnel and health officials in poor countries can begin to scale up the deployment of ARV treatments—creating and refining the necessary infrastructure, supply chains, and administrative protocols as they go. The clinical skills, laboratory equipment and procedures, supply networks, and management systems that will come into being to ensure the effective delivery of ARVs will enhance health care systems in low-income countries. The delivery of treatment creates and consolidates infrastructure, improving both individual patient outcomes and the health system as a whole.

Fears About Drug Resistance

The third major concern about the provision of AIDS treatment in poor countries is the fear of drug resistance. The dramatic success of AIDS therapy in wealthy countries is increasingly threatened by the emergence of forms of HIV that are resistant to existing ARVs.[33] Many believe that an effort to introduce these drugs on a mass scale in the developing world would open a virological Pandora's box. Three possible sources of drug resistance have been cited: incorrect prescribing or mishandling of medications, patients' failure to adhere to treatment regimens, and drug supply interruptions. Problems in any of these areas would create conditions in which drug-resistant variants of HIV might appear and spread.

Anxiety about the emergence of HIV strains that are resistant to current ARVs is, unfortunately, far from unreasonable. The danger is real and must be guarded against wherever ARV treatment is made available. Yet there are ways to address each of the potential sources of drug resistance and to minimize the risks as ARVs are distributed more widely in low-income settings. We discuss each of the major problem areas in turn. Additionally, we present arguments from an increasing number of health experts who claim that the best way to avoid large-scale drug misuse and consequent resistance is not by trying to prevent poor people from gaining access to ARVs, but instead by creating rational, equity-based mechanisms to manage the supply and distribution of the drugs.

In the absence of treatment, HIV can multiply rapidly in the bloodstream of an infected person. ARVs act to inhibit the process of viral multiplication. Unfortunately, HIV can become resistant to any single drug via mutations, yielding new viral strains less susceptible to the drug's specific action. When this occurs, drugs are rendered less effective against these resistant forms of the virus. Resistance develops quickly in patients taking only a single drug (monotherapy) or even two ARVs (dual therapy).[34] Indeed, acquired resistance is probably inevitable in even the best of settings. However, the use of combinations of three or more differently acting drugs creates a multipronged attack on the virus, making it much more difficult for resistant forms of HIV to emerge.

The area of the world where the greatest amount of resistance to AIDS medications occurs is not in poor countries, where the medications have, until recently, been virtually impossible to obtain. Rather, the majority of drug resistance is found in the major urban centers of wealthy countries. These resistant strains are in many cases the lingering result of widespread mono- and dual therapy, which was the standard approach to care in wealthy countries before HAART became available in 1996. In cities such as San Francisco, drug resistance is reaching troubling proportions, and there are increasing reports of drug-resistant HIV strains being transmitted to previously uninfected people.[35]

The lesson to learn from countries with experience in treating HIV/AIDS with ARVs is that, to be effective in the long term, combination therapies of at least three drugs must be used from the beginning of treatment. For this reason, the WHO guidelines advise against dual drug regimens, instead recommending the use of triple therapy.[36] To prevent the mishandling of drugs, patients receiving ARV therapy must necessarily be under the care of a trained health provider who follows established protocols. Monitoring the progress of treatment is critical, not only from the perspective of each patient's welfare, but also as a means to control the problem of drug resistance. When a patient no longer responds to treatment, it may be a sign that the virus is getting out of control and may be an indication of acquired drug resistance. Locally appropriate guidelines to recognize treatment failure must be made available to health providers. Also, secondary (or salvage) regimens must be defined so that patients may be switched to an alternative drug regimen when necessary.

In the absence of organized treatment programs, people who are ill may purchase ARVs privately or acquire them by illicit means. The possibilities of unregulated dissemination of ARVs through pilfering and black market sales are very real concerns. A recent report in the medical journal *Lancet* cites a study on ARV utilization in Harare, Zimbabwe, which the author describes as "retroviral anarchy."[37] In this study, 27 percent of retail pharmacists were found to be stocking ARVs, and at least 17 percent of patients were taking AZT monotherapy.[38] The study reported, "prescribers and dispensers were utilising any [antiretroviral drug] that they could lay their hands on. It appeared that no effort had been made to develop treatment guidelines."[39] Based on these considerations, some health experts warn that time for preventing widespread evolution of drug-resistant HIV may be running out. And some are arguing that ARV treatment should not be provided in an ad hoc manner, but should be integrated into national HIV/AIDS control programs, especially in high-prevalence countries.[40]

Compliance

Starting patients on an appropriate drug regimen is only the first step in implementing a good treatment program. Effective suppression of viral reproduction also depends upon maintaining therapeutic drug levels in the patient's body. Even a minor drop in drug levels may allow the virus an opportunity to replicate and increase the chance of drug resistance. Thus, a key to minimizing drug resistance is rigorous adherence to the prescribed treatment regimen—in other words, taking the right amounts of the drugs at the right times. Decreases in adherence by as little as 10 percent have been associated with a doubling of viral load (the amount of virus in a patient's bloodstream).[41] In other words, to keep the virus under control, patients need to take their medications correctly at least 90 percent of the time.

Adherence to lifelong drug regimens is difficult under the best of circumstances, leading many to argue that adherence will be even more problematic in settings where poverty, lack of education, and stigma pose additional challenges. To some extent, these arguments are based on earlier experiences with ARV treatment. Just a few years ago, many people living with AIDS in the US were prescribed as many as 33 pills per day. But new generations of less toxic medications are now available, enabling patients to adhere to their drug regimens by reducing side effects and pill count. Today, one of the most common drug regimens requires just one tablet in the morning and four at night, and the streamlining process continues.[42] Another fixed-dose combination permits patients to take one pill twice a day; several once–a–day regimens have also been shown to be effective. Nonetheless, adherence remains an ongoing concern that must be addressed in the planning and implementation of all AIDS treatment programs.

The first indications from developing countries are encouraging on this point. Preliminary results from pilot programs in low-income countries have shown levels of patient adherence comparable to those seen in wealthier settings. In an AIDS treatment project conducted by MSF in Khayelitsha, outside of Cape Town, South

Africa, the survival rate among 300 patients has been 90 percent, in spite of the advanced stage of disease among many of them upon entry.[43] At the end of six months of treatment, 90 percent of patients had undetectable viral loads, indicating effective viral suppression. Another South African program, affiliated with the University of Cape Town, showed that, among 104 patients who had completed 48 weeks of therapy, adherence was 89 percent.[44] In a Senegalese treatment program, 87 percent of patients achieved the target of 80 percent adherence, and 59 percent had undetectable viral loads after 18 months of therapy.[45] Reports on patient adherence from the US are no better, and in some cases worse, than the levels of drug adherence found in these and comparable studies.[46]

Managing Drug Supplies

A viable system for managing supplies of ARVs is essential to ensure uninterrupted provision of medications to people on therapy and to avoid widespread unregulated availability of drugs. Some experts have been looking at tuberculosis control programs as a model for delivery of ARVs on a large scale. Like AIDS treatment, TB therapy requires close supervision of patients, precise record keeping, reliable supply mechanisms, and skilled laboratory support. WHO recommends DOTS (directly observed treatment, short course) as its preferred TB treatment strategy. In addition to specific treatment policies, the prerequisites for a DOTS control program include government commitment to nationwide coverage, establishment of a system of regular drug supply, and establishment and maintenance of a monitoring system. Many countries have developed significant infrastructure for the treatment and management of tuberculosis. Countries that have developed DOTS-based national TB programs have in effect already created the foundation for an effective response to the challenge of AIDS treatment.

This concept is at the core of the Haitian program described above, and is also central to a recent proposal by Anthony Harries of Malawi's National Tuberculosis Control Program.[47] Harries and colleagues aim to link the provision of ARV treatment for HIV disease in African countries to health delivery infrastructure already established (or in the process of taking shape) for national tuberculosis control. The potential public health synergy is clear. Epidemiologically, Africa's TB and HIV epidemics are deeply intertwined. Coordinated action against the two diseases is a necessity. Anchoring ARV provision in existing TB control infrastructure would be efficient and cost-effective, avoiding unnecessary duplication of services, procedures, and personnel. As Harries and colleagues observe: "Good national tuberculosis control programmes have the experience of providing, monitoring, and supervising care of patients for long periods of time, and are in a position to develop and implement a structure within which antiretroviral drugs can be safely and effectively administered."[48]

It simply no longer makes sense to talk about the distribution of ARVs in poor countries, as some still wish to do, in a hypothetical mode ("Should we or shouldn't we?"). This way of posing the problem is rapidly being overtaken by the facts. Antiretrovirals are beginning to reach people with HIV/AIDS who live in developing countries through a variety of largely unregulated channels, and this pattern is certain to intensify as awareness of the medicines and demand for them rise. In other words, it is no longer a question of *whether* ARVs will be made available in poor countries, but only of *how* the drugs will reach these countries and their stricken populations. Will ARVs be administered through rational, sustained, and inclusive programs that aim to respect equity and the rules of good medical practice? Or will the drugs circulate chaotically, with no central oversight and administration, no quality control, no mechanisms to achieve distributional equity, and little or no qualified supervision of patients and their treatment regimens?[49] These are the real choices: the delivery of HAART through rational, coordinated programs on one side, "antiretroviral anarchy" on the other.[50]

High costs, inadequate infrastructure, and the dangers of drug resistance are regularly cited as reasons why HAART cannot or should not be provided in resource-poor settings. Each of these issues points to a legitimate area of concern for AIDS treatment programs. Yet, under scrutiny, these arguments against the rapid deployment of ARV treatment in developing countries collapse. Today, momentum for treatment is building, as evidenced by widespread support for WHO's call to have three million people in developing countries on ARVs by 2005. This "three by five" challenge has become a rallying cry for many activists and members of the international health community.[51]

The technical obstacles to treatment and strategies for overcoming them are now widely discussed. Ultimately, of course, these discussions are affected by moral orientations and political interests, avowed or implicit. In the past, the burden of proof has fallen on the sick, the poor, and their allies to demonstrate that providing high-quality medical treatment in poor communities is feasible, appropriate, and sustainable. It is time for that to change. Perhaps skeptics should bear the burden of explaining why poor people in Khayelitsha or the Haitian Central Plateau should not receive the same life prolonging treatment received by hundreds of thousands in affluent countries.[52]

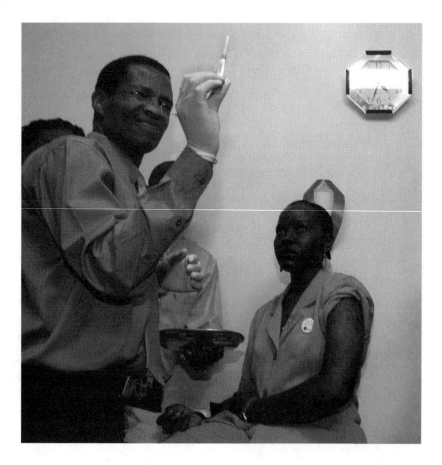

Woman participates in AIDS vaccine trial in Nairobi, Kenya in 2001. The first human trials took place in 1987.

MYTH SIX:
Vaccines

Myth: Promising reports about AIDS vaccines undergoing human trials mean that a vaccine will soon be available to prevent HIV infection. Once a vaccine against HIV is successfully developed, the AIDS crisis will be solved.

Response: A September 2001 *USA Today* article, describing the promise of AIDS vaccines now in human trials, carried the headline: "Researchers Feel They'll Beat the Virus."[1] In April 2002, a popular online health magazine compared creating an AIDS vaccine to NASA's moon landing program, and reported that scientists are on the verge of an AIDS vaccine breakthrough, a medical "giant leap for mankind."[2]

Similar stories surface recurrently in mainstream media, fueling hopes that medical research may soon yield a vaccine capable of stopping AIDS. A vaccine able to prevent HIV infection would constitute an epoch–making medical triumph. Yet to focus on vaccines as a "magic bullet" against AIDS can have dangerous consequences. Premature celebration may encourage perilous complacency about AIDS. Likewise, optimism about the pace of vaccine research may harden reluctance on the part of political and economic leaders to adequately fund other forms of prevention, and to back AIDS treatment for the developing world.

Are claims of an HIV vaccine on the near horizon justified? Will a vaccine solve the AIDS crisis? To answer these questions, we examine: (1) the grounds for some experts' cautious optimism about HIV vaccines; (2) the formidable scientific obstacles still to be overcome; and (3) reasons why, even when a workable vaccine emerges, we will still be far from having beaten AIDS.

Progress on Vaccines

A safe, effective vaccine would be a uniquely powerful tool in the fight against AIDS—in the long run, it is probably the only hope for the complete conquest of the disease. After the discovery of HIV in 1983, many scientists anticipated the rapid development of a vaccine. The first human trial of a candidate vaccine took place in 1987. But initial optimism dissipated as scientists learned more about HIV's remarkable capacity to evade the body's defensive systems—including the virus's ability to invade some of the very cells the immune system utilizes to fight off infections. Some questioned the very possibility of creating a vaccine capable of preventing infection with HIV.[3]

Now a new generation of research has brought renewed optimism. An upbeat mood marked the September 2001 international HIV vaccine conference in Philadelphia. "We have reached a new level of acceleration, not only in what we're doing, but in the promise of what can be done," Anthony Fauci, director of the National Institute of Allergy and Infectious Diseases (NIAID), told journalists.[4]

Support from governments for AIDS vaccine research has been stepped up. The US National Institutes of Health (NIH) is the largest funding agency for HIV vaccine research worldwide, operating mainly through the NIAID. The NIH budget for HIV vaccine research increased from roughly $100 million in 1995 to $180 million in 1999 to an estimated $357 million in 2002.[5] NIAID supports investigators—in the US but also in other countries throughout the world—who are working on studies ranging from basic research to testing different vaccine strategies in animal models and human volunteers. In 2000, NIAID combined its domestic and international clinical trials programs to form the HIV Vaccine Trials Network (HVTN), a global research network able to quickly evaluate promising vaccine candidates.

New international vaccine research partnerships have blossomed in the rich world and in developing regions. The African AIDS Vaccine Programme (AAVP) is a network of researchers from countries throughout Africa with the goal of accelerating development of vaccines. In addition to fostering regional and international scientific collaborations, AAVP is focusing on capacity building and addressing ethical and legal issues related to conducting vaccine trials.[6] Within South Africa, a similar effort to promote HIV vaccine research began in 1999 with the formation of the South African AIDS Vaccine Initiative (SAAVI). SAAVI has set a 10-year timetable for the development of an effective, affordable vaccine for the southern African region.[7] Founded in 1996, the New York–based International AIDS Vaccine Initiative (IAVI) has created a series of vaccine development partnerships linking researchers from universities and biotechnology companies in affluent countries with clinical researchers and vaccine manufacturers in developing countries.[8] Today, AVI is set to expand its efforts, galvanized by a $100 million pledge from the Bill & Melinda Gates Foundation. In Uganda and Kenya, AVI-sponsored candidate AIDS vaccines have already entered human clinical trials.[9]

Vaccines are not as commercially lucrative as many other pharmaceutical products. Unlike drugs which people take repeatedly when they get sick, a vaccine is usually administered to each person only once or a few times in a lifetime to induce immunity. The challenges of vaccine development and the lingering possibility of unforeseen adverse effects when a vaccine is widely distributed imply greater potential risks for investors.[10] Accordingly, the large international drug companies have been slow to commit themselves to AIDS vaccine research. Today, however, some leading companies are turning increased attention to the problem, and new forms of public-private partnership have emerged to mobilize the commercial sector.

In 2001, Merck's CEO spoke optimistically of "recent scientific advances in understanding the biology and immunology of HIV infection" and promised an expansion of the company's HIV vaccine program.[11] Merck currently has two different candidate vaccines in early safety trials in human volunteers.[12] One of these has been able to slow disease progression in monkeys infected with a virus similar to HIV that causes an AIDS-like disease.[13] The company recently entered into collaboration with HVTN to initiate human trials of the two vaccines together, in what has been called a "prime-boost" strategy.[14] In early 2002, another international pharmaceutical giant, Glaxo Smith Kline, announced a collaboration with HVTN to carry out safety trials in humans of a candidate vaccine that also showed an ability to slow disease in laboratory-infected monkeys.[15]

Researchers Face Scientific Challenges

New partnerships, fresh ideas, and increased funding flows have boosted AIDS vaccine research. Yet renewed optimism must be tempered by recognition of the enormous scientific challenges still to be met before effective vaccines become a reality.

Despite gains in research, significant gaps remain in our understanding of fundamental biological and immunological issues connected with HIV and its effects on the human body. Most important, scientists have yet to identify what are called the "correlates of immunity": the immune system responses necessary to confer protective immunity against HIV. With most other infectious diseases, some fraction of people who get sick are able to mount a successful immune response to combat the infection. Even for potentially devastating diseases like cholera or bacterial meningitis, there are patients who fully recover, often acquiring long-term immunity in the process. This is the principle on which a number of successful vaccines are based.[16]

For example, the oral polio vaccine (OPV) works by causing a mild infection with a polio virus that has been altered to weaken its pathogenic capabilities, leaving it unable to cause serious symptoms of disease and readily susceptible to attack and elimination by the body's immune system. As a result of OPV vaccination, some cells of the immune system retain a "memory" of the first infection and become primed to act rapidly and aggressively if they ever encounter a fully virulent polio virus. Although most people with HIV infection mount a vigorous immune response, there have been no cases of HIV-infected individuals who were able to completely eliminate the virus from their bodies. This makes the task of vaccine design very difficult, because it is not clear what sort of immune response would be beneficial.

An equally daunting obstacle is the diversity of the virus and its ability to mutate at dizzying rates. HIV's diversity is demonstrated by the appearance of multiple variants in one infected person. To give some perspective, HIV has been compared with influenza virus, another virus with an impressive capacity for mutation. The number of different influenza viruses circulating throughout the world during a flu epidemic can be fewer than the number of HIV variants represented in a single HIV-infected human being.[17] Rapid mutation gives the virus an excellent means to evade the immune system by altering those portions of its structure that are recognized by "memory cells."

Across populations, the diversity of the virus is reflected in the geographical distribution of distinct HIV subtypes. In the course of its deadly progression through human populations, HIV has diverged into at least nine different subtypes, or clades, labeled A–K.[18] Different HIV subtypes predominate in different regions of the world, provoking an ongoing debate about whether or not a vaccine developed against HIV strains predominant in North America and Europe would be equally effective against strains found in other parts of the world.[19] If regionally specific vaccines are required, the implications for production and delivery systems (and therefore for cost) will be grave.

Complexities in the way HIV replicates and persists in humans also contribute to problems in AIDS vaccine development. HIV circulates in the body in two different forms: as free virus and within infected cells. The immune system tends to use alternate response pathways for eliminating freely circulating virus and virus-infected cells of the body. A successful AIDS vaccine will likely need to stimulate both of these pathways in order to confer long-term protection against HIV. To complicate matters further, the virus can enter the body by different transmission routes, and different types of immune responses may be needed to protect from infection, depending on which "path" the virus follows. The two major routes of infection are (1) introduction directly into the bloodstream by needle injection; and (2) introduction via the mucosal membranes of the genital tract, the rectum, or the mouth, as in sexual transmission.[20]

Ideally, an AIDS vaccine would stimulate the appropriate immune response to give protection from infection through every potential transmission route. The optimal AIDS vaccine would also protect against infection by all variants and subtypes of the virus. In practice, it may not be possible to accomplish every desired purpose with a single vaccine. Some of the research community's challenges lie in deciding what vaccine characteristics are most critical and should be prioritized in research.

Vaccines in the Pipeline?

When the press reports that an experimental AIDS vaccine has "entered human trials," or is about to do so, can we assume researchers are making strides toward a solution? It is tempting to believe that if scientists have reached the stage of testing these products on human beings, they must be confident they are on a promising track.

However, such inferences must be drawn cautiously. To assess the significance of reports about AIDS vaccine trials (or other potential medical and scientific breakthroughs), we need to understand the stages of testing established for vaccines and other new medicines by the US Food and Drug Administration (FDA). Looking at the structure of clinical trials gives us a clearer picture of the time frame and the formidable costs involved in vaccine development, conveying a sense of the distance AIDS vaccine research still has to cover.

Between the identification of a disease agent and the arrival of an effective product on the market, developing a safe and effective vaccine can take anywhere from 10 to 50 years.[21] FDA-regulated vaccine or drug development is divided into four progressive stages: preclinical, Phase I, Phase II, and Phase III trials.[22] Before proceeding to clinical testing in humans (Phases I–III), researchers must carry out preclinical trials to show safety and promising results in one or more animal models of the disease. Phase I clinical trials test for safety and the potential for adverse reactions in a small number of closely supervised human subjects, about 20 to 50 people.[23] Phase II trials are conducted with a larger population of up to several hundred people and provide further information about safety and preliminary data on subjects' immunological responses (i.e., whether the drug seems to produce at least some of the beneficial effects vaccine designers had intended). The final stage of efficacy testing for a candidate vaccine is a Phase III clinical trial, involving several hundred to several thousand people.[24] Costs rise steeply when moving from Phase I/II trials into Phase III trials.[25]

The FDA monitors each step of the vaccine testing process, referred to as the "pipeline." As a candidate vaccine moves forward in the pipeline, progress to the next stage of testing is predicated upon a successful outcome from the previous one. Sometimes, a product will be put through two or more rounds of a particular phase of clinical testing as a means of examining the responses of different populations. For example, if regional differences are thought to have a potential impact on the outcome, then multiple trials of the same vaccine may be carried out in alternative locations. The majority of candidate products drop out of the pipeline after unsuccessful Phase I or II trials. Ultimately, a small fraction of the total candidate vaccines that go into clinical trials make it into Phase III testing.

The strategy of starting with small studies on safety and scaling up to large studies on efficacy is intended to protect human subjects and ensure that vaccines are not released into large-scale distribution until any potentially harmful effects can be identified. Although the process can be sped up in some ways, for instance by conducting multiple trials simultaneously in different populations, safety considerations limit how rapidly these operations can proceed. Activists are now pressuring researchers and government agencies to move new candidate vaccines into Phase II and Phase III trials quickly, but pushing products that do not perform well in early trials into more advanced trials is not necessarily wise. First of all, such a practice is ethically dubious. Moreover, if large Phase III trials of poor vaccines end up having negative health effects on many trial participants, the outcome may damage relations with communities and jeopardize volunteer recruitment for later trials of more genuinely promising vaccines.

Such risks must be considered especially carefully in developing countries, where many people already feel suspicion toward medical and scientific researchers from rich countries, and where significant differentials in power, wealth, and social prestige separate the researchers organizing trials from the local volunteers participating in them.[26] The best way to get more promising vaccines into Phase III trials is to increase the number of candidates going into the pipeline at the preclinical stage.

To date, about 40 different candidate AIDS vaccines have been tested in over 70 Phase I/II trials, involving more than 10,000 volunteers.[27] Clinical trials are taking place in both rich and poor countries and are targeting the specific subtypes of HIV most prevalent in the area. Thus far, studies have been conducted in the US, several European countries, Brazil, China, Cuba, Haiti, Thailand, Trinidad and Tobago, and Uganda. The rate of candidate vaccines entering Phase I trials has increased during the last few years.[28] Yet from all these early trials, only one candidate has so far proceeded to Phase III trials.[29]

The candidate vaccine, known as AIDSVAX, was designed by the California biotechnology firm VaxGen. It is currently involved in two simultaneous Phase III trials. While an interim analysis in November 2001 indicated that AIDSVAX is safe, there was not enough data to show evidence of any efficacy.[30] The study is slated to continue until the end of 2002, when final results will be available.[31] Many leading scientists in the field have already expressed skepticism about the ability of AIDSVAX to mount a protective immune response on the basis of both theoretical considerations and earlier trials data.[32] The NIH is planning to begin another phase III trial around 2003 of a vaccine strategy, currently in phase II testing, that uses a candidate from the pharmaceutical company Aventis Pasteur in combination with VaxGen's AIDSVAX. However, some scientists are already expressing skepticism about the combined product based on the results of earlier rounds of testing.[33] Unfortunately, as a result of slow momentum in the AIDS vaccine field, there are few other candidates waiting in the wings to soon move into Phase III trials.

Beyond the daunting scientific challenges and the rigors of the FDA's testing process, the internal political schisms of the research community itself further obstruct efficient vaccine development. Critics point out that the field of AIDS vaccine research is hampered by a lack of coordination and overall planning.[34] The sheer number of groups now operating in the field adds to the confusion. "Today there are more players in HIV vaccine development than ever before, and this diversity can accelerate research," according to the Washington-based AIDS Vaccine Advocacy Coalition (AVAC). Yet without leadership and coordination, the multiplication of groups pursuing vaccine research may not in itself increase efficiency or accelerate progress.[35] Partnerships such as SAAVI, AAVP, and AVI and those now being fostered by the NIH and HVTN are promoting greater integration within the research community, but insufficient communication and territorial rivalries persist.

In the clinical testing of prototype vaccines, the lack of coordination is exacerbated by differentials in financial power. The power of money and a candidate vaccine's apparent scientific promise do not always align, and valuable time and resources can be wasted. As the research community tries to decide which vaccines deserve efficacy trials, money can distort the picture. Jon Cohen, author of a comprehensive historical study of AIDS vaccine research, points to VaxGen's AIDSVAX as an example. The biotech company used its formidable financial resources to move AIDSVAX into the Phase III efficacy trials currently underway despite the widespread skepticism about the vaccine and NIH officials' decision not to fund the trials. "Now the world can of course just test everything that has financial backing and appears safe and at least scientifically rational, but that approach, I suspect, will hit the wall somewhere," Cohen observes.[36]

"Partially Effective" Vaccines

The enormous difficulties confronting vaccine research have led some scientists to doubt our capacity to create, at least in the near term, a vaccine able to fully prevent HIV infection.[37] The first AIDS vaccines deployed will almost certainly be of relatively low efficacy. As an indication of where the bar is being set, researchers involved in testing AIDSVAX have said they would consider 30 percent efficacy a successful outcome.[38] In stark contrast, the polio vaccine mentioned previously is felt to have more than 95 percent efficacy.

Positive results in some recently reported animal studies have identified vaccine strategies that can mitigate the impact of disease but cannot prevent infection.[39] With such a vaccine, people could still be infected with HIV after being vaccinated, but their immune systems would be primed to fight the infection better, reducing viral load and delaying progression to full-blown AIDS. Although it would not stop transmission altogether, this type of vaccine could have a tremendous impact on morbidity and mortality, improving the lives of those infected and increasing their life spans. Moreover, by reducing viral load in vaccinated individuals who become infected, such a product could lower their chances of transmitting HIV to others, potentially slowing the pandemic's spread.

What these discussions boil down to is that even when we do finally have a vaccine, the product alone will probably not be potent enough to guarantee protection against infection. Other prevention strategies will continue to be crucial to HIV/AIDS control programs. The discovery of an HIV vaccine will not abrogate the need to expand voluntary counseling and testing in poor countries and to invest in the development and distribution of women-centered protection tools, such as female condoms and microbicides.

Prevention education may even need to be intensified to counterbalance the false sense of security that could come with the availability of a partially effective vaccine. As public health officials have observed in some US and European communities since the introduction of highly active antiretroviral therapy (HAART), a general perception—however unfounded—that AIDS has been "solved" can lead to increases in risky behavior.[40] Jose Esparza, coordinator of the WHO/UNAIDS HIV Vaccine Initiative, has argued, "We should not expect that a future HIV vaccine, especially one with only moderate efficacy, will be a 'magic bullet' that replaces other preventive interventions. Instead, vaccines will be part of comprehensive HIV prevention packages that also include health promotion and behavioral interventions."[41]

The Distribution Time Gap

While AIDS vaccine research has made progress, a safe, effective vaccine is not yet in our grasp, and it is even further from being in the grasp of the millions of people in poor communities most immediately at risk for contracting HIV disease. Leading scientists predict that in all probability another seven to ten years will pass before an effective vaccine can be developed and tested, and considerably longer before it becomes available for large-scale distribution in developing countries.[42] Ten years does not seem excessive as a time frame for a major scientific breakthrough. Yet this figure takes on a different weight when we again remind ourselves of the urgency of the AIDS crisis. Every day, more than 8,000 people die of AIDS, and 14,500 men, women, and children are newly infected with HIV, most of them in regions where no effective treatment is available. As we look forward to a vaccine, we must not overlook the humanitarian catastrophe continuing to unfold as vaccine candidates are designed, tested, and (possibly) deployed.

Once an effective HIV vaccine has passed through all necessary stages of clinical testing, further challenges will remain. Scientists, industry, and health officials will have to confront the enormous logistical task of manufacturing the new medicine in adequate quantities, educating the public, and delivering the vaccine to poor people in the developing world. As AVI's experts point out, the global track record in dealing with similar challenges is scarcely encouraging. "The historical paradigm for fostering use of new vaccines in developing countries has been a public health failure."[43] After making it through the approval process, all modern-day vaccines have been marketed first in industrialized countries at high prices, allowing the sponsoring firms to recoup their research and development costs and realize profits. Only with a lag time of approximately a decade have relatively cheap versions of the products made their way into developing countries. Avoiding a repetition of this scenario in the case of AIDS vaccines must become a key priority of global AIDS activists.

According to Malegapuru William Makgoba, president of the Medical Research Council of South Africa, considerable groundwork remains to be done, both to build partnerships between rich and poor countries so that AIDS vaccine trials can proceed in an atmosphere of trust and mutual respect, and to create mechanisms for the efficient manufacture and distribution of vaccines, once they have been proven to be safe and effective. Rules to govern access and distribution of vaccines must be determined in advance and must take into account that most of the initial use of an AIDS vaccine will be in high-prevalence countries that do not have the resources to buy and distribute the vaccine without support from the international community. The most effective channels for such support, including possible purchase guarantees from rich-country governments to the private sector, should be hammered out now, to avoid unnecessary delays later.[44]

AVAC confirms that preparatory work has been woefully inadequate, both in building trust with communities where future trials will take place, and in planning for vaccine distribution in poor countries. Policy makers acknowledge that extensive AIDS vaccine education campaigns will be needed to promote vaccines and explain their limitations to people in communities hard hit by AIDS, both in the US and abroad. Only well-planned education and outreach can guarantee adequate recruitment for vaccine trials and build solid relationships between vaccine researchers and affected communities. But, according to AVAC, thus far community education has lagged.[45]

Internationally, government officials, private sector donors, and a variety of NGOs and other agencies have begun to discuss the issues that will affect the accessibility of HIV vaccines, such as the need to create a bulk-purchasing mechanism. But the talk has brought little in the way of action. Rich countries have not done enough to support health infrastructure projects in the developing world that might smooth the road for effective vaccine delivery. Nor has the US government endorsed tiered pricing (differential pricing schemes that would mandate steep discounts on vaccine sales to poor countries). No credible purchasing mechanism for AIDS vaccines has yet been established, raising the specter of long delays in getting the medicine to the poor world. "When a vaccine is developed, funding to purchase HIV vaccines for poor countries must be in place," AVAC analysts warn, or we risk witnessing a repetition of the tragic history of "decade or longer delays in delivering new vaccines to the developing world."[46]

The American government, along with other large industrialized democracies and relevant international agencies, should be working to develop strategies for rapid distribution of successful vaccines in the developing world. Strategies should include insuring sufficient production capacity, commitments to tiered pricing, and the design and implementation of appropriate intellectual property agreements. The US Trade Representative can and should advocate for special international patent arrangements designed both to reward vaccine research and to guarantee that the end products of the research remain affordable.

The most urgent task is the establishment of a multibillion-dollar bulk purchasing facility for vaccines against HIV, malaria, and tuberculosis. By guaranteeing a market for successful vaccines, a purchasing mechanism funded by wealthy governments could stimulate vaccine research. Once vaccines become available, they could then be channeled rapidly to the developing world. The US government must lead the way in creating such a mechanism and guaranteeing its credibility and sustainability.

A truly effective AIDS vaccine would unquestionably rank as one of the most important medical breakthroughs of our era. However, there are limits to the positive effects it would yield. We must keep these limitations in mind, even as we campaign for expanded support for vaccine research and development, doing everything possible to back scientists in their efforts to bring useful vaccines online rapidly. In the meantime, we must not let premature reports of successful vaccines diminish interest in other important arenas.

In particular, there is a risk of diminished support for antiretroviral programs, because of the costs involved and the still-widespread perception that a choice must be made between prevention and treatment. When AVI president Dr. Seth Berkeley affirms that "a vaccine is our only realistic hope for ending this epidemic, especially in developing countries where costs of treatment are prohibitive," activists' reaction is divided.[47] Yes, in the long term, a vaccine (as part of a comprehensive prevention and treatment program) may offer the best prospect for ending the pandemic. Vaccine work should proceed as rapidly as possible. But, lack of access to AIDS treatment in developing countries must not be seen as an immutable fact. The absence of antiretroviral (ARV) treatment programs in much of the poor world is a deplorable political and moral failure of the international community. This failure must be corrected even as vaccine research moves forward aggressively.

Attention must be focused on the more than 42 million people currently carrying the virus and the millions more who will be infected before an even partially effective vaccine can be made available in the developing world. For these people, the appearance of a vaccine a decade down the road will mean little. What they require is treatment with the current panoply of ARVs and the best new drugs medical science can continue to devise.[48] As increased investment in AIDS vaccine research must not come at the expense of other forms of prevention, so it must not blunt our determination to extend treatment as rapidly as possible to poor countries beleaguered by HIV/AIDS.

One positive note is that constructive synergies may emerge between efforts to widen access to treatment, expand prevention programs, and conduct vaccine trials in resource-poor settings. Vaccine trials depend upon the creation and maintenance of reliable infrastructure for screening and monitoring trial participants. Much of the same infrastructure could also be used to extend treatment and voluntary counseling and testing capabilities. Community education is essential to prepare for vaccine trials, to ensure truly informed consent from participants, and to mitigate any potential misunderstandings about the trial.[49] Input from participating communities should be enlisted in these efforts to be sure that all operations are conducted with the highest ethical standards and within appropriate cultural contexts.[50] This type of education could be coordinated through local prevention programs, thus expanding AIDS awareness.

As we discussed in Myth 4, the availability of treatment can be a means to strengthen prevention programs by encouraging people to come in for voluntary counseling, testing, and support. Similarly, linking prevention and treatment can provide greater opportunities for community education and outreach around vaccine and clinical trials. If the political will and the necessary resources can be mobilized, these key elements of a fully developed AIDS control program—prevention, treatment, and vaccine research—will reinforce one another.

Clinic in Tijuana, Mexico, which depends on drug donations from the US, provides free treatment to people with HIV/AIDS.

MYTH SEVEN:
Drug Company Profits vs. Poor People's Health

Myth: Activists' moral pleas for treatment equity are no match for the pharmaceutical industry's political power and drive for high profits. If millions of middle-class Americans cannot obtain substantially reduced prescription drug prices despite years of lobbying, there is little chance the drug companies will change their pricing policies to help poor people with AIDS in the developing world.

Response: Major research-based pharmaceutical companies such as Glaxo Smith Kline, Merck, Boehringer-Ingelheim, and Pfizer are among the most profitable and politically influential corporations in the world. Any realistic effort to control the AIDS crisis must reckon with both the unparalleled scientific capabilities and the political weight of the drug industry. However, that the major drug companies wield great power does not mean that other stakeholders in the AIDS field are helpless. The history of the AIDS activist movement since the early 1980s proves otherwise.

For those committed to fighting AIDS, the primary objective is not attacking companies, the patent system, or corporate-driven globalization per se (though many of us may support those agendas) but finding answers to practical questions: (1) How can people at increased risk for HIV best be enabled to protect themselves from infection? (2) How can we best ensure that *all* people with AIDS in *every* country, regardless of income or wealth, obtain access to a reliable supply of safe, effective, affordable medicines? These questions should be the touchstones that determine our strategies vis-à-vis the major drug companies. Drug companies can be allies or foes of people with HIV/AIDS and AIDS advocates, depending on whether companies' actions enable satisfactory solutions to these questions or instead place obstacles in the way.

We should not underestimate the economic and political power of the pharmaceutical industry, but we should also not be intimidated by it. The task is to identify the sources of that power, discern its limits, and demand that the exercise of industry prerogatives be subordinated to the goal of equity in AIDS control and global health. We begin with a brief overview of the industry and an assessment of current intellectual property rights structures that secure brand name drug companies' profitability and political influence. Then we look at episodes from the history of AIDS activism, showing how activists have been able to confront the power of big drug companies and gain important victories. Finally, we consider concrete policy suggestions to address the urgent needs of AIDS' poorest victims, while acknowledging the interests and contributions of the research-based pharmaceutical industry.

Pharmaceuticals and Intellectual Property Rights

The modern pharmaceutical industry developed in the decades after World War II, buoyed by a succession of dramatic discoveries, from early antibiotics such as penicillin and streptomycin to today's cancer chemotherapies and antidepressants. These new medicines revolutionized health care and contributed to dramatic improvements in health and life quality for millions of people.[1]

Today, the pharmaceutical industry is among the world's most profitable. The research and development expenses needed to bring a new drug to market are high; industry estimates range from $250 million to over $800 million per agent.[2] But the return on investment is impressive as well. Successful preparations often generate annual revenues in excess of $1 billion for a sustained period. There are currently 29 drugs on the market, bringing in over $1 billion each in annual sales. Such "blockbuster" medicines have propelled leading drug makers to levels of profitability envied by other industries in 2001. The 10 drug companies on the Fortune 500 list earned an average profit of 18.5 cents for every dollar of sales—eight times the Fortune 500 median profit margin of 2.2 cents.[3]

Drug companies can be divided into two categories: research-based or "innovator" firms, which conduct significant original laboratory research to pioneer and patent new medicines, and generic firms, which produce and sell versions of existing drugs. As with most industries reliant on sophisticated technology, the research-based pharmaceutical sector is largely concentrated in wealthy countries. A few poor and middle-income countries—India, China, Mexico, and Brazil, for example—have some innovative capacity in the pharmaceutical sector. However, drug companies in most developing countries are limited to generic production of existing medicines. Most low-income countries, unfortunately including some of the countries hardest hit by AIDS, have either no domestic pharmaceutical industry at all or rudimentary facilities unable to produce generic copies of complex compounds such as antiretroviral drugs.

The research-based pharmaceutical companies are collectively represented by powerful trade associations such as the Pharmaceutical Research and Manufacturers of America (PhRMA) and the Geneva-based International Federation of Pharmaceutical

Manufacturers Associations (IFPMA). These groups conduct policy research, publish reports, and employ large numbers of political lobbyists to influence legislation in Washington and other power centers on issues affecting the industry's interests. Prescription drug price reform in the US constitutes one example, international trade regulations another.

According to industry representatives, high profit margins on successful drugs are needed to reward companies for the difficulties and risks of innovation, which include numerous compounds that fail to yield marketable products despite long periods of costly research. On the other hand, critics observe that the industry spends more on advertising than on research. In 2001, the drug company Pharmacia, for example, spent 44 percent of its revenues on marketing, advertising, and administration, versus 16 percent on research and development. The ratios for other large firms were similar.[4]

Executive salaries and compensation packages take on formidable proportions within the drug industry. The Panos Institute reports that in 2001 alone, the five highest-paid pharmaceutical company executives received over $183 million in compensation, not including unexercised stock options, "considerably more than the entire health budget of many impoverished nations."[5] It is also worth noting that publicly-funded research, for example through the National Institutes of Health, contributes significantly to the development of many of the pharmaceutical industry's profitable products, including leading AIDS medications.[6]

The mechanism that ensures major pharmaceutical companies' high profits on successful medicines is the patent system. The industry's power stems in large part from the patent protections mandated by current national and international rules governing intellectual property (IP).[7]

Intellectual property rights are designed to protect the interests of inventors and to reward original research. They stipulate that the holder of a patent on a particular device or process (such as a newly approved medication) has exclusive rights to produce and sell that item during a certain fixed period. Anyone who imitates or otherwise appropriates the inventor's original idea must obtain authorization from the patent holder and pay some form of royalty. The effects of patents on prices can be seen in the price change of a drug when its patent protection expires and generic versions of the medication enter the market. For example, compare the price of CVS or RiteAid generic ibuprofen to the brand drug, Advil. In the US, the average generic medication sells for 48 percent less than the same drug under patent.[8] Worldwide, according to the World Health Organization (WHO), generic medicines generally sell at prices 30 to 50 percent lower than their branded equivalents.[9]

Intellectual property rules vary greatly from country to country, and the US and other major powers have a history of altering their patent laws over time to further their own economic interests at different stages of their industrial development.[10] Indeed, it is worth noting that some European countries did not recognize patents until well into the 20th century and that Japan introduced patent protection for pharmaceutical products as late as 1976.[11]

Since the 1970s, a major effort has been underway, led by affluent countries and their successful corporations, to standardize IP rules at the international level and bring individual countries' regulations into line with globally agreed norms. The promotion of a uniform international IP framework is the goal of the World Intellectual Property Organization (WIPO) and a major policy objective of the World Trade Organization (WTO).

The centerpiece of current international IP rules is the Trade Related Aspects of Intellectual Property Rights (TRIPS) agreement, signed in 1994. World Trade Organization membership is conditional upon a country's acceptance of TRIPS regulations on patents, copyrights, and other IP rights issues. TRIPS statutes granting patent holders exclusive rights for 20 years were based to a considerable extent on the very strong US patent regime, which covers both products and processes. Industry interests, and especially the pharmaceutical sector, exerted a strong influence on the TRIPS agreement negotiations, and many civil society groups and consumer interest advocates argue that TRIPS was designed largely to protect the interests of established, successful corporations.[12]

Two features of the TRIPS agreement have been central to recent international IP rights debates. First, a delayed-implementation clause has allowed many countries a grace period postponing full application of TRIPS standards to pharmaceutical products. For most countries that did not have pharmaceutical patent protections before 1995, this grace period is set to expire in 2005. (The world's lowest-income countries now have until 2016 to become compliant.) Second, the TRIPS policy explicitly authorizes countries to suspend patent protections under conditions of national emergency.

Some developing nations, such as Brazil and India, have taken advantage of the delayed-implementation clause as a window to increase the production of generic versions of medicines still under patent in developed countries. Brazil has invested heavily in the state-sponsored production of generic medicines and uses the savings to fund, among other things, a universal-access antiretroviral (ARV) therapy program.[13] India has not provided subsidized AIDS drugs to its own population, but numerous Indian firms have capitalized on the delay in the country's full implementation of TRIPS regulations to produce generic versions of key AIDS drugs and other medications. Indian companies such as Cipla, Ranbaxy, and Aurobindo have been able to offer antiretrovirals (ARVs) at a fraction of the cost of brand-name medicines from major research-based manufacturers.

In 2001, Cipla offered a three-drug ARV cocktail in Africa for $300 a year, a 97 percent price drop from the $10,000 per patient per year charged for the corresponding brand-name cocktail in the US.[14] Price competition on ARVs from generic firms has fundamentally transformed the terms of debate around AIDS treatment in sub-Saharan Africa and elsewhere, forcing price drops from innovator companies, dynamizing static markets, and opening up the possibility of large-scale treatment of poor people with AIDS.

Activists, health care providers, and policy makers advocating access to ARVs have focused on the sections of the TRIPS agreement dealing with national emergencies. The agreement explicitly allows for deviations from ordinary patent rules when the health and safety of a country's people are threatened. Two intellectual property (IP) mechanisms for responding to grave public health challenges are especially relevant: parallel importation and compulsory licensing.

Parallel importation involves purchasing a product in a country where the price is low, and distributing or reselling it in another country where the price was originally higher. Because of the often considerable differences in the price at which a drug is sold in different countries, poor countries could use parallel importation to search world markets for the lowest prices available on key medicines. Parallel importing in pharmaceuticals is legal under specific conditions and routinely practiced—even in the absence of an emergency—in parts of the developed world, for example in Europe.[15]

Under compulsory licensing, a government can order a patent

holder to license the right to make, use, sell or import its patented product (e.g., an AIDS drug) to a government agency, different company, or other third party. The new producer then manufactures and distributes the item, paying the innovator a reasonable royalty. By introducing a generic competitor to the patent-protected drug, compulsory licensing often causes the price of the original drug to drop dramatically in the local market, in some cases by 95 percent or more.[16] Compulsory licensing mechanisms have been used frequently by rich-country governments, including the US and UK.[17] The US government threatened to authorize a compulsory license for the antibiotic ciprofloxacin during the anthrax attacks of September and October 2001. In May 2002, Zimbabwe became the first nation in sub-Saharan Africa to announce the intention to apply compulsory licensing in the context of AIDS. Implementation has been delayed, and the effects on the country's epidemic remain to be seen.[18]

Although compulsory licensing and parallel imports are legal under WTO rules, the US government (through its trade representatives, who are heavily lobbied by the pharmaceutical industry) has often used its influence to attempt to dissuade poor countries from adopting these policies. For example, some US political leaders initially supported several major pharmaceutical companies in an effort to preempt possible use of parallel importation and compulsory licensing by South Africa under that country's 1997 Medicines Act.[19] In another high-profile case, in January 2001, the US lodged a WTO complaint challenging the legality of Brazil's decision to authorize generic production of patented AIDS drugs.[20] With international public opinion strongly endorsing the Brazilian position, a settlement was reached and the complaint withdrawn in June 2001.

Activism, "Big Pharma," and the Interests of the Poor

Since the emergence of organized AIDS activism in the early 1980s, tensions and antagonism—but also patterns of strategic alliance—have characterized the activist community's interactions with government, the biomedical establishment, and the drug industry. The power of the major drug companies to shape national and global AIDS policy is considerable. Yet the history of AIDS activism confirms grassroots movements' capacity to influence corporate and governmental agendas.

Here, we focus on three examples: (1) shifts in US AIDS policy at the end of the Clinton era; (2) pharmaceutical manufacturers' lawsuit against the South African government; and (3) the WTO Doha declaration on TRIPS and public health. These cases bring concrete evidence that drug company power has its limits. Advocates for the rights and interests of poor people with HIV/AIDS can generate change by claiming a place at the table in policy debates while simultaneously mobilizing public awareness through education and direct action.

"Zapping" AIDS Policies in the US

The late 1990s saw a series of bold actions by US and international AIDS activists. Advocates for AIDS treatment equity fought to expose and undo the unfair pricing practices of pharmaceutical companies and the US government's AIDS policies. In the process, they joined forces with an international movement of resistance to corporate-driven globalization.

Among the most highly publicized of these activist interventions were the "zaps" of Al Gore's presidential campaign speeches by members of ACT UP (the AIDS Coalition to Unleash Power). ACT UP aimed to challenge the Clinton-Gore administration's support for pharmaceutical companies' efforts to block compulsory licensing initiatives that could cut the cost of AIDS medicines in Africa. ACT UP veteran Eric Sawyer writes:

> We had obtained a copy of what we call the "smoking gun memo." Dated February 5, 1999, the memo was written by a State Department staff member and was prepared to convince a New Jersey Congressional Representative that the Clinton-Gore administration was doing everything in its power to support the interests of several big international pharmaceutical firms in their battle to prevent the South African government from producing its own generic versions of AIDS drugs. This memo listed courses of action, including threats to withhold trading rights and foreign aid to South Africa.[21]

ACT UP responded by shaming Gore at his presidential campaign kickoff in June 1999 with chants of "Gore's Greed Kills." Several subsequent campaign events were similarly disrupted.

ACT UP's challenge to Gore gained a wider resonance in November 1999, when 25,000 protesters converged on the WTO Ministerial Conference in Seattle, paralyzing the meetings.[22] When the World Bank met the following spring in Washington, DC, protesters again overwhelmed the event.[23] Visibly affected by the outpouring of emotion surrounding issues of trade policy and widening global inequalities, President Bill Clinton dramatically changed the administration's stance on access to medicines, indicating that his government would no longer interfere with poor countries' rights to give primacy to public health concerns in interpreting the TRIPS agreement.[24] This concession, announced on May 11, 2000, was followed one day later by a statement from PhRMA that leading drug companies had resolved to implement an AIDS drug donation program through the United Nations.[25] The Accelerating Access Initiative, as it has become known, was the first effort at improving access to ARVs in the developing world.[26]

Treatment advocates firmly believe that the timing of events in spring 2000 was not coincidental. Without the zaps of Al Gore's campaign appearances and the massive civil unrest surrounding the WTO, the Clinton administration would never have begun its tentative steps towards policy reform. In turn, PhRMA announced its new access program just 24 hours after reports of the administration's change in position. Charlene Barshevsky, the Clinton Administration's trade representative, confirmed that "it was the activities of ACT UP and the AIDS activists that galvanized our attention that there was an absolute crisis."[27] Activists' bold interventions had raised public consciousness around an issue previously seen as marginal and catalyzed a dramatic reversal in US government policy, precipitating a shift in the pharmaceutical industry's pricing practices on AIDS drugs.

AIDS Treatment on Trial in South Africa

The efforts of US-based activist groups were part of a wider international movement pressing for access to ARVs for the poor. The movement's most highly publicized confrontation with the pharmaceutical industry culminated in 2001, as a consortium of leading drug manufacturers pressed a lawsuit against the South African government to preempt the potential use of compulsory licensing and parallel importation of AIDS drugs. Activists in South Africa and around the world took up the cause, mobilizing international public opinion. The suit, which the drug makers had hoped to keep low profile, instead became an international *cause célèbre*.

In 1997, South Africa, struggling with the transition from apartheid rule to multiracial democracy and reeling under the impact of one of the world's most severe HIV/AIDS epidemics, passed the Medicines and Related Substances Control Amendment Act. The legislation authorized the use of compulsory licensing and parallel importation in response to a national health emergency. Although the South African government stated from the outset that it would shape its pharmaceuticals policy under the new act strictly in accordance with WTO rules, major multinational drug manufacturers began to pressure South Africa to repeal the legislation. In addition to the immediate threat to their profits in the South African market, pharmaceutical companies saw the Medicines Act as a dangerous precedent. In particular, they feared that the new act could: (1) pave the way for wider incursions of generic drugs manufactured in countries such as India and Brazil and (2) encourage a "back flow" of cheaper drugs into US and European markets. In 1998, the Pharmaceutical Manufacturers' Association of South Africa (PMASA), a body representing local subsidiaries of 39 major international drug firms, filed a lawsuit against the South African government, alleging that the Medicines Act was unconstitutional and in violation of international intellectual property rights accords.

South Africa's Treatment Action Campaign (TAC) led the international response to the suit. Activists employed a wide variety of strategies, ranging from classic letter writing, petitioning, and public education campaigns to provocative street theater, civil disobedience, and the takeover of corporate offices. On July 9, 2000, on the eve of the XIII International AIDS Conference in Durban, South Africa, a coalition of South African and international activist groups led by TAC mobilized 5,000 people on the streets of Durban to demand debt cancellation for developing nations, lower prices for AIDS medications, and the withdrawal of the PMASA suit. The event was the largest AIDS protest ever organized by civil society. In the US, groups like ACT UP took the protest to the centers of corporate power, staging repeated demonstrations at company headquarters and other facilities belonging to pharmaceutical manufacturers such as Pfizer, Bristol-Myers Squibb, and Glaxo Smith Kline. On February

20, 2001, ACT UP protesters took over the investor relations office of Glaxo Smith Kline on Park Avenue in New York. Activists chained themselves to desks in the office, and six were arrested.[28]

International solidarity actions multiplied. Médecins Sans Frontières launched a global "Drop the Case" petition, garnering signatures from 285,000 people in 130 countries. In February 2001, TAC formally entered the legal proceedings in Pretoria in the role of *amicus curiae*, bringing the voices of poor people with AIDS directly into the court chambers. TAC's press declaration affirmed: "This case is about greed. For the companies, their right to profiteer is non-negotiable. For TAC, the rights to life, dignity, access to health care services and the best interest of children are non-negotiable. These are the grounds that we place before the Court."[29]

On April 19, 2001, facing a growing public relations disaster, the 39 pharmaceutical companies withdrew their lawsuit. An international activist mobilization had irrevocably altered the context of the dispute, focusing global public attention on the moral disparity between companies' zeal to safeguard profits and the suffering and death of impoverished South Africans. The companies had been unprepared for the scale of the activist response and the international backlash generated by the case. Rick Lane, president of Bristol Myers Squibb, admitted, "I think we underestimated the capacity to be made villains."[30]

The Doha Declaration on TRIPS

An additional victory for activists came at the November 2001 meetings of the WTO Ministerial Conference in Doha, Qatar, where TRIPS regulations were under review in preparation for a proposed new round of international trade talks. A policy declaration hammered out during intense negotiations in Doha reaffirmed the right, under TRIPS, for countries in the grip of major health emergencies to practice parallel importation and to issue compulsory licenses for the generic production of patented drugs. The Doha Ministerial Declaration did not, technically speaking, add new content to the TRIPS framework. However, the declaration established an important rule of interpretation by affirming that "the TRIPS agreement does not and should not prevent [WTO] Members from taking measures to protect public health."[31] Public heath needs are recognized as a key normative lens through which TRIPS statutes are to be read. Following Doha, the WTO's dispute resolution panels and appellate body "must interpret the [TRIPS] Agreement and the laws and regulations adopted to implement it in light of the public health needs of individual Members."[32]

While pharmaceutical industry lobbyists criticized the decision, the numerous AIDS activists who had converged on Qatar celebrated. The *Wall Street Journal* observed that the pharmaceutical industry had been visibly "outmaneuvered by activists."[33] For Jamie Love, director of Ralph Nader's Consumer Project on Technology, "It's like the WTO looked at the signs of the demonstrators on the street, and then put them in a declaration and adopted it."[34]

Unfortunately, the victory in Doha was far from complete. While the Doha declaration confirmed poor countries' right to manufacture generic drugs under compulsory licenses in a health emergency, it did nothing to provide them with the economic and technical resources required to exercise this right. Article 31(f) of the TRIPS agreement requires that a product manufactured under a compulsory license be supplied primarily to the licensee's domestic market (i.e., that the product not be exported). For countries like Brazil and India, with substantial domestic pharmaceutical manufacturing capabilities, this restriction poses no difficulties. However, large numbers of developing countries, including many of the sub-Saharan African countries where HIV/AIDS burdens are highest, lack the capacity to manufacture complex medicines on their own, or else constitute such small markets that domestic manufacturing under a compulsory license might not be economically viable.[35]

The Doha declaration recognized this as a potential obstacle to an effective use of TRIPS compulsory licensing provisions, and Paragraph Six of the declaration instructed the WTO's Council for TRIPS to "find an expeditious solution to this problem...before the end of 2002."[36] However in December, 2002, negotiations broke down as the US government, dismissing the appeals of developing countries and international health organizations, fought to limit the diseases that would be covered by a new agreement and restrict the number of countries which would automatically benefit. At the end of the talks, only the US rejected a compromise solution; all 140 other WTO member states supported it. According to *The Lancet*, the US position was "undoubtedly in line with the desires of industry." Many viewed the US stance as a sign of contempt and disregard of poor countries' public health needs.[37]

New Agendas for AIDS Drug Access

The collapse of post-Doha negotiations on TRIPS deepened antagonism between AIDS treatment activists and the drug industry. Yet strategic cooperation remains necessary to advance the interests of those confronting the fatal synergy of poverty and AIDS.

Poor people with AIDS have a vital interest in obtaining existing AIDS drugs at affordable prices—which for many people means free of charge—and in gaining access to new, better medications. The research and development capabilities of major pharmaceutical companies are unrivaled, and the industry's continued participation in AIDS drug work is indispensable, if new medications are to be made available rapidly.

We will not present a fully fleshed-out action plan for expanding access to AIDS drugs in poor countries here.[38] However, we can indicate some of the options such a comprehensive plan will include:

• In the short term, low- and mid-income countries should make full use of all mechanisms, including parallel importation and compulsory licensing, to obtain AIDS medicines for their people at the lowest possible cost. Citizens of high-income countries should pressure political representatives to allow poor countries to use TRIPS-permitted policy tools. In light of the failed December 2002 negotiations on changes to TRIPS, people in the US have a special responsibility to challenge their government's efforts to weaken the Doha declaration.

• Wealthy countries and donor organizations should fully fund the Global Fund to Fight AIDS, Tuberculosis and Malaria (GFATM) committing the $9–10 billion international health experts have estimated would be required annually to mount an effective global effort against the three great infectious killers, AIDS, tuberculosis, and malaria. Drug procurement for the Global Fund will generate significant revenues both for established research-based pharmaceutical companies and companies capable of producing high-quality generics. The presence of such a guaranteed market outlet for massive quantities of AIDS, TB, and malaria medicines will help stimulate investment in new medicines to address these illnesses.

• In connection with the GFATM, the possibility of a global bulk-purchasing mechanism for ARVs and other HIV/AIDS-related medications should be studied. Such a procurement facility would purchase large quantities of high-quality medicines from both research-based and generic suppliers and make the drugs available to poor countries at reduced prices. Comparable international bulk supply mechanisms already exist for TB medicines, and have helped sharply reduce prices of TB medicines.[39]

• Activists should lobby governments to bolster support for public-private partnerships such as the International AIDS Vaccine Initiative (AVI). Such partnerships attempt to combine the strengths of the public sector, NGOs, and private industry. Public-private ventures can prioritize equity concerns industry alone would be unlikely to embrace. By supporting public-private partnerships, governments can help harness the power and resources of the private sector in ways that will more effectively serve the interests of poor people infected with or at risk for HIV.

• With the participation of the research-based pharmaceutical industry, a global system of differential pricing could be formalized for those medicines—including ARVs—sold in both industrialized countries and developing world markets. Differential pricing for pharmaceutical products would mean that prices for key drugs in developing countries could be reduced to near the level of marginal cost, while companies would continue to earn profits on the same medications in affluent markets. Since developing-country markets represent only a tiny share of major pharmaceutical companies' global earnings, such an agreement is not unrealistic. In April 2001, the concept of a formalized system of differential pricing was broadly endorsed by participants at a joint World Health Organization (WHO) and World Trade Organization (WTO) conference on the financing of essential drugs.[40] Technical challenges and details of implementation have been analyzed in a number of scholarly papers.[41] According to health economists, the research-based pharmaceutical industry is increasingly prepared to embrace a system of differential pricing.[42]

• Technical assistance and funding from public and foundation sources could be mobilized to support the creation of a not-for-profit drug industry for diseases of poverty. Several efforts have been launched to work toward this goal, most prominently the

Drugs for Neglected Diseases Initiative (DNDi) spearheaded by Médecins Sans Frontières (MSF). In contrast to a public-private partnership, the DNDi aims to move a portion of research on drugs for diseases of poverty entirely out of the private for-profit sector, relying exclusively on support from public and nonprofit entities. Participating organizations to date include the Pasteur Institute, the Indian Council on Medical Research, the Brazilian government pharmaceutical laboratory, Fiocruz, and the Special Program for Research and Training in Tropical Diseases (a joint undertaking of the World Bank, the United Nations Development Programme, and WHO). Philippe Kourilsky, director general of the Pasteur Institute, has stated that if successful, the DNDi will achieve "nothing short of creating a global, not-for-profit pharmaceutical industry."[43] Meanwhile, the Gates Foundation has funded the recent launch of the San Francisco–based Institute for OneWorld Health, a nonprofit drug company also committed to research targeting diseases disproportionately prevalent in the developing world.[44]

• The lower AIDS drug prices obtained through international generic competition may be threatened after 2005, when countries like India and Brazil are expected to comply fully with TRIPS agreement regulations in the pharmaceutical sector. The impact of the 2005 deadline on drug supplies for AIDS treatment programs worldwide must be examined and immediate measures must be taken to ensure that the global application of TRIPS standards does not further restrict developing countries' capacity to respond to HIV/AIDS and other public health crises.

• In the long term, the international community should be prepared to undertake a thorough reevaluation of existing global intellectual property rights structures, including the TRIPS agreement, in light of credible evidence that these structures, while beneficial to wealthy countries, damage the interests of developing countries in areas such as agriculture and health.[45]

The key objective of AIDS activists is to find answers to the two questions posed at the start of this chapter, and to see those answers put into action: (1) How can people at increased risk for HIV best be enabled to protect themselves from infection? (2) How can the global community best ensure that *all* people with AIDS, particularly the poor, obtain access to a reliable supply of safe, effective, affordable medicines? These problems have no simple solutions, and specific strategies are subject to intense debate. We do know some things, however. The major pharmaceutical manufacturers are immensely powerful, and corporations are designed to maximize profit, not to value justice and compassion. Drug companies, like other corporations, *can* enable social and economic justice, but they will not pursue this agenda spontaneously. They must be led to do so by outside forces—through informed public debate, legal and political constraints, and sustained vigilance from civil society. Despite the wealth, power, and political reach these companies enjoy, motivated activists can set ethical limits on corporate prerogatives.

Fourteen year-old girl, one of more than 13 million children who have lost their parents to AIDS, cares for her family near Johannesburg, South Africa.

MYTH EIGHT:
Limited Resources

Myth: Financial resources for global health are extremely limited, so public health officials in poor countries should prioritize programs that address basic needs, such as nutrition, clean water, maternal health, and childhood immunization. Trying to provide costly, complicated AIDS treatment will divert an incredible share of countries' health budgets toward the needs of a few, while failing to deliver significant benefits for the rest of the population.

Response: First diagnosed in the early 1980s, AIDS was classified as a "new" or "emerging" disease. Yet health workers know well that most sickness and death in poor countries still stems from frustratingly "old" ailments. Tuberculosis (TB) kills nearly two million people worldwide every year. A staggering 300 to 500 million clinical cases of malaria occur annually, with more than one million deaths, the overwhelming majority of them in poor regions.[1] Respiratory infections, diarrheal disease, and measles continue to kill children in poor communities throughout the world. A large fraction of the world's population lacks access to adequate food, clean water, and decent housing, dramatically worsening health outcomes. Accordingly, some public health specialists argue that the health benefits of antiretroviral therapy are insufficient to justify the costs when measured against the potential payoffs from comparatively inexpensive interventions that directly affect larger segments of the population, such as vaccination and maternal health campaigns.[2]

In terms of years of life saved per dollar spent, antiretroviral (ARV) treatment will never compare favorably with interventions such as food security and nutrition programs, maternal health interventions, and childhood vaccinations.[3] Nonetheless, comparatively costly health interventions can still be highly desirable for ethical and humanitarian reasons or for the economic and social benefits they bring (positive "externalities," in economic parlance). We aim to show that, despite its relatively high cost, ARV treatment in poor countries today does not privilege the interests of a few at the expense of the many. AIDS treatment is an essential part of rational strategies to limit the damage of a plague that increasingly threatens the health, security, and stability of entire societies.

Several considerations must be addressed when evaluating the role of ARV therapy in poor countries' health agendas: (1) the distribution of AIDS among different population groups and its impact on life expectancy; (2) the consequences of AIDS on food production and nutrition; (3) the relationship between AIDS and other infectious diseases; (4) the AIDS orphan crisis; and (5) the impact of HIV/AIDS on poor countries' health care systems. Taken together, analysis of these issues suggests that AIDS treatment will bring critical economic, social, and health benefits for wide segments of the population in developing countries, and that ARV therapy will reinforce rather than undermine other parts of countries' health agendas.[4]

AIDS treatment must not replace efforts against other forms of illness in the developing world. AIDS control programs, including antiretroviral therapy, should be added to existing public health agendas. But where will the money come from? In concluding this chapter, we consider one proposal that would shift the parameters of the discussion on "limited resources" for global health.

HIV/AIDS Demographics

Two features of HIV/AIDS' demographic distribution underscore why treating AIDS in developing countries should be an economic and public health priority.

Many of the world's deadly ailments (e.g., diarrheal diseases, measles) kill mainly children. In contrast, AIDS predominantly kills young adults: the most productive members of families and society, and often those on whom others depend for support. The majority of AIDS victims are struck down in the prime of their years of work and parenting. Young adult AIDS victims have often had time to absorb significant investment on the part of society (for example via education) but have not yet lived long enough to repay that investment through work and other social contributions. Sickness and mortality among young adults in what should be the most vigorous and productive phase of their lives inflict severe economic damage on affected countries. This pattern also produces vast numbers of orphans, with the grave social, economic, and health consequences that follow. (See discussion of the orphan crisis, below.)

As a killer of young adults in their prime years, AIDS has provoked catastrophic declines in life expectancy. From 1950 to 1990, progress in the fight against infectious diseases and other health threats raised average life expectancy in developing countries from 40 to 63 years. During this period, the gap between average life expectancies in the developing world and in industrialized countries was halved, from 25 to 13 years.[5]

The explosion of AIDS has reversed these gains in high-burden countries, most shockingly in Africa. In Zimbabwe, average life expectancy in the absence of AIDS would be 70 years. It is 38 and falling.[6] Botswana, Mozambique, Rwanda, Zambia, and Zimbabwe all now have average life expectancies below 40 years of age. Without AIDS, people in these countries could have expected to live to 50 or beyond. By 2010, many countries in southern Africa will have life expectancies falling close to age 30, levels unknown for a century.[7] Life expectancies in high-burden countries outside Africa are also declining as a direct result of AIDS. In the Bahamas, average life expectancy is now 71; without AIDS it would be 80. In Haiti, the pandemic has pushed life expectancy down from 57 to 49. Thailand, Cambodia, and Burma have all lost three years in average life expectancy due to AIDS.[8]

Economists observe a strong relationship between a country's average life expectancy and its capacity to generate economic growth, suggesting HIV/AIDS will have devastating long-term effects on developing countries' economies.[9] HIV prevention must be intensified to protect future economic stability. But rapid deployment of ARV treatment in countries with high HIV/AIDS prevalence is vital to check this demographic disaster in the short and medium term, keeping infected young adults healthy and productive longer and inhibiting further economic erosion. Economic conditions influence many aspects of people's health.[10] By stabilizing the workforce, slowing the loss of skills through illness and death, and helping secure the requirements for improved economic performance, AIDS treatment will benefit all of society and enable progress in other areas of health work.

HIV/AIDS, Agriculture, and Famine

One of the economic sectors most gravely threatened by HIV/AIDS is agriculture. Particularly in regions like Africa, agriculture's role in economic development and health is critical. In some countries, agriculture directly generates only 20 percent of gross domestic product (GDP), but agricultural work directly or indirectly provides livelihoods for as many as 80 percent of the population.[11] Meanwhile, disruption of food production can have devastating long-term consequences for all aspects of health by undermining the nutritional status of a population.

Worldwide, according to the United Nations Food and Agriculture Organization (FAO), seven million farm workers have died of AIDS-related causes since 1985, and 16 million more are expected to die in the coming 20 years.[12] Rising mortality among young farm workers has disrupted the transmission of agricultural knowledge and land management skills from one generation to the next.

When a farm worker becomes ill, labor-intensive cash crops are often neglected as the family concentrates its efforts and resources on providing care for the sick member.[13] Other family members may have to repeatedly take time away from their farming work to accompany the sick person to a medical clinic or traditional healer. When the patient's condition worsens during key phases of the agricultural cycle, such as clearing, sowing, or harvest, both the sick person's absence and the work time lost by caregivers can lead to irrecoverable losses in production.

A recent survey in the rural Bukoba district of Tanzania found that women whose husbands were sick spent 60 percent less time on agricultural activities than they ordinarily would.[14] In Thailand, about one-third of rural households that had experienced an AIDS-related death reported that their agricultural production dropped by half, with a similarly drastic decrease in household income.[15] After farm family breadwinners fall ill, subsistence food must be purchased, and family members may even have to sell off farm equipment or household goods to survive.[16] The sustainability of livestock suffers. Often, animals are sold to pay for funeral expenses, to support orphaned children, or because there is no one to look after them.[17]

Researchers have begun to measure AIDS-related losses in food production at national levels. Over the past five years, agricultural output has been halved in Zimbabwe, with a significant portion of the losses due to HIV/AIDS.[18] The maize harvest has declined by 54 percent, and marketed output has dropped by 61 percent.[19] Today, Zimbabwe and other countries in southern Africa face the double scourge of AIDS and hunger. In September 2002, UN officials estimated that more than 14 million people in six southern African countries could be in imminent danger of starvation as a result of food shortages exacerbated by HIV/AIDS' effects on agriculture.[20] As the number of productive individuals decreases and the amount of land under cultivation dwindles, experts have warned, regions with high HIV/AIDS prevalence could confront chronic food crises in the years ahead.

Rapidly expanding the availability of ARV treatment must be part of the response to this double crisis. In agriculture as in other critical economic sectors, AIDS treatment that keeps skilled workers strong and active longer will bring social utility well beyond the benefits to individual patients. It is literally a matter of survival for families and communities. Far from taking resources away from other, more fundamental health objectives, AIDS treatment in agricultural areas with high HIV/AIDS prevalence is necessary to ensure that people can meet the most basic health goal of all: getting enough food to eat.

Interactions between AIDS and Tuberculosis

For some observers, AIDS treatment threatens to compromise other health initiatives by absorbing a disproportionate share of poor countries' health budgets. However, to accurately gauge the costs and benefits of ARV treatment, we should note that wide deployment of AIDS treatment will actually strengthen efforts to control other infectious illnesses, most importantly tuberculosis.

Today, in countries from South Africa to Russia to Haiti, HIV and TB have forged a deadly synergy, and HIV/AIDS is fueling a TB explosion. In 2000, 12 percent of the global TB burden was associated with HIV, up from just four percent in 1995.[21] According to the World Health Organization (WHO), "Up to 70 percent of patients with sputum smear-positive pulmonary TB are HIV-positive, and up to half of people living with HIV develop TB."[22] WHO has called HIV the "single most important factor" determining the increased incidence of TB in Africa over the past decade.[23] Worldwide, according to World Bank projections, 25 percent of the HIV-positive people who will die of tuberculosis in 2020 would not have been infected with TB in the absence of HIV/AIDS.[24]

About two billion people (one-third of the world's population) carry the disease-causing bacterium, *Mycobacterium tuberculosis*, but the vast majority of these people remain free of active TB because a healthy immune response keeps the bacteria contained. However, HIV weakens the immune system and can break down this containment. HIV-positive people become much more likely to pass from latent to active tuberculosis, in which TB bacteria are released into their lungs and multiply.[25] In the active phase, people become not only sick, but also highly contagious.[26]

HIV/AIDS' role as an accelerator of TB makes anti-AIDS efforts indispensable for effective TB control. ARV treatment should be a component of clinical strategies to break the two diseases' deadly synergy. Technical arguments for allying ARV treatment with DOT (directly observed therapy) programs for TB were discussed in Myth 5. Previous experience with the management of TB drug regimens can pave the way for efficient delivery of ARVs. But, reciprocally, the availability of AIDS treatment will also enhance health systems' abilities to combat TB. A recent South African study found that highly active antiretroviral treatment (HAART) reduced the incidence of TB by more than 80 percent among a cohort of HIV-positive patients in a region where both diseases are endemic.[27]

Just as important, at the community level, offering AIDS treatment can play a role in the expansion of health-promoting attitudes. Increasing people's willingness to be tested for TB and HIV and curbing stigma associated with both illnesses are fundamental to controlling the epidemics.[28] Evidence suggests the availability of AIDS treatment will draw greater numbers of people into health facilities for HIV and TB testing and will help reduce stigma and fear in the community.[29] The capacity to provide highly active antiretroviral treatment (HAART) can also improve the motivation of health care providers exhausted and demoralized by a prolonged losing battle against the twin epidemics. South African researchers argue that "HAART can have a critical role in addressing the therapeutic nihilism surrounding the HIV-1 and tuberculosis co-epidemic in South Africa and other African countries."[30]

Household Dynamics and Children's Health

Children's health constitutes another channel through which AIDS treatment will bring significant gains for the wider population in high-prevalence countries, not just for the people living with HIV/AIDS who receive the drugs. As noted, AIDS tends to strike adults in their prime, often when they are raising children and are at or near the height of their capacity for generating income.[31] For families in developing countries, the sickness and death of a young adult member often shatters household financial security and puts other family members, especially children, at risk. Rapidly declining household economic conditions can lead to hunger, domestic conflict, lost educational opportunities, forced migration, family disintegration, and the economic exploitation of those who normally depend on others for income—especially children and the elderly. Sapping the capacity of families and communities to take care of children, AIDS exacerbates a whole range of childhood health problems.

Consider Botswana, where adult HIV prevalence is currently the highest in the world, at 36 percent.[32] The Botswana Institute of Development Policy Analysis predicts that within 10 years, a quarter of all households in the country will lose at least one income earner to AIDS.[33] With the combined effects of a declining productive population and an expanding dependent population, each surviving income earner will have to provide for an average of four additional dependents because of HIV/AIDS.[34] Whether directly or indirectly affected by AIDS, households under financial duress are likely to (1) liquidate assets (such as livestock or furniture) to meet the immediate needs of caring for sick family members and covering funeral costs; and (2) decrease food consumption in an effort to reduce household expenditure.[35] The resulting reduction in nutrition increases health risks for family members in all age groups, above all for children.

Conditions in other countries are hardly less troubling. A 1997 study in Thailand found that households affected by an AIDS-related death earned half the income of those that were unaffected.[36] Moreover, of the affected households, 15 percent had to withdraw their children from school, and 43 percent of elderly people were left to take care of themselves.[37] In urban households in Ivory Coast, the presence of an adult with AIDS corresponds to a 50 percent decrease in food consumption, a 41 percent decrease in expenditure on education, and a fourfold increase in spending on health care.[38]

Children whose parents have been struck by AIDS may face an

increased risk of succumbing to common childhood diseases. When parents are ill, children are less likely to be brought to clinics or health posts to be vaccinated against measles and other common illnesses. Similarly, children whose parents are sick or dead may have no one to help them obtain medical care for acute health episodes such as severe malaria, raising the probability that more children will die of readily treatable infections. Infant diarrhea, a major killer in poor regions, can be managed by providing drinking water and adequate food. Yet simple care does require an active caregiver. If no competent caregiver is available, children die.[39]

The Orphan Crisis

As discussed in previous myths, AIDS is producing millions of orphans—children and young people who face psychological suffering, deprivation, social exclusion, and multiple health risks. Before AIDS, about two percent of all children in developing countries were orphans (defined as children who, before the age of 15, have lost either their mother or both parents). By 1997, the proportion of children with one or both parents dead had shot up to seven percent in many African countries and in some areas reached an astounding 11 percent. By the end of 2000, there were more than 12 million AIDS orphans in Africa alone.[40] The total number of orphans in Africa is expected to reach 40 million by 2010.[41]

In most societies, extended families have traditionally assumed responsibility for orphans. But in some countries with severe AIDS epidemics, the disease is generating orphans so quickly that family structures can no longer cope. Child-headed homes are becoming increasingly common in high-prevalence countries. It is estimated that 0.4 percent of households in Zimbabwe are child headed, with rates reaching up to three percent in the Rakai district of Uganda. Among orphan-headed households, only three percent have a family member classifiable as a "breadwinner in employment."[42] The loss of parents and family support strips children of the basic necessities and forces many into the street. A recent study in Zimbabwe found that half of street children are orphans, the majority as a result of AIDS.[43]

Orphans in developing countries must cope with severe economic, social, health, and educational disadvantages. Many orphans must leave school in order to work because school fees are no longer affordable. In Uganda, the school attendance of children who have lost one or both parents is almost halved, and those who do go to school spend less time there than they used to. [44] Orphaned girls are more likely to become sexually active at a much younger age because of pressing economic circumstances, rape, or lack of parental supervision. Meanwhile, children who have lost a mother or both parents to AIDS face an even bleaker future than other orphans. An analysis in Ivory Coast found that extended families have more difficulty finding substitute parents for children orphaned by AIDS than for other orphans.[45] A 1999 joint report by UNICEF and UNAIDS revealed that AIDS orphans are at greater risk of malnutrition, illness, abuse, and sexual exploitation than children orphaned by other causes.[46]

The many health risks and forms of abuse and social exclusion suffered by AIDS orphans constitute a strong argument for including ARV treatment in AIDS control strategies in high-prevalence countries. The longer HIV-positive parents can remain healthy and productive, able to work and raise their children, the greater the chance that the children can avoid suffering, marginalization, denial of opportunities, and potentially deadly health problems. The relatively high cost of antiretroviral medications for parents with AIDS may be counterbalanced by significant benefits, not only for individual parents and children, who would be able to sustain their relationships over a longer time, but also for the community as a whole, whose stability would be enhanced by the reinforcement of family structures and the availability of greater material and social support for young people within families.

Impact of HIV/AIDS on Health Care Systems

Today, the battle against HIV/AIDS is exhausting the health care systems of countries on the front lines of the pandemic, most of which have not yet attempted to introduce large-scale treatment programs using ARVs. A case can be made that implementing effective AIDS treatment, far from imposing unmanageable additional burdens on health systems, will in the long run help reduce the pressure on key health facilities in high-prevalence regions.

In the countries hardest hit by the pandemic, stopgap efforts to cope with the consequences of HIV/AIDS are currently overwhelming hospitals and other health facilities and absorbing much of the time and energy of medical personnel.[47] Patients with HIV/AIDS now occupy half the beds in the Provincial Hospital in Chiang Mai, Thailand, and almost three-quarters of the beds in the Prince Regent Hospital in Bujumbura, Burundi, for example.[48] The 2001 Swaziland Human Development Report estimated that patients with HIV/AIDS filled half the beds in some of that country's health centers.[49]

The overload within individual hospitals and clinics is mirrored at the level of national health budgets. A study examining public health spending in 16 African nations found that spending for AIDS alone was more than 2 percent of GDP in seven countries. Moreover, in these countries, 40 to 66 percent of the total funding budgeted for health care was going to AIDS.[50]

Even as struggling health systems and hospitals devote greater portions of their budgets, staff, materials, and bed space to HIV/AIDS, the level of care they are able to provide for all illnesses deteriorates. As

HIV-positive patients fill hospitals, people seeking help for other conditions are being crowded out or forced to wait longer for attention and treatment. As a result of AIDS, the Kenyan hospital sector has seen "increased mortality among HIV-negative patients, who are being admitted at later stages of illness."[51] AIDS is also killing health workers in high-prevalence areas at appalling rates and contributing to burnout among workers who survive; skilled health sector employees were among those hardest hit during the plague's early spread through southern Africa. Says one physician in Zaire,

> Before training we thought of doctors as supermen. Now we realize that our expectations to be held in high esteem [are] not the case...I have no plan for the future. Life has lost meaning...Life is strange—you are supposed to go from birth to death...[now] we are only mortuary attendants.[52]

To address these challenges, countries need aggressive HIV prevention programs to reduce new infections. Wider availability of ARV treatment for AIDS will also relieve the pressure on health systems. Untreated HIV leaves patients vulnerable to a wide array of opportunistic infections that can require long hospitalizations and expensive therapies. ARV therapy strengthens patients' immune systems and enables them to fight off many infections more effectively, cutting the need for extended hospital stays and other forms of medical treatment.

Data from Brazil show that the country's universal ARV access program has dramatically reduced the number and cost of AIDS-related hospitalizations, freeing hospital beds, medical staff, and other resources to provide better care to patients with non-AIDS-related conditions. The Brazilian Ministry of Health estimates that the universal free provision of HAART prevented 234,000 AIDS-related hospital admissions in the period 1997–2000, resulting in a US$677 million savings for Brazil's Unified Health System.[52] Funds spent on antiretrovirals are partially recouped through decreased demand for other medicines. For example, by treating AIDS patients with ARVs, the Brazilian health system was able to reduce its need for the drug ganciclovir, used to treat cytomegalovirus infection, by 69 percent over a two-year period, saving US$34 million.[53] The Ministry of Health has estimated total savings obtained through the universal provision of ARV treatment at close to US$1.1 billion.[54]

This evidence is significant. It suggests that HAART does not undermine other programs, and that ARV therapy may reduce stresses on health systems where it is universally available. Of course, Brazil's results will not be immediately replicable in much poorer countries with significantly higher rates of HIV/AIDS and lower per capita health spending. Yet the Brazilian success does set a target for other countries to aspire to, and helps leverage national and international support for AIDS treatment.

A Global Strategy for Poor People's Health

The investment in HAART brings significant benefits for communities and society as a whole, in addition to extending the lives of people living with HIV/AIDS. The deployment of ARV treatment in poor countries will promote a range of crucial health and societal goals. AIDS must be addressed within an integrated health and social justice agenda, and, conversely, no comprehensive, equitable health and development agenda can neglect the provision of AIDS treatment.

Antiretroviral therapy must not supplant efforts against other illnesses. AIDS therapies should be added to existing public health agendas, as part of an across-the-board effort to improve the health of poor people in the developing world. Yet if developing countries' health systems are already overburdened, how will they fund the additional capacities required to deliver ARVs? Recently, ̖ the world's leading economists, health experts, and development specialists have turned their attention to the problem of new approaches to health and health financing in developing countries. The landmark 2001 report of the WHO Commission on Macroeconomics and Health (CMH) offers a credible blueprint for an integrated global health and antipoverty agenda incorporating ARV therapy for AIDS.[55]

The authors argue that ARV therapy, despite the high expense, is cost-effective in resource-poor settings when reckoned against the immense social and economic costs of not treating millions of people with HIV/AIDS.[56] The commission's policy design integrates the progressive rollout of ARV treatment into a framework addressing the full spectrum of diseases and dangers that most seriously compromise health and economic productivity in poor communities: HIV/AIDS, tuberculosis, malaria, childhood diseases, unsafe pregnancy and delivery, infant illness at the time of delivery, and tobacco-related illnesses (all exacerbated by malnutrition). The report shows how resources can be mobilized and programs designed so that developing country public health officials will be forced to choose between necessities (either AIDS treatment or measles vaccination) less often and instead can implement integrative strategies enabling across-the-board progress in health.

The precondition for an integrated offensive against the major health threats in poor countries is significantly increased international investment in health. Under the commission's proposal, official development assistance for health care allocated by affluent countries for resource-poor countries would increase from current levels of around $6 billion per year to $27 billion by 2007. Low- and middle-income countries would in turn step up their own domestic health spending, while working to increase transparency and accountability in governance and to promote active community and civil society involvement in health campaigns. The humanitarian benefits of such a program would be vast. And, the commission's analysts argue, improving the health of the poor would spur global productivity and generate significant gains for the world economy. By 2015–2020, increased total health spending of $66 billion per year above current levels could generate global economic gains of $360 billion annually, a sixfold return on investment.[57]

The investment required is substantial. However, the resources do exist. The problem is not immovable structural constraints nor material scarcity, but how the affluent choose to spend money. In the US, when vast sums must be mobilized to prop up the airline industry, subsidize American agriculture, or wage "preemptive wars," the needed funds flow without delay. To overcome the tension between AIDS treatment and other public health goals, we must challenge political and economic power holders in wealthy countries to dramatically expand funding for global efforts against disease, including but not limited to HIV/AIDS.

Increased international donor support for health programs in the developing world is a goal both AIDS activists and health economists can endorse.[58] While striving to make the most effective use of available resources, we have an obligation to press basic questions about how resources are allocated. Why are resources severely constrained in some areas, such as health care for the poor, while appearing virtually without bounds in others, such as US military spending? Today US foreign assistance is miserly; as a percentage of GDP, it continues to be the smallest contribution made by any of the major industrialized nations. Yet, even as American politicians plead poverty when it comes to foreign aid, President George W. Bush recently ordered the construction—at an estimated cost of $17.5 billion over two years—of a missile defense system many experts regard as deeply flawed. The Bush administration is also stepping up preparations for a war in Iraq whose total cost, some economists calculate, may reach almost $2 trillion.[59] Such resource–allocation decisions, enacted in our name, should engage our moral responsibility. Does the current distribution of public spending on health and the military accurately reflect our values? If not, we must question the choices and act to bring change.

President Bush's January 2003 pledge to increase support for the global AIDS fight could mark the beginning of a shift in US priorities. Yet sentimental expressions of "compassion" for the victims of AIDS are not yet an adequate policy. Activist pressure will be more vital than ever in the coming years to ensure that the administration carries through on and expands its HIV/AIDS commitments. And while demanding greater US engagement on AIDS and global health, we must prevent modest increases in AIDS funding from functioning as moral cover for a wider US politics of aggression and domination.

World AIDS Day demonstrators in New York City carry signs
with names of people afflicted with AIDS.

MYTH NINE:
Nothing To Gain

Myth: People in the US and other wealthy countries have nothing to gain by fighting AIDS in the developing world. American contributions to the global AIDS effort are acts of charity. They help poor foreigners while yielding little benefit for Americans. Since the disease does not affect their constituents, it is normal that politicians in wealthy, powerful countries consider global AIDS a low-priority issue.

Response: US contributions to international efforts against AIDS have been minimal, relative to the country's power and wealth. American lawmakers' reluctance to fund global AIDS work reflects the perception that the pandemic has no impact on American interests. Current evidence disproves this assumption. Affluent Americans and Europeans are not insulated from the growing biomedical and social fallout of the AIDS crisis. The continued spread of the disease in the developing world may significantly compromise our interests on a variety of fronts. The best arguments for American involvement in international AIDS work are moral. But an effective case can also be made that helping to check the global spread of HIV/AIDS will bring long-term gains for the US in three major areas: (1) public health; (2) the economy; and (3) security. We discuss these areas in turn and then look at moral arguments for an intensified US commitment. When lobbying lawmakers, AIDS advocates may find that moral arguments alone often have little impact. But moral reasoning tied to the prospect of tangible payoffs can provide a powerful motive for change. While our discussion focuses on the US, many of the points are applicable to other high-income countries.

HIV/AIDS and Global Health Equity

In an era of global trade and tourism, widespread labor migration, and frequent cross-border refugee flows, health protection must be understood in global terms. The historic importance of globalization can be easily overstated. Yet the rapid circulation of people and goods across national and continental boundaries poses significant challenges for public health officials today. The implications for the control of infectious diseases in particular are far-reaching. Theoretical modeling by epidemiologists has shown that even modest increases in international linkages between populations (for example through tourism, migration, or business travel) may substantially increase rates of infectious disease transmission.[1] Recent outbreaks of West Nile virus across the US and of multiple-drug-resistant tuberculosis in New York City attest to the transcontinental mobility of pathogens.[2] In the words of one bioethicist, we are witnessing the "microbial unification" of the world.[3]

Wealthy countries will attempt to shield their populations from this international proliferation of infectious agents with intensified policing of their national boundaries, for example through immigration restrictions against people with HIV, like the ones currently in place in the US. The success of such policies—to say nothing of their moral legitimacy—will be partial, at best. Exploding HIV/AIDS epidemics in Africa, South Asia, the Caribbean, and Eastern Europe pose an ongoing health threat to US citizens traveling or working abroad, and infections will continue to make their way onto American soil.

Moreover, because of the particular nature of HIV disease and its effects on the human immune system, HIV/AIDS poses a multipronged health threat. We saw earlier (see Myth 8) that AIDS can exacerbate the impact of other deadly infectious diseases, especially tuberculosis (TB). As the AIDS pandemic rages, it raises global TB risks. In regions where an underlying HIV/AIDS epidemic has not been addressed, efforts against TB have also stagnated. HIV promotes TB's progression from latent infection to active disease, and as the number of HIV-positive people with active TB increases, the danger of contracting TB rises for all members of the community, regardless of HIV status.[4] Because *Mycobacterium tuberculosis* is an airborne pathogen, merely being in a room with or taking an airplane with a person carrying active TB can create sufficient opportunity for exposure and transmission. The HIV and TB epidemics now exploding in the Russian Federation and Ukraine show that technologically advanced countries, not just poor nations, are vulnerable to the combined assault of these killers.

To protect ourselves against TB effectively, the best policy is to ensure that the intertwined TB and HIV epidemics are controlled on the global level. Infectious pathogens ignore human-made borders. Infectious disease surveillance and treatment systems must do the same. In the words of Nobel Prize–winning microbiologist and geneticist Joshua Lederberg, "We arrive at the realization that world health is indivisible, that we cannot satisfy our most parochial needs without attending to the health conditions of all the globe."[5] Particularly for a country like the US, historically dependent on immigrant labor and committed to free trade and global economic integration, defending citizens against infectious killers requires active collaboration and support of other countries' efforts to overcome epidemics.

Upgrading infectious disease surveillance and control

mechanisms in the developing world will both assist poor countries immediately in their fight against AIDS and bring lasting benefits for the US and other wealthy countries. The primary obstacle is the initial funding needed for the necessary infrastructure, a category of "global public goods," defined by economists as those "whose benefits reach across borders, generations, and population groups."[6] These goods tend to be undersupplied by the market precisely because of their public character—once they are in place, everyone can freely benefit from them, and those who may have invested in their creation enjoy no special privileges in their use.[7] Individual state actors will always be discouraged from investing in a global public good since much of the eventual benefit from the investment will accrue beyond a country's borders.[8]

With this in mind, leaders like UN secretary general Kofi Annan and the economists of the World Health Organization's (WHO) Commission on Macroeconomics and Health have stressed the necessity of international coordinating mechanisms to generate and manage investment in global efforts against infectious disease. Structures like the Global Fund to Fight AIDS, Tuberculosis, and Malaria (GFATM) have emerged from this concern. Recognizing that stronger international infectious disease control will serve all countries' interests, but that individual states face disincentives against unilateral investment, wealthy countries like the US should take the lead in supporting the creation and expansion of international mechanisms to reinforce infectious disease infrastructure in the developing world.

The gains accruing to high- and low-income countries from this intensified public health investment will include not only more-effective measures against current crises (AIDS and TB) but also the capacity to mount a rapid, coordinated response to future infectious disease threats, which some scientists argue may be imminent.[9]

Economic Impact of HIV/AIDS Pandemic

An effective global fight against AIDS will benefit the US and other wealthy countries economically. When lobbying lawmakers in the US and other high-income countries, AIDS advocates can show that controlling AIDS in the developing world will save both lives and money. Of course, many people will understandably question the need to point beyond the health of people to the well-being of markets and corporations as a reason to fight AIDS. However, showing that AIDS and other infectious diseases threaten economic interests is a useful way of capturing the attention of lawmakers.

Arguments that wealthy countries will gain economically by helping control AIDS in the developing world can focus on the pandemic's effects on corporate profitability, and the impact of HIV/AIDS at regional and international levels.

Major international companies doing business in regions with high HIV-prevalence are increasingly concerned about the effects of AIDS on productivity and profitability, as the disease ravages workforces, including highly trained cadres.[10] *The Economist* reported that some multinational corporations operating in South Africa must hire three workers for every skilled position to ensure that replacements are on hand when trained workers die.[11] In some hard-hit African countries, AIDS has cut overall worker productivity in half.[12]

The impact of AIDS on the corporate bottom line provoked concern at the meetings of the World Economic Forum in February 2002. International health officials and heads of major corporations discussed new public-private partnership initiatives to respond to HIV/AIDS's growing economic and social fallout. Göran Lindahl, chairman-designate of the Anglo American Mining Corporation and private-sector representative to the GFATM, stated that companies now see reducing the burden of disease as a "critical factor for business success in developing countries."[13]

Some businesses have moved from words to actions. For example, Volkswagen Brazil introduced a successful company-wide prevention and treatment program that has raised worker awareness of the AIDS threat, reduced the number of infections among workers, and cut HIV/AIDS-related absenteeism by 90 percent.[14] A pilot partnership between the NGO Family Health International and South Africa's Harmony Gold Mining Company dramatically reduced the incidence of sexually transmitted infections (STIs) among Harmony workers at the Virginia mine in Free State province. The initiative saved the company an estimated US$540,000 in medical costs and lost productivity in just a nine-month period and provided a model for other mining firms to follow.[15] Coca-Cola, the largest foreign employer in Africa, has begun to use its delivery trucks to distribute AIDS information and condoms.[16]

Meanwhile the Coca-Cola case crystallizes some of the ambiguities of corporate involvement in the AIDS fight. Coca-Cola has garnered praise for good corporate citizenship as a result of its condom distribution efforts and because it offers HIV/AIDS health coverage—including antiretroviral drugs on a need basis—to its "direct employees" in Africa. Yet activists, in particular Health Global Access Project (Health GAP), revealed that the company counted only 1,500 people on the African continent as direct employees—neglecting the 100,000 men and women who bottle and distribute Coke in Africa under subcontracting and licensing arrangements. In April 2002, activists gained access to Coca-Cola's shareholder meeting at Madison Square Garden in New York and publicly challenged the company's leadership to extend full HIV/AIDS health benefits to all its African workers.

The Coca-Cola case underscores the limits to the coincidence of corporate interests and those of poor and working people with AIDS. When common ground exists, it should be exploited. But the core question for global AIDS activists—What will best serve the interests of poor people with AIDS?—does not enter into the logic of profit maximization that governs corporations. However, this should not stop AIDS advocates from making strategic use of economic arguments to broaden debate and highlight the multiple dimensions of the crisis.

The regional and global macroeconomic effects of the AIDS plague fall most heavily on poor and vulnerable communities in the developing world, but they also have serious implications for wealthy countries. The findings of WHO's Commission on Macroeconomics and Health and other recent scholarship show that AIDS and the other infectious diseases primarily afflicting the poor have a significant negative impact on global economic performance. Taking action to reduce the burden of these diseases will bring long-term economic benefits not only for poor countries but for the US and other established market economies.

The macroeconomic burden of AIDS in the worst affected areas has assumed overwhelming proportions. Though the numbers have been subject to much debate, a range of studies indicate that the impact of the pandemic on per capita gross domestic product (GDP) growth in high-prevalence countries is substantial.[17] Some economists have forecast that many African economies may suffer up to a 25 percent decrease in GDP growth rates over the next 20 years, largely as a result of AIDS.[18] By 2010, South Africa will face a real annual GDP 17 percent smaller than it would be in the absence of AIDS.[19] In some severely affected African countries, AIDS in

2002, slashed annual GDP growth by four percentage points, from five percent to one percent per year.[20]

Health economists often quantify the socioeconomic impact of disease in terms of Disability Adjusted Life Years (DALYs) lost because of sickness and premature death. To obtain a rough estimate of the aggregate economic loss inflicted by a disease, economists multiply the number of DALYs claimed by the illness by a coefficient calculated to represent the economic value of a year of healthy life. In 1999, an estimated 72 million DALYs were lost in sub-Saharan Africa due to AIDS. If each DALY is valued extremely conservatively at the level of annual per capita income in the region, the economic value of lost life years in 1999 due to AIDS would be 11.7 percent of the total gross national product of sub-Saharan Africa. Using a more realistic economic valuation of each DALY at three times per capita income, the losses are 35.1 percent of GNP.[21]

The social and economic damage now being inflicted on southern Africa will spread to other regions if the pandemic is not controlled. As AIDS makes increasing inroads in Asia, Eastern Europe, and the Caribbean, its effects will undermine economic growth and potential prosperity across growing areas of the world. Research at the University of the West Indies has predicted that AIDS could cause an annual five percent loss in GDP in Jamaica and Trinidad and Tobago by 2005. One study has found that for the whole Caribbean region, AIDS could reduce the expected GDP by 4.2 percent.[22]

Given the gravity of the threat posed to global prosperity and economic development by AIDS and other diseases primarily affecting the poor, some economists maintain that massive increases in global health spending by high-income countries can be justified not only on humanitarian grounds but also in terms of rich countries' economic self-interest. Looking at AIDS, TB, malaria, and other diseases of poverty as obstacles to economic development, WHO's Commission on Macroeconomics and Health argues that by raising their grant funding in the international health sector to $22 billion per year by 2007 and $31 billion yearly by 2015, wealthy donor countries would enable 8 million lives per year to be saved by 2010, with the progress in health translating directly into significant global economic gains.[23] Counting contributions from all sources (including poor countries themselves), the commission calculates that by 2015–2020, increased health investments of $66 billion per year above current spending will generate at least $360 billion annually in direct and indirect gains for the world economy.

Of course, most of the direct economic benefit of controlling AIDS will accrue initially outside US and European borders, in developing countries themselves. Yet northern powers' foreign aid and development policies have always relied on the idea that heightened prosperity in developing regions will benefit wealthy countries, too. As poor countries develop and prosper, they become more reliable trading partners and stronger markets for the goods and services US workers and firms produce. It is worth recalling that nearly half of the US' total exports go to developing countries. In some recent years, the US has exported more to Africa than to the former Soviet Union.[24] Additionally, the US imports nearly 20 percent of its oil and mineral resources from Africa. Should AIDS cause the economies of poor countries to deteriorate further, wealthy economies will lose already important trading partners.

Political leaders in the US and other high-income countries have routinely asserted the benefits of an African economic resurgence for industrialized countries and African peoples alike.[25] Bland and insubstantial as such rhetoric may be, this nominal commitment by American policy makers provides AIDS activists with an opening to press a claim that stemming the disease's devastating socioeconomic effects is not charity, but a necessary investment in the global economic future.

AIDS as a Security Issue

While political leaders in affluent countries are often reluctant to allocate funds for humanitarian causes, they are willing to spend very large sums on initiatives that promise to strengthen national and global security. This emphasis has become even more pronounced following the attacks of September 11, 2001. Responding to the current climate, some AIDS advocates have emphasized the pandemic's potential security implications.

This line of argument uncovers important truths, but it also involves risks. To invoke the notoriously amorphous concepts of national and global security may lend unintended support to regressive forces and attitudes in American politics.[26] Security concerns could be cited to legitimize US military intervention or covert CIA operations in poor countries, as well as to argue for expanded HIV/AIDS work there. Indeed, the track record suggests that discussions of security among American foreign policy specialists are more likely to lead to military solutions than to strengthened humanitarian efforts. But if the security theme is linked to a strong moral and human rights stance, it can help clarify the enormous stakes at play in the world's response to AIDS.

Security includes economic, social, political, and military factors. For some, it is under this heading that the multidimensional threat posed by AIDS becomes most apparent. By diverting scarce public resources; creating millions of orphans; incapacitating adult men and women; and decimating the recruitment pool for militaries, government administrations, the health professions, and other vital sectors, AIDS attacks the very structure of society.[27] The consequence is an increasing destabilization of institutions and processes needed to maintain security and civil order at all levels, from households and villages to nations and regions.

In hard-hit African countries, ministries of defense now confront HIV infection rates of 20 to 40 percent among soldiers. These rates reach as high as 50 to 60 percent in countries where HIV/AIDS has been present for more than a decade.[28] Civilian law enforcement is also compromised. AIDS is estimated to account for up to three-quarters of all deaths in the Kenyan police force, for example.[29] As military and police personnel become ill and die, governments' ability to maintain peace, stability, and the rule of law may deteriorate, with severe consequences for national and regional security and development opportunities. Simultaneously, the pandemic's wider socioeconomic effects constrain states' ability to meet citizens' needs for food, housing, and education, leading to a loss of faith in political and social institutions.[30] The corrosion of security and governance institutions provoked by AIDS in parts of sub-Saharan Africa today sounds an alarm for other regions where the epidemic is spreading rapidly.

A heavy disease burden among a country's population is strongly correlated with political instability. According to the CIA Task Force on State Failure, high infant mortality (a leading indicator of overall disease burden) is one of the three most powerful predictors of the breakdown of state structures.[31] Additionally, as AIDS decimates older adult populations of affected countries, an increasing percentage of the population is aged between 15 and 24. This demographic shift is an important predictor of internal violence, in turn closely correlated with state collapse and pressures for military intervention by the international community.[32]

Recognizing the risks, in 2000 the American government officially designated the global AIDS pandemic as a threat to US national security, the first time in history a disease has been added to a list that includes terrorism and weapons of mass destruction. A January 2000 CIA report stated that in the next 20 years new and reemerging infectious diseases including HIV/AIDS will "pose a rising global health threat and will complicate US and global security....These diseases will endanger US citizens at home and abroad, threaten US armed forces deployed overseas, and exacerbate social and political instability in key countries and regions in which the US has significant interests."[33] In a 2000 interview, national security advisor Samuel Berger explained the government's unprecedented decision to label a disease as a national security threat, citing the proportions of the global pandemic and its capacity to sap the social, political, and economic foundations of entire regions. "If we don't address this as an urgent problem, we're going to have increasing instability, increasing conflict and an implosion of many of the countries in the developing world," Berger said.[34]

Unfortunately, some US policy makers may interpret this data—that AIDS threatens less affluent countries' governance capabilities, economic viability, and social cohesion—as justification for more aggressive American intrusions, perhaps through military force, in their internal affairs. Conversely, others may view the magnitude of the AIDS crisis and its socioeconomic and security fallout as a good reason for the US to *disengage* from heavily affected regions, in particular sub-Saharan Africa. A more reasonable response to AIDS as a security issue is neither isolationist disengagement nor further efforts to manipulate and dominate developing countries. The message that AIDS threatens national, regional, and global security must be linked to arguments for a humanitarian response respectful of human rights and other countries' sovereignty.

The Moral Stakes

Fighting HIV/AIDS in the developing world will bring benefits for the US and other wealthy countries in the areas of public health, the economy, and security. Yet the strongest argument for wealthy, powerful countries to commit themselves to the global AIDS effort is based not on self-interest but on morality.

Contemporary American society is characterized by an uneasy moral pluralism, the coexistence of multiple, in some cases mutually unintelligible moral "languages." But limited consensus across the boundaries of moral value systems is possible.[35] When presented with the facts, people from very different ethical and social horizons can recognize the egregious injustice embodied by the global AIDS crisis. A deadly but preventable infection spreads across widening regions of the developing world; countries with vast financial and technological resources like the US stand by as passive spectators. The amount of money required to fight the pandemic more effectively has been calculated; wealthy countries refuse to contribute their share.[36] A relatively simple intervention can often prevent the transmission of the virus from a pregnant woman to her baby; each year tens of thousands of infants still contract the disease because poor countries lack the money, medicines, and technical support to implement this procedure universally. People in high-income countries are successfully treated for the illness as a matter of routine; in poor countries, only a minute fraction of those who need treatment can obtain medicines. Human beings with identical medical conditions are enabled to live—or condemned to die—because of their income.

HIV/AIDS health care issues can be framed in terms of human rights; indeed, access to the highest attainable standard of health care is an inalienable right for all persons.[37] This is articulated in the foundational text of international human rights law, the 1948

Universal Declaration of Human Rights. Article 25 affirms: "Everyone has the right to a standard of living adequate for the health and well-being of himself and his family, including food, clothing, housing and medical care...."[38] Therefore, nonaccess to effective AIDS prevention and treatment violates the basic rights of millions of people in the developing world.

Furthermore, the World Health Organization Constitution states that "the enjoyment of the highest attainable standard of health is one of the fundamental rights of every human being."[39] Thus, violating the human rights of poor Africans, Asians, or Latin Americans is as serious as breaching the rights of affluent Americans. Today, the vocabulary of human rights is routinely employed by global leaders in medicine and public health, as well as by people living with HIV/AIDS and their advocates.[40]

For example, Costa Rican human rights NGOs helped an HIV-positive college student bring a suit to the country's Supreme Court requesting government assistance in paying for antiretroviral medications the student could not afford. The court ruled in the student's favor, sparking a wave of similar petitions. The Costa Rican government then ordered the national social security system to develop a plan for the provision of highly active antiretroviral therapy (HAART) to all citizens living with AIDS.[41] In Venezuela in 1997, a consortium led by the NGO Acción Ciudadana Contra el SIDA filed a suit on behalf of a group of poor people living with HIV/AIDS who were unable to afford antiretroviral therapy.

Citing rights guaranteed in the National Constitution, the American Convention on Human Rights, and other international conventions signed and ratified by Venezuela, the suit maintained that the HIV-positive claimants were being denied their right to proper medical care because they could not obtain HAART. The court ruled in the plaintiffs' favor and ordered the social security system to provide them with free antiretroviral treatment.[42] Such cases show that rights language offers more than noble abstractions. Human rights discourse can be operationalized on the ground, translating moral conviction into legal and political action that effects change.

The US frequently uses human rights arguments and standards to criticize other countries (e.g., Cuba, China, Iraq). If Americans applied a rigorous rights-based ethical and legal analysis to US foreign policy in areas such as international health, the results would be dramatic. One outcome would be a drastically stepped-up American commitment to the global fight against AIDS and other diseases of poverty.

An American marching in Global Day of Action
in New York City.

MYTH TEN:
Nothing We Can Do

Myth: Even with good intentions, ordinary people in rich countries can do little to help in the struggle against AIDS in poor countries.

Response: Among the many myths spawned by the global AIDS crisis, the belief that there is "nothing we can do" is one of the most destructive. If it cannot be overcome, then the other ideas brought forward in this book mean little.

It is not hard to understand how this myth has taken hold. The AIDS crisis just seems too big. Each day 14,000 people contract HIV, while underfunded prevention programs languish. Each day AIDS kills 8,500 human beings, while treatment remains beyond the reach of all but a minute fraction of those who are infected.

The numbers and the enormous suffering they represent should convince us of the need to act without delay, but may instead induce paralysis. Witnessing the unfolding of such a catastrophe may push us toward resignation and despair. But if a dawning awareness of the pandemic provokes hopelessness, a greater understanding of the disease and its spread takes us beyond resignation to action. We can overcome fatalism and powerlessness by: (1) looking back at what activists have already accomplished, and (2) looking ahead to the actions that we, as citizens and residents of affluent countries, can undertake in the global battle against HIV/AIDS.

Looking Back

Important victories by earlier anti-AIDS activists provide inspiration for today's movement. In the US, organized AIDS activism began soon after the disease was detected, before the epidemic even had an official name, and has continued for more than 20 years.[1] Refusing to be labeled as "patients" or "victims," early activists living with HIV/AIDS helped permanently alter relations among doctors, biomedical and government institutions, and ordinary people fighting for their lives.[2]

Starting in the early 1980s, AIDS activists in the US, led by groups like the AIDS Coalition To Unleash Power (ACT UP), took on the Food and Drug Administration (FDA) and the medical establishment, picketed the drug companies, and publicly challenged and shamed politicians when budget cuts threatened AIDS services. Activists took their demands to the streets and into corporate boardrooms and FDA research labs. Pressure from AIDS activists accelerated FDA drug-testing protocols; increased access to experimental AIDS drugs for people willing to try the drugs but not selected for participation in a clinical trial; and secured a place at the table for people living with HIV/AIDS and grassroots community representatives when officials met to decide upon AIDS research agendas and public health spending priorities. Actions such as the October 11, 1988 protest at FDA headquarters in Rockville, Maryland, in which more than a thousand demonstrators participated and hundreds were arrested, generated so much public attention that the government could no longer downplay the crisis or ignore those living with the virus.[3]

Early activists achieved their aims by using a two-pronged approach: (1) mobilizing large groups on the street for provocative public protests; and (2) learning the languages of the boardroom and medical literature, so that their representatives could dialogue persuasively conduct a dialogue with physicians, scientific researchers, public health specialists, and politicians.[4] The enduring lesson of the early AIDS movement is that both deadly diseases and oppressive political forces can be strongly challenged. Ordinary people—men and women with little or no prior training in the relevant medical, scientific, legal, and political issues—can acquire the necessary scientific knowledge and political skills to help redefine agendas in health policy and treatment research.

For many in the US, the primary motive for AIDS activism receded in 1996 when combination antiretroviral therapies became available. Nevertheless, activists with a wider vision understood that the success of highly active antiretroviral therapy (HAART) in affluent countries meant that the next and greater challenge for activism was just beginning. The task was to seek ways to bring the same level of AIDS care now available in the US to the millions of infected people in the developing world. This necessarily meant forging a political-economic critique of the structural forces driving the worldwide epidemic and blocking equity in treatment access. At the 1996 International AIDS Conference in Vancouver, ACT UP cofounder Eric Sawyer publicly denounced those in high-income countries who believed that access to antiretrovirals for a handful of the world's most privileged citizens signified the end of AIDS. Sawyer challenged drug companies to implement differential pricing for poor-world markets, urged rich-world governments to multiply their foreign assistance budgets for HIV/AIDS treatment and prevention, and ended his speech by leading the conference's thousands of participants in a group chant: "Greed kills! Access for all!"[5]

Four years later, at the 2000 International AIDS Conference in Durban, South Africa, activists from wealthy and poor countries joined forces to press their demands for treatment equity:

The countries hardest hit by the epidemic [have] made their position clear: access to treatments, including antiretrovirals, is indispensable for their populations and must be established on a permanent basis. That means that pharmaceutical companies must yield to public health priorities and adapt their prices to the countries' payment capacities or allow these countries to produce and import treatments at lower cost in accordance with legal stipulations included in international agreements. Northern countries, particularly the US and the European Union, must stop subjecting poor countries to pressure and blackmail and must help to finance the development of access to treatments.[6]

Since the Durban conference, activists have continued to build local and international alliances. ACT UP and Health Global Access Project Coalition (Health GAP), in particular, have maintained their confrontational stance toward the pharmaceutical industry, shaming companies for their pricing practices on AIDS–related medications in the domestic market and overseas. Activist agitation and provocation at events like Al Gore's presidential campaign kickoff rally embarrassed top American leaders and forced changes in US trade practices, particularly the withdrawal of American support for the controversial lawsuit brought by international pharmaceutical companies against the South African government. (See Myth 7.)

When the consortium of multinational drug giants abandoned its suit in April 2001, the victory belonged to the Treatment Action Campaign (TAC), South Africa's pathbreaking AIDS activist organization. Yet the resolute, highly publicized solidarity shown by activists in the US, Europe, and elsewhere played a crucial supporting role. American and European activists staged marches, teach-ins, and demonstrations in solidarity with the TAC effort and supported the South African group's fight with petitions and letter writing campaigns to the pharmaceutical companies and US politicians. As activists focused international attention on "Big Pharma's" court action, negative publicity and consumer disapproval in affluent countries helped force a change in the companies' policy. A TAC statement on the case underscored that a "global effort and the dedication of thousands of volunteers" had enabled success.[7]

Some Americans who played a key role did not have decades of prior activism and organizing experience. The heroes of the campaign included Amy Kapczynski, a Yale University law student then in her early twenties. Kapczynski attended the Durban conference and was inspired by the courage and political sophistication of the South African treatment activists she met. The attitude of South African activists, demanding justice and rejecting pity, struck Kapczynski's imagination. "It's not about feeling bad and doing things out of guilt. People have a right to medication. They have a right to dignity and to...the highest attainable standard of health," Kapczynski later told journalists.[8] Returning to the US, Kapczynski teamed up with activists from Médecins Sans Frontières (MSF) to launch a US-based campaign challenging corporations' and research institutions' policies on intellectual property and AIDS drug access. Kapczynski was instrumental in driving the campaign that ultimately led Yale University and Bristol Myers Squibb to pledge not to enforce the patent on d4T — a key antiretroviral drug — in South Africa. In turn, the actions by Yale and Bristol Myers Squibb helped precipitate the pharmaceutical manufacturers' decision to abandon their South African lawsuit.[9]

The history of AIDS activism demonstrates that ordinary people have made a difference in the global fight against AIDS. Yet the activist push must intensify in the coming years. The power of ordinary people to effect change, though limited, is real. And as we link our efforts and resources, that power grows. There are many ways in which people in wealthy countries can get involved in the global AIDS struggle. (See "Resources for Activism" at the end of the book.) And in several of these areas, our participation is not only possible but essential if the worldwide effort is to succeed.

What Can Be Done

Some will want to fight AIDS directly by participating in treatment and prevention programs in poor countries. Those who have medical or public health skills, or who are being trained, might volunteer with MSF, the Red Cross or Red Crescent, or another medical relief organization or nongovernmental organization (NGO). In many regions impacted by the crisis, qualified medical and paramedical personnel—physicians, nurses, public health workers, trainers and counselors, social workers with health expertise, or students in these and related fields—are in short supply because of budget cuts, a longstanding "brain drain," and because local health workers are falling victim to the disease. The contributions of foreign health professionals and volunteers will continue to be important in many poor countries grappling with AIDS.

In addition to direct clinical practice, health workers can also help in designing and administering public health programs, AIDS research studies, and prevention campaigns. Non-clinicians can have an especially important role in the areas of prevention and data collection. Effective training of community health workers is vital to the success of community-based AIDS prevention and care programs, and volunteers with some experience in teaching can be active in this area.

Many poor and middle-income countries have good reason to be suspicious of foreigners' offers of aid, whether in health care or other sectors. South Africa, for example, has made a policy of seeking to reduce the number of foreign doctors in the country. Yet numerous opportunities for constructive cooperation remain. Those looking to participate in health work (and specifically HIV/AIDS work) in developing countries should assess how specific programs are run, and examine what provisions are made to retain or guarantee local ownership and decision-making powers.

People with medical training are not the only ones who can make meaningful contributions. Throughout this book, we have insisted that HIV/AIDS transmission intertwines with social, economic, and political factors such as poverty, gender inequality, access to education, civil conflict, and the presence or absence of effective governance and sound legal structures. People with skills or interests in economics, finance, education, gender issues, computer science, law, and agriculture can pursue their work in poor countries in ways that will contribute, directly or indirectly, to the fight against AIDS.

For example, those working with international development organizations (e.g., the Peace Corps) can build AIDS education and prevention efforts into their projects. Even projects tangentially related to the health sector can and should integrate HIV/AIDS work. In regions like sub-Saharan Africa, international development and service organizations have made AIDS prevention a central assignment for an increasing number of field workers. The Peace Corps has identified HIV/AIDS as a special organizational focus area and is providing its volunteers in Africa with basic training in HIV/AIDS education and prevention, so they can take this knowledge into the communities they serve—whatever their specific job responsibilities. Many Peace Corps volunteers engage in AIDS prevention work in schools and other community settings, often in cooperation with local, national, or international organizations, including ministries of health, AIDS service organizations and other health NGOs, groups working with orphans, and advocacy groups led by people living with HIV/AIDS.[10]

People with a legal background can be highly useful to the struggle for equity in AIDS treatment access. Amy Kapczynski's organizing efforts provide one example. Toby Kaspar, another young American with legal skills and a commitment to social justice, was instrumental in developing the legal arguments to enable MSF South Africa's importation of generic ARV medications from Brazil.[11] Many North American students have participated in internships at the AIDS Law Project at the University of the Witwatersrand in Johannesburg, South Africa. Others have interned at TAC and put their legal and medical research skills and computer knowledge to good use. These internships are an important means of building international understanding, solidarity, and in some cases, sustained collaboration.

Scientific Research on HIV/AIDS

The front lines of the AIDS fight also include laboratories where new tools for treatment and prevention are being developed. Here, people trained in biological sciences, and those who are still students, can work to overcome AIDS and other infectious killers.

People without formal scientific training can get involved in cutting-edge AIDS research by volunteering to participate in an AIDS vaccine clinical trial. Developing an effective vaccine is, in the long run, the best way to beat AIDS, and vaccine research cannot move forward without volunteer trial subjects. Those interested in enrolling in a vaccine clinical trial can visit IAVI's website (www.iavi.org), which includes links to several major vaccine testing projects. The National Institute of Allergy and Infectious Diseases (NIAID) is also seeking volunteers for its vaccine research program. "A large HIV vaccine trial will require thousands of participants of all races, genders, and socioeconomic backgrounds," NIAID officials note. While thousands of people have already volunteered to take part in HIV vaccine studies, many more volunteers will be needed in the coming years.[12]

Medical and research work is vital, but doctors, nurses, and vaccine researchers cannot win the fight against HIV/AIDS by themselves. Virologists studying HIV, community prevention educators, and AIDS doctors cannot fully use their specialized skills without solid political backing grounded in grassroots support. The work of generating and maintaining such support is where the rest of us can get involved. *Our* efforts should comprise at least four major approaches: education, organizing, advocacy, and financial support.

Activism through Education

One of the most essential tasks for activists and aspiring activists is to educate *ourselves, our communities*, and the wider public, about the HIV/AIDS crisis. *We* need to learn the facts, and to share and disseminate those facts as widely as possible. Much of the inertia on AIDS in wealthy countries stems from plain ignorance about the scope of the crisis, the factors driving it, and the possibilities for intervention and change.

As we have argued in this book, AIDS education among affluent first-world citizens must often begin with challenging prevalent myths and undoing specious conventional wisdom about AIDS.[13] Fortunately, a large number of worldwide activist groups and advocacy organizations have raised public awareness and created a knowledge base for an international grassroots response to AIDS. *Global AIDS: Myths and Facts* is a part of that movement, as are the efforts of groups like ACT UP, the Global AIDS Alliance, Health GAP, MSF, Physicians for Human Rights

(PHR), the Student Global AIDS Campaign (SGAC), and Treatment Action Group (TAG). The continued growth of this movement is evidence of an intensified global concern about the devastation AIDS is inflicting on poor countries.

AIDS advocacy organizations based in schools and on college campuses have made education about the global crisis a top priority. Founded in 2001, SGAC has created a network of students at more than 200 high schools, colleges, and graduate schools across the US. The alliance has staged teach-ins, outreach efforts, and conferences for student activists from around the country. It has also lobbied lawmakers, networked with international youth activist groups, and organized its first national student AIDS conference in Washington, D.C. in early 2003. SGAC members were among those arrested in a civil disobedience action at the White House in November 2002, shaming the Bush administration for its tepid response to the AIDS crisis.[14]

Mobilizing and Organizing

Power often grows with numbers, and an effective way to make your voice heard is to join (or create) an organization. AIDS activist groups reflect a wide spectrum of political views, class, racial and ethnic constituencies, and institutional philosophies. For example, in recent years the Philadelphia chapter of ACT UP has become an exceptionally vibrant activist center. ACT UP Philadelphia has thrived by reaching beyond a white, gay, male, and middle-class population—the group's original base in the 1980s and 90s—to connect with the poor communities of color where the US epidemic is increasingly concentrated. At the same time, ACT UP Philadelphia has also focused increasing attention on the global AIDS crisis. Members from poor urban neighborhoods in Philadelphia recognize that the spread of the plague in the developing world is driven by the same kinds of socioeconomic forces that increase their own risk and disempower their communities.

The Stop Global AIDS Campaign takes a different but complementary approach to organizing. It uses the mass audience appeal of pop stars like Alicia Keys and the glitz of settings like the MGM Grand Hotel in Las Vegas to attract mainstream media attention and raise awareness. Linking students, celebrities, the music industry, religious groups, and humanitarian agencies, the campaign melds pop culture with politically substantive analysis of the AIDS crisis. One of the participating groups, Artists Against AIDS Worldwide (AAAW) built a compelling information campaign aimed at young people based on Marvin Gaye's Motown classic "What's Going On?" The video, featuring musicians like Bono, Alicia Keys, Gwen Stefani, and Wyclef Jean, was frequently played on MTV, and some of the proceeds from CD sales went to AIDS-related advocacy groups, including the Global AIDS Alliance. Led by Dr. Paul Zeitz, the Alliance used the campaign's official launch at the Fox Billboard Bash in Las Vegas as a platform for the release of a research report, "Pay Now or Pay More Later," a detailed study analyzing the economics of the global crisis.[15]

Other mobilizations are tailored for more specific constituencies. For example, Physicians for Human Rights (PHR), recipient of the Nobel Peace Prize for its anti-landmine project in 1997, encourages health professionals in affluent countries to become political players in the worldwide fight against AIDS. In fall 2001, PHR teamed with Partners In Health (PIH) to launch a nationwide campaign to engage US health care providers in the political and economic dimensions of the struggle against global AIDS. Because doctors are respected as authorities in the health field, PHR and PIH argue that they can and should mobilize media coverage, galvanize political debates, and bring new vigor to the anti-AIDS agenda in the US and the world. The vision statement for the campaign, the "Health Professionals' Call to Action on AIDS," signed by prominent physicians and public figures, demands specific policy changes, including a renewable US government commitment of $2.5 billion per year to the Global Fund to Fight AIDS, Tuberculosis, and Malaria (GFATM).[16]

Lobbying Policymakers

The history of AIDS activism and other successful social and political movements teaches that sustained pressure from the grassroots is required to make politicians engage seriously with complex and morally troubling issues like HIV/AIDS. Accordingly, letter-writing, petitioning, education, and lobbying campaigns led by groups such as ACT UP, the Global AIDS Alliance, Health GAP, PHR, and the Student Global AIDS Campaign have been instrumental in beginning to convince Washington lawmakers that ordinary Americans want to see more of our public funds allocated to global AIDS work.

President George W. Bush's January 2003 State of the Union address, containing promises of substantially increased funding for US engagement in the international AIDS fight, was seen by many as a watershed moment. Yet behind the dramatic unveiling of a possible shift in US government AIDS policy lay years of determined lobbying and direct action by advocacy organizations. (See Myth 7.) For example, in November 2002, two months before the President's speech, activists from ACT UP, Health GAP, SGAC, and other groups were arrested in the course of a nonviolent civil disobedience action at the White House. During the protest, activists chained themselves to the fence of the presidential mansion to protest the Bush administration's inaction on AIDS.[17]

Moreover, as veteran policy analysts and activists are aware, the *real* work of lobbying and educating lawmakers really begins now. We must ensure that the promising commitments on AIDS funding articulated in President Bush's address are not quickly eclipsed by other priorities in the Bush agenda, particularly massive tax cuts for the wealthy, the "war on terrorism," and military action against Iraq. The President's promises on AIDS must make it through Congress in order to become reality, and the legislative process involves numerous opportunities for commitments to be watered down and proposed budget allocations to shrink. Activists' vigilance and involvement will be more crucial than ever in the months and years ahead, as advocates seek to engage politicians and make sure that emotive evocations of America's "compassion" are translated into real laws, real money, and real action on the ground.

Raising Money

A health crisis of this scale and complexity cannot be addressed without very large sums of money. Expanding access to ARV treatment, strengthening education and prevention initiatives, building health infrastructure in the poor world, accelerating AIDS vaccine research are *all* vital, and will demand enormous outlays of capital in the coming years. Stephen Lewis, UN special envoy for HIV/AIDS in Africa, has argued that we already have the knowledge to turn the pandemic around in poor countries. What is missing, most fundamentally, is money.

> We know how to decrease mother-to-child transmission dramatically. We know how to do testing and counseling. We know how to undertake prevention of many kinds through the schools and targeted at vulnerable groups. We know how to do antiretroviral therapy—initially limited, of course, but available to us. We know what it means to find a way of integrating orphans back into the

community when their parents have died. We have all over the [African] continent individual projects and programmes that are successful. The frustration lies in our inability to take them to scale....What [is really needed] is...dollars. This is the single most inhibiting factor.[18]

Adequate funding for the different aspects of the international AIDS fight will be crucial to making this fight successful. Here again, as citizens of rich countries, we are in a uniquely favorable position to do something about the problem.

As simple as it sounds, it is money that often makes the difference between adequate prevention programs and poor ones, between treatment and no treatment, between life and death. For this reason, cutting-edge AIDS activism in the US began early on to target the exploitative pricing policies on AIDS medicines by pharmaceutical companies. Early activists also demanded the creation of government programs to help poor people with HIV or AIDS get the drugs they required and assistance with other major expenses, like housing. For the same reason, a primary focus of most American activist groups' political lobbying is securing adequate funding—for AIDS services, research, and the annual contribution to the Global Fund.

The level of US support to the GFATM is crucial in many ways. On the one hand, it has an immensely important symbolic value. It announces the seriousness (or lack thereof) of US commitment to solidarity with developing countries struggling against a public health disaster unprecedented in modern times. A more substantial American contribution to the GFATM would almost certainly spark greater support from other donors. But beyond symbolism, the money flowing to the GFATM and other financial clearinghouses for the AIDS fight will buy better chances for survival and dignified, productive lives for millions of men, women, and children.

As citizens and residents of rich countries, we have access to money, directly and indirectly, through personal resources and simply by virtue of our education, our social connections, our citizenship status, our access to communications and lobbying tools. For many of us, money is not an overwhelming problem, so we can underestimate its importance. A good portion of our work as activists can and should be focused on the task of channeling as many dollars as possible to the GFATM, vaccine research programs, and NGOs doing effective local prevention work and delivering ARV treatment in poor settings. By taking on these responsibilities, we are doing things that are relatively easy for us. Such sacrifices of time and money would be difficult, however, for the vast majority of persons living with HIV/AIDS, most of whom confront the deadly synergy of HIV/AIDS *and* poverty. Sitting down at the computer to write a letter to your senator requesting money for the Global Fund seems fairly mundane, compared with volunteering at an AIDS clinic in Tanzania or Thailand. But without consistent financial support from rich countries though multilateral programs like the Global Fund, many AIDS programs in places like Tanzania and Thailand will cease to exist. Dollars alone will not treat or cure AIDS, but without dollars, there will be no treatment and no cure.

The funding problem must be addressed from a number of different angles at once. We can start close to home by making personal donations to groups working on different aspects of the AIDS challenge. We can launch fund drives through our mosques, temples, churches, or other religious groups; through our schools; or through other community organizations to which we belong. We can use any connections we may have to corporations, foundations, or other potential donor agencies to educate these groups about the AIDS crisis and encourage contributions. Most importantly, we can and must keep the pressure on the President and on our representatives in government to ensure that the US and other rich countries increase financial support for the GFATM and other AIDS initiatives to a level commensurate with the economic power and global leadership position our countries enjoy.

Our Challenge

We have looked back briefly at the history of AIDS activism and suggested ways to get involved in the ongoing effort. We have also argued that activism by citizens and residents in wealthy countries is crucial, as substantial funding will be needed for years to come in the fight against the pandemic. The tasks ahead are daunting, but the history of the movement shows that informed, determined activism can make a difference. By itself, indignation does little good, but focused, collective passion can move formidable obstacles.

The global AIDS struggle is multifaceted, and the different dimensions interpenetrate and support each other: prevention and treatment efforts on the front lines; laboratory research; vaccine trials; grassroots education and mobilization; political lobbying; and generating and channeling financial resources. The examples we have discussed here are not exhaustive. Readers will find many additional ways to become involved.

Whatever approach *you* choose, the key is to recognize the urgency of the challenge and make a commitment to participate, effectively using the time, skills, and resources you can contribute. AIDS activism may not become the center of your life. But it can, and should, be a part of what all of us do and think about on a daily basis. Other problems and concerns cloud our awareness moment by moment. But future generations, with the clearer vision conferred by a historical perspective, may judge us above all on how we responded—or failed to respond—to the AIDS crisis. What were we doing, they will ask, while tens of millions of our fellow human beings became infected with a virus whose transmission we knew how to prevent, and died of a disease we had drugs to treat? Looking back, they will see clearly the limits of our capacities, but also how much lay within our power to change.

CONCLUSION

This book has addressed widespread misconceptions about the HIV/AIDS pandemic and what can be done to fight it. As we responded to the myths, a series of key points emerged:

• HIV/AIDS is a global crisis, and tackling it effectively demands a global response. So far, AIDS has taken its most devastating toll in sub-Saharan Africa, but the disease is advancing rapidly in other parts of the world, including South Asia, China, the Caribbean, and Eastern Europe.

• The socioeconomic, political, and environmental devastation inflicted on Africa by centuries of slave trafficking and colonial exploitation created the conditions for HIV's rapid spread through the continent.

• Along with low-income countries' enormous foreign debt burdens, economic policies mandated during the 1980s and 1990s by the World Bank and International Monetary Fund have hampered efforts to control AIDS in developing regions.

• AIDS continues to ravage communities of color and poor communities in the US. Public health experts report alarming signs of a resurgent HIV/AIDS epidemic in several key sectors of the American population.

•Investment in AIDS prevention programs should be dramatically expanded. To succeed, prevention efforts must take into account the socioeconomic forces that tend to constrain peoples' choices about sex, drug use, and other issues. Factors such as poverty, economic inequality, gender dynamics, racism, labor migration, and armed conflict reduce people's autonomy and force them into situations of heightened risk.

• Corruption and governmental inertia have hampered the fight against AIDS. However, results in Thailand, Uganda, and Brazil show that effective AIDS control can proceed despite corruption. Meanwhile, global efforts against corruption are making gains, opening the way for increased transparency and efficiency in AIDS work in developing countries.

• Intensified prevention is vital to control the AIDS crisis, but prevention alone is not enough. To focus exclusively on prevention would be to pronounce a death sentence on the 42 million women, men, and children already living with HIV/AIDS.

• AIDS prevention is enhanced when treatment is available. Without the possibility of obtaining effective treatment, people have little motivation to get tested for HIV. Without widespread counseling and testing, prevention efforts fail.

• Successful pilot programs in developing countries, including Haiti, South Africa, and Uganda, prove that AIDS treatment with antiretroviral medicines (ARVs) can be administered successfully in resource-poor settings. Brazil has shown that a middle-income country can successfully implement a national ARV treatment program with universal coverage.

• A vaccine remains the best hope to control AIDS in the long term. Support for vaccine research should be sharply increased. However, most scientists believe a vaccine is at least 7 to 10 years away and may have only partial efficacy. Conventional prevention programs and treatment for the millions already infected will be essential, even after a vaccine is introduced.

• The research-based pharmaceutical companies are immensely powerful. Their pricing policies have often made them adversaries rather than allies of people with AIDS. Yet history proves that grassroots activists can change the behavior of drug companies and political authorities through creative direct action and determined negotiation.

• Poor countries face many public health challenges, including malnutrition, tuberculosis, malaria, and childhood killers such as measles and diarrheal disease. AIDS treatment cannot replace other health interventions; it must be added to existing programs, in the framework of a comprehensive global effort to fight the full spectrum of diseases that disproportionately affect the poor.

• Although some international health experts continue to argue that AIDS treatment is not cost-effective in resource-poor settings, such analyses often fail to take into account the enormous indirect costs and consequences of the AIDS pandemic. When weighing the costs and benefits of AIDS treatment, we should consider that ARV therapy will reduce the number of orphans, cut AIDS-related hospitalizations, and contribute to the well-being of the wider population by improving life expectancy, economic stability, food production, tuberculosis (TB) control, and children's health.

• Some view wealthy countries' contributions to the global AIDS fight as acts of charity. In reality, controlling AIDS in the developing world will directly serve the interests of the citizens of industrialized countries by improving international public health, strengthening the global economy, and countering threats to national and global security.

• HIV/AIDS demands a multidimensional response involving collaboration and cooperation among countries and the active participation of the public and private sectors, including health, agriculture, education, industry, the arts, and above all, civil society.

• Many key organizing and advocacy tasks connected with global AIDS can and must be accomplished by ordinary citizens of wealthy countries like the US.

Today, in a world fraught with armed conflict, we need the vision to imagine a different kind of struggle: a nonviolent campaign whose success would be measured not by the body count of slaughtered enemies, but by the number of human lives saved from deprivation and disease.

HIV and the social and economic inequalities that have driven its spread are worthy adversaries against which to measure our collective courage and strength. It is time to declare a global war on AIDS and other diseases of poverty and to pour into that campaign resources on a scale too often reserved only for military purposes. To win the war against AIDS would bring about, not the subjugation of one human group by another, but greater freedom and security for all people. Precisely because the HIV/AIDS pandemic has so starkly underscored the world's social and economic divisions, defeating the disease would be a vital step toward healing schisms of inequality and exclusion. The vision of a shared, nonviolent struggle against disease, injustice, and unnecessary suffering can spark the imagination of people around the world and unite polarized communities. This could be a new form of globalization, one that is driven by civil society instead of by corporate agendas, and that seeks collaborative responses to human needs that transcend borders.

Speaking on Capitol Hill to the Congressional Biomedical Research Caucus in September 2001, Paul Farmer began to articulate a new vision: "...what I am pleading for are new instruments of mass salvation, rather than weapons of mass destruction. Imagine if the can-do mentality and scientific sophistication that gave us, in short order, a weapon of mass destruction were to be turned to the promotion of global health equity. Imagine a Manhattan Project for the diseases of the poor."

The broad intellectual blueprint for the effort has been drawn up in work such as that of World Health Organization's (WHO) Commission on Macroeconomics and Health, with its call for dramatically scaled-up international investment to address the health needs of the developing world, including AIDS prevention and treatment. But without grassroots organization and sustained citizen pressure in wealthy countries, the ideas of policy experts will have little effect. Economists know how to calculate resource needs, and health workers on the front lines know how to use resources to save lives. But the gap between these two can only be bridged by a collective political commitment to move the resources from where they are disproportionately concentrated to where they are desperately needed. To build that commitment, nothing is more effective than the determination of ordinary people willing to invest their energy in organizing, education, and advocacy.

Certain decisions indelibly mark a community's or nation's moral character and impart an orientation to its collective life that afterward proves difficult to alter. Our choice with regard to the AIDS crisis belongs to this category. As we in the world's wealthier societies weigh whether to commit ourselves to scaled-up global efforts against HIV/AIDS, we are helping determine whether millions of men, women, and children in developing countries will live or die. We are also deciding our own destiny. Consciously or not, we are choosing the fundamental principles we will live by and, ultimately, what our lives will mean and how we will be remembered by history. We can commit ourselves either to human solidarity as a fundamental value or to the pursuit of individual well-being and comfort, even when such comfort can only be secured by turning away from suffering people who will die without help.

We can elect to continue with our lives, detached while millions of human beings perish for want of preventive and therapeutic tools our affluent societies possess in abundance. Or we can take action to overcome this fatal imbalance and assist people in need, affirming a human community committed to fairness, compassion toward the vulnerable, and equality of access to the basic goods that enable a healthy, dignified life. To choose the latter course is not to practice charity but to recognize and act upon human interdependence. Human beings are separated by drastic material inequalities but linked by common vulnerabilities that prompt us to cooperate for the common good. By the choices we make with respect to AIDS, we are defining our moral selves, and determining the ethical character of the world we will inhabit and leave to future generations.

RESOURCES FOR ACTIVISM

Whether you are a student, volunteer, activist, or physician, this guide is intended to give you ideas on how to become involved in the struggle against AIDS. This is not an exhaustive list. Our aim in preparing this guide was to compile a representative sampling of organizations and other resources with considerable emphasis on advocacy and activism. Many of the following websites include lengthy lists of links to other AIDS-related organizations.

FOR INFORMATION

A Closer Walk

Documentary film (2001) conceived by the late Jonathan Mann, a crusader against AIDS and champion for human rights, and filmmaker Robert Bilheimer, reveals the local effects of HIV/AIDS in the US, the Caribbean, Africa, and Asia through interviews with people living with HIV/AIDS, physicians, activists, and other witnesses. For more information, visit www.thebody.com.

A & U, America's AIDS Magazine

25 Monroe Street, Suite 205, Albany, NY 12210-2743
phone: 888-245-4333
website: www.aumag.org
A nationally distributed magazine with interviews, advice, and public interest articles aimed at readers with HIV.

AIDS Education Global Information Systems

website: www.aegis.org

Online knowledge base that provides access to more than 750,000 documents on living with AIDS, prevention, treatment, news stories, legal resources and publications, and an extensive list of links.

AIDS Treatment News—AIDS.ORG

7985 Santa Monica Blvd, #99, West Hollywood, CA 90046

website: www.aids.org

Offers an extensive list of online fact sheets on subjects such as testing, prevention, and treatment, with an emphasis on women and pediatric AIDS. *AIDS Treatment News*, an online publication, is a resource on new therapies.

The Body

Body Health Resources Corporation, 250 57th St., New York, NY 10107

website: www.thebody.com/index.shtml

Educational website that aims to demystify AIDS by providing resources on quality of life, government and advocacy, and religion and spirituality. Sponsors interactive forums and bulletin boards for community workers, health care providers, activists, and people living with HIV/AIDS.

Centers for Disease Control & Prevention (CDC)

National Center for HIV/AIDS and TB Prevention

1600 Clifton Road, Atlanta, GA 30333

phone: 404-639-0900; fax: 404-639-0910

website: www.cdc.gov

Aims to reduce HIV- and TB-related illness and death, in collaboration with community, national, and international partners. The website is a resource for fact sheets, general information, and statistics.

Child Rights Information Network—HIV/AIDS
17 Grove Lane, London SE5 8RD, England
phone: (44) 207-716-2240; fax: (44) 207-793-7628
website: www.crin.org
Global network that disseminates information about the Convention on the Rights of the Child through databases, newsletters, and list servs. The HIV/AIDS database provides news, documents, abstracts, and events.

Health Care Information Resources
McMaster University Health Sciences Library, 1200 Main St.
W. Hamilton, ON, Canada L8N 3Z5
phone: 905-525-9140, ext. 22321; fax: 905-528-3733
website: www.hsl.mcmaster.ca
Information on health and disease, an extensive list of AIDS-related links, with an emphasis on international health and Canadian organizations.

HIV InSight
4150 Clement St., Building 16, VAMC 111V–UCSF
San Francisco, CA 94121
fax: 415-379-5547
website: www.hivinsite.ucsf.edu
Comprehensive resource, including the University of California San Francisco's online textbook about AIDS care, prevention, and policy. Also offers an extensive list of links. Information also available in Spanish.

Johns Hopkins AIDS Service
website: www.hopkins-aids.edu
Website for physicians treating patients with HIV or AIDS. Includes information on guidelines, clinical trials, and prevention tools, and provides listings of upcoming conferences and events.

Joint United Nations Programme on HIV/AIDS (UNAIDS)

20, Avenue Appia, CH-1211 Geneva 27, Switzerland

phone: (41) 22-791-4570; fax: (41) 22-791-4187

website: www.unaids.org

Funds projects, disseminates educational and statistical information, and co-sponsors the World AIDS Campaign, World AIDS Day, and the Global Fund to Fight AIDS, Tuberculosis, and Malaria. Website includes a database of international best practices, fact sheets, and academic resources.

Journal of the American Medical Association
HIV/AIDS Resource Center

website: www.ama-assn.org/special/hiv

Resource for physicians, health professionals, students, and the general public with an extensive collection of articles and reports from *Journal of the American Medical Association* and other professional sources.

Medscape—HIV/AIDS

website: www.medscape.com/hiv-aids.home

Scans news sources and academic journals for the latest scientific news. Includes a database of national and state hotlines, national professional groups, service organizations, and US government agencies.

National Institutes of Health (NIH)

Office of AIDS Research, Bethesda, MD 20892

phone: 301-496-4000

website: www.nih.gov/od/oar

Responsible for planning, coordinating, evaluating, and funding all NIH AIDS research. Its website provides updates and public information on AIDS research and funding, links to other NIH AIDS sites, and Web broadcasts.

Positive Nation

250 Kensington Lane, London SE11 5RD England

phone: (44) 20-7564-2121; fax: (44) 20-7564-2128

website: www.positivenation.co.uk

Published bya coalition of people living with HIV and AIDS in the UK.

POZ

1 Little W. 12th St., 6th Floor, New York, NY 10014

phone: 212-242-2163; fax: 212-675-8505

Largely political publication for HIV-positive readers, with sliding scale subscription rates.

ORGANIZATIONS

ACT UP/New York—AIDS Coalition To Unleash Power

332 Bleecker St. Suite G5, New York, NY 10014

phone: 212-966-4873

website: www.actupny.org

A diverse, nonpartisan group of individuals united in anger and committed to direct action to end the AIDS crisis.

ACT UP/Philadelphia—AIDS Coalition To Unleash Power

PO Box 22439, Land Title Station, Philadelphia, PA 19110-2469

phone: 215-731-1844; fax: 215-731-1845

The Philadelphia branch of the New York–based organization.

Action for Reach Out—Hong Kong

G/F, 21 Portland St., Yaumatei, Kowloon, Hong Kong

phone: 852-2770-1065; helpline telephone: 852-2770-1002

website: http://www.geocities.com/wellesley/8140

Action was developed to assist women working within the commercial sex industry (CSI) in Hong Kong, including women coming to Hong Kong from other countries. Its main goal is encouraging women to form support networks among themselves.

African American AIDS Policy and Training Institute

1833 W. 8th St., Suite 200, Los Angeles, CA 90057-4257

phone: 213-353-3610; fax: 213-989-0181

website: www.blackaids.org

Dedicated to the fight against AIDS for people of African descent. Projects include the Simon Nkoli Exchange, a Peace Corps-type exchange program for US and African front line HIV/AIDS workers. The institute also sponsors training for peer treatment educators.

AIDS Action

1906 Sunderland Place NW, Washington, DC 20036

phone: 202-530-8030; fax: 202-530-8031

website: www.aidsaction.org

A network of 3,200 AIDS service organizations across the US dedicated solely to responsible federal policy for improved HIV/AIDS care and services, vigorous medical research, and effective prevention.

AIDS Action Committee of Massachusetts

131 Clarendon St., Boston, MA 02116

phone: 617-437-6200; fax: 617-437-6445; TTY: 617-450-1423

website: www.aac.org

A New England organization that advocates for fair and effective AIDS public policy and funding, educates the general public and health care providers, and provides services to people with AIDS and those who care for them. You can participate in action alerts and legislative alerts online.

AIDS Memorial Quilt

The NAMES Project Foundation

PO Box 5552, Atlanta, GA 31107

phone: 404-688-5500; fax: 404-688-5552

website: www.aidsquilt.org

The quilt is a large, ongoing community arts project, which provides creative means for remembrance and healing while increasing public awareness of AIDS. You can volunteer to help at a local chapter or to host a display in your community or school.

AIDS Ride

2719 Media Center Dr., Los Angeles, CA 90065

phone: 800-825-1000

website: www.aidsride.org

Pallotta Team Works organizes four AIDS rides across the US. It also sponsors several other programs in Europe, Canada, and Africa. Proceeds go to AIDS service organizations working within the communities the ride passes through.

American Academy of HIV Medicine

836 N. La Cienega Blvd., Suite 303, Los Angeles, CA 90069-4708

phone: 866-241-9601; fax: 800-793-2604

website: www.aahivm.org

Independent organization of HIV specialists dedicated to promoting excellence in HIV/AIDS care. Committed to supporting specialists in HIV medicine and to ensuring better care for those living with HIV/AIDS through advocacy and education.

AVERT

4 Brighton Rd., Horsham, West Sussex, RH13 5BA, England

phone: (44) 140-321-0202; fax: (44) 140-321-1001

website: www.avert.org

UK-based organization that undertakes a wide range of educational and medical research work with the aim of prevention, improvement of the quality of life of those already AIDS-infected, and medical research toward a cure. Also operates international care and support centers.

Buddhist AIDS Project

phone: 415-522-7473

website: www.buddhistaidsproject.org

An all-volunteer, nonprofit affiliate of the Buddhist Peace Fellowship, BAP serves anyone living with HIV/AIDS, including family, friends, caregivers, and people who are HIV-negative. Based in San Francisco, BAP highlights HIV/AIDS news, with links to local, national, and international resources.

Canadian AIDS Society

309 Cooper Street, Ottawa K2P 0G5, Canada

phone: 613-230-3580

website: www.cdnaids.ca

Coalition of 115 community-based AIDS organizations across Canada. CAS advocates on behalf of people and communities affected by HIV/AIDS, facilitates the development of programs, services, and resources for their member groups, and provides a national framework for community-based participation in Canada's response to AIDS.

Department of Health and Human Services
Office of HIV/AIDS Policy
HHS Building 716 G, 200 Independence Ave., SW
Washington, DC 20201
phone: 202-690-5560; fax: 202-690-7564
website: www.hhs.gov
Coordinates HIV/AIDS policy for all Department of Health and Human Services agencies (CDC, NIH, FDA, SAMHSA, HRSA, HIS) and serves as liaison to the White House Office of National AIDS Policy.

Global AIDS Alliance
P.O. Box 820, Bethesda, MD 20827-0820
phone: 202-397-7700
website: www.globalaidsalliance.org
Campaign for better access to HIV/AIDS medications and cancellatioin of multilateral debt of impoverished countries. Sign up to receive action alerts and get involved by writing letters or donating money.

Global Health Council
HIV/AIDS Program, 1701 K St., NW, Suite 600
Washington, DC 20006
phone: 202-833-5900, fax: 202-833-0075
website: www.globalhealth.org
Creates networks of domestic and international nonprofit organizations to share information and influence global AIDS policy issues. Provides advocacy tools and publishes *Global AIDS Directory 2000,* which includes details on more than 250 AIDS-related agencies.

Harvard AIDS Institute

651 Huntington Ave., Boston, MA 02115

phone: 617-432-4400, fax: 617-432-4545

website: www.hsph.harvard.edu/hai

Dedicated to conducting and catalyzing research to end the worldwide AIDS epidemic. Also sponsors academic training programs, conferences, and the publication *Harvard AIDS Review.*

Health Global Access Project Coalition (Health GAP)

511 E. 5th St., #4, New York City, NY 10009

phone: 212-674-9598; fax: 212-208-4533

website: www.healthgap.org

Web-based organization that aims to bridge the gap in access to HIV/AIDS medications internationally. Get involved by signing petitions, participating in marches, or contributing to the Global AIDS Fund. The website contains an extensive HIV/AIDS news listing.

Health Resources and Services Administration

HIV/AIDS Bureau, Department of Health and Human Services

Health Resources and Services Administration

Office of Communications, 5600 Fishers Lane

Rockville, MD 20852

phone: 301-443-3376

website: www.hrsa.gov

Provides federal funding for HIV/AIDS care to low-income, uninsured, and underinsured individuals. The website provides information about CARE Act programs and funding and grant opportunities.

International AIDS Candlelight Memorial

Global Health Council, 1701 K St., NW Suite 600

Washington, DC 20006-1503

phone: 202-833-5900, ext 224; fax: 202-833-0075

website: www.candlelightmemorial.org

The world's largest and oldest grassroots HIV/AIDS event shows support for those living with HIV/AIDS, raises awareness, and mobilizes community involvement.

International AIDS Society

P.O. Box 4249, Folkungagatan 49 SE-102 65, Stockholm, Sweden

phone: (46) 8-556-970-50; fax: (46) 8-556-970-59

website: www.ias.se

Contributes to the control of HIV infection and AIDS through advocacy, education, facilitation of scientific networks, and support for best practices in research, prevention, and care.

International Association of Physicians in AIDS Care

33 North LaSalle Street, Suite 1700, Chicago, Illinois 60602-2601

phone: 312-795-4930, fax: 312-795-4938

website: www.iapac.org

Provides HIV clinical management updates and timely public health policy information for physicians and health care providers.

International Community of Women Living with AIDS

2C Leroy House, 436 Essex Rd, London N1 3QP, United Kingdom

phone: (44) 207-704-0606; fax: (44) 207-704-8070

website: www.icw.org

UK-based charity run by and for HIV-positive women. Sets up local support networks to reduce the isolation of women living with HIV/AIDS.

International Council of AIDS Services Organizations
399 Church St., 4th Floor, Toronto, Ontario M5B 2J6, Canada
phone: 416-340-2437; fax: 416-340-8224
website: www.icaso.org
Aims to mobilize and strengthen communities' and their organizations' ability
to deal with the prevention, care, treatment, and research of HIV/AIDS. Publishes reports, organizes conferences, and provides information and resources
on programs such as UNGASS, the Global Fund, and vaccine policies.

Médecins Sans Frontières
Campaign for Access to Essential Medicines
6 East 39th St., 8th Floor, New York, NY 10016
phone: 212-655-3764; fax: 212-679-7016
website: www.doctorswithoutborders.org
International humanitarian agency that provides emergency medical care
to endangered peoples across the world. The Campaign for Access to Essential Medicines is working to increase access to essential medications for
HIV/AIDS and other diseases in poor countries.

National Catholic AIDS Network
P.O. Box 422984, San Francisco, CA 94142-2984
phone: 707-874-3031; fax: 707-874-1433
website: www.ncan.org
National organization devoted to helping the Catholic Church respond in
an informed and compassionate manner to the challenges presented by the
HIV/AIDS pandemic. Provides educational materials for youth, individuals, and parishes about understanding AIDS.

National Minority AIDS Council

1931 13th St. NW, Washington, DC 20009

phone: 202-483-6622; fax: 202-483-1135

website: www.nmac.org

Develops leadership within communities of color to address challenges faced by people of color with HIV/AIDS. Produces educational materials, sponsors conferences. Website offers job database and organizational links.

OneWorld International

Floor 17, 89 Albert Embankment, London, SE1 7TP, England

phone: (44) 207-735-2100; fax: (44) 207-840-0798

website: www.oneworld.net

A coalition of over 1,000 organizations working for social justice. Hosts the "AIDS Channel," a multimedia web portal, which focuses on HIV/AIDS as development, social, economic, and human rights issue.

Partners In Health

641 Huntington Avenue, Boston, MA 02115

phone: 617-432-5256

website: www.pih.org

Partners In Health is a nonprofit organization that works in Latin America, the Caribbean, Eastern Europe, and the United States. PIH links the resources of wealthy medical and academic institutions withthe experience and aspirations of people living in poverty. Its goal is toovercome health problems conventional wisdom currently deems "insoluable."

Physicians for Human Rights

Health Action AIDS, 100 Boylston St., Suite 702, Boston, MA 02116

phone: 617-695-0041; fax: 617-695-0307

website: www.phrusa.org

Works to end the global AIDS pandemic by mobilizing health professionals, students, and the general public. Organizes an annual "Student Week for Awareness and Action" each April.

Physicians Research Network

20 W. 22nd St., 11th Floor, New York, NY 10010-5804

phone: 212-924-0857; fax: 212-924-0759

website: www.prn.org

A nonprofit organization that provides support for professionals who care for people with, or at risk for, HIV in the New York City area.

Student Global AIDS Campaign—Global Justice

30 Brattle Street, 4th Floor, Cambridge, MA 02138

phone: 617-495-2090

website: www.fightglobalaids.org

Student network devoted to combating the global AIDS crisis and changing the US AIDS policy through conferences, media outreach, and political advocacy. You can create or join an SGAC chapter at your school or university.

Treatment Action Campaign

P.O. Box 74, Nonkqubela, 7793, South Africa

phone: (27) 21-788-3507; fax: (27) 21-788-3726

website: www.tac.org.za

Campaigns against the view that AIDS is a 'death sentence' by lobbying for greater access to treatment for all South Africans by raising public awareness about the availability, affordability, and use of treatments.

United Nations Children's Fund (UNICEF)

UNICEF House, 3 United Nations Plaza, New York, NY 10017

phone: 212-326-7000; fax: 212-887-7465

website: www.unicef.org

Advocates for the rights of children living in poverty in developing countries. A co-sponsor of UNAIDS, UNICEF is dedicated to the prevention of infection and the support for women and children living with HIV/AIDS.

United States Agency for International Development (USAID)

Division of HIV/AIDS

1300 Pennsylvania Avenue, 3rd Floor, Washington, DC, 20201

phone: 202-712-0676; fax: 202-216-3046

website: www.usaid.gov/pop_health/aids

Supports multilateral efforts and runs its regional and bilateral programs in more than 40 countries.

World Health Organization (WHO)

20, Avenue Appia, CH-1211 Geneva 27, Switzerland

phone: (41) 22-791-4613; fax: (41) 22-791-4834

website: www.who.int/en

WHO's mission is to ensure that all people attain the highest possible level of health. WHO defines health as a state of complete physical, mental, and social well-being and not merely the absence of disease or infirmity.

NOTES

INTRODUCTION

1 UNAIDS, *Report on the Global HIV/AIDS Epidemic: December 2002* (Geneva: UNAIDS, 2002), p. 33.

2 In June 2001, Andrew Natsios, administrator of the US Agency for International Development, said that many Africans "don't know what Western time is. You have to take these [AIDS] drugs a certain number of hours each day, or they don't work. Many people in Africa have never seen a clock or a watch their entire lives." Speaking to the *New York Times,* a senior Treasury Department official, who wisely wished to remain anonymous, concurred that Africans lack a "concept of time." See J. Donnelly, "Prevention Urged in AIDS Fight," *Boston Globe,* 7 June 2001, p. A8; J. Kahn, "Rich Nations Consider Fund of Billions to Fight AIDS," *New York Times,* 29 April 2001, p. 10.

3 See A.D. McNaghten, D.L. Hanson, J.L. Jones, et al., "Effects of Antiretroviral Therapy and Opportunistic Illness Primary Chemoprophylaxis on Survival After AIDS Diagnosis," *AIDS* 13 (1999):1687–95; A. Mocroft, C. Katlama, A.M. Johnson, et al., "AIDS Across Europe, 1994-8: The EuroSIDA Study," *Lancet* 356 (2000): 291–296; and G.J. Dore, Y. Li, A. McDonald, et al., "Impact of Highly Active Antiretroviral Therapy on Individual AIDS-Defining Illness Incidence and Survival in Australia," *Journal of Acquired Immune Deficiency Syndromes* 29, no. 4 (2002): 388–395.

4 D. Pedersen and E. Larsen, "Too Poor to Treat: States Are Balking at Paying for Pricey AIDS Drugs," *Newsweek,* 28 July 1997, 60.

5 See Paul Farmer, Margaret Connors, and Janie Simmons, *Women, Poverty and AIDS* (Monroe, Maine: Common Courage Press, 1996); Paul Farmer, *AIDS and Accusation: Haiti and the Geography of Blame* (Berkeley: University of California Press, 1992).

6   For critical examinations of early theories about the origins of AIDS, see, for example Paul Farmer, "AIDS and Accusation: Haiti, Haitians and the Geography of Blame," in D. Feldman, ed., *AIDS and Culture: The Human Factor* (New York: Praeger Scientific, 1990), 122–150; Mirko Drazen Grmek, *History of AIDS: Emergence and Origin of a Modern Pandemic,* trans. Russell C. Maulitz and Jacalyn Duffin (Princeton, NJ: Princeton University Press, 1990); Edward Hooper, *The River: A Journey to the Source of HIV and AIDS* (Boston: Little, Brown, 1999); Paula Treichler, *How to Have Theory in an Epidemic: Cultural Chronicles of AIDS* (Durham, NC: Duke University Press, 1999). For conspiracy and denialist views, one can begin with the influential formulations of Peter Duesberg, e.g., P. Duesberg, "HIV Is Not the Cause of AIDS," *Science* 241 (1988)514–517; P. Duesberg, *Inventing the AIDS Virus* (Washington, DC: Regnery Publishing, 1996). Representative conspiracy theses include: Alan Cantwell, *AIDS and the Doctors of Death: An Inquiry into the Origin of the AIDS Epidemic* (Los Angeles: Aries Rising Press, 1988); John Lauritsen, *The AIDS War: Propaganda, Profiteering and Genocide from the Medical-Industrial Complex* (Pagan Press, 1993). A wide selection of denialist literature is available through websites such as *"Virusmyth,"* < http://www.virusmyth.net/aids/index.htm>.

HIV/AIDS Basics

1   Contents of this section draw from the following sources: *"AIDS Basics," HIV InSite* <http://hivinsite.ucsf.edu/InSite.jsp?page= FAQ>; Centers for Disease Control and Prevention, Divisions of HIV/AIDS Prevention, *Fact Sheets and General Information,* <http://www.cdc.gov/hiv/general.htm>; National Institute of Allergy and Infectious Diseases, "HIV Infection and AIDS: An Overview," August 2002 <http://www.niaid.nih.gov/factsheets/hivinf.htm>; National AIDS Treatment Information Project, *Index of NATIP documents,* < http://www.natip.org/index2.html>; and *Overview of HIV Disease* <http://www.natip.org/overview.html>.

MYTH ONE: AIDS and Africa

1   UNAIDS, *AIDS Epidemic Update December 2002* (Geneva: UNAIDS, 2002), 34-36.
2   We use "Africa" to refer to sub-Saharan Africa throughout the book.
3   For a historical background, see Walter Rodney, *How Europe Underde-*

veloped Africa (Dar es Salaam: Tanzania Publishing House, 1972).

4   In the early 1890s, rinderpest, a virulent infectious disease of cattle, destroyed 95 percent of eastern and southern Africa's cattle herds. Milk and beef disappeared from the diet, causing widespread malnutrition. The return of grazing land to bush created new breeding areas for the tsetse fly, and an epidemic of sleeping sickness ensued. These agricultural and ecological disasters severely weakened populations and rendered them more vulnerable. Brooke G. Schoepf, Claude Schoepf, and Joyce Millen, "Theoretical Therapies, Remote Remedies: SAP's and the Political Ecology of Poverty and Health in Africa," in *Dying for Growth: Global Inequality and the Health of the Poor,* Jim Kim, Joyce Millen, Alec Irwin, and John Gershman, eds. (Monroe, Maine: Common Courage Press, 2000), 91-125; see also Adam Hochschild, *King Leopold's Ghost* (Boston: Houghton Mifflin, 1999).

5   Schoepf, Schoepf, and Millen, "Theoretical Therapies, Remote Remedies," 91–125; Steven Feierman and John M. Janzen, eds., *The Social Basis of Health and Healing in Africa* (Berkeley: University of California Press, 1992); Meredeth Turshen ed., *Women and Health in Africa* (Trenton, NJ: Africa World Press, 1989).

6   John Gershman and Alec Irwin, "Getting a Grip on the Global Economy," in Kim, Millen, Irwin, and Gershman, eds., *Dying for Growth*, 11-43; cf. Michel Chossudovsky, *The Globalisation of Poverty: Impacts of IMF and World Bank Reforms* (London: Zed Books, 1997).

7   Schoepf, Schoepf, and Millen, "Theoretical Therapies," 98-125.

8   World Bank, *Accelerated Development in Sub-Saharan Africa: An Agenda for Action* (Washington, DC: World Bank, 1981).

9   See Schoepf, Schoepf, and Millen, "Theoretical Therapies, Remote Remedies," Peter Lurie, Percy Hintzen, and Robert A. Lowe, "Socioeconomic Obstacles to HIV Prevention and Treatment in Developing Countries: The Roles of the International Monetary Fund and the World Bank," *AIDS* 9, no. 6 (1995): 539–546; Leon Bjilmakers, Mary Bassett, and David Sanders, "Health and Structural Adjustment in Rural and Urban Settings in Zimbabwe: Some Interim Findings," in *Structural Adjustment and the Working Poor in Zimbabwe*, ed. Peter Gibbon (Uppsala: Nordiska Afrikaininstitutet, 1995), 215–282; Stephan Moses et al., "Impact of User Fees on Attendance at a Referral Centre for Sexually Transmitted Diseases in Kenya," *Lancet* 340, no. 8817 (1992): 463–466.

10   Oxfam, "Debt Relief and the HIV/AIDS Crisis in Africa," Oxfam Briefing Paper 25, July 2002, <http://www.oxfam.org.uk/policy/pap

ers/25aidsdebt/25aidsdebt.html> (21 November 2002).

11   UNAIDS and World Health Organization, *AIDS Epidemic Update December 2002* (Geneva: UNAIDS, 2002), 12.

12   Ibid., 34-35.

13   Clara Ferreira-Marques, "World AIDS Epidemic on Rise, E. Europe Cases Swell," (Reuters, 28 November 2001), <http://www.aegiscom /news/re/2001/RE011146.html> (15 October 2002).

14   National Intelligence Council, *The Next Wave of HIV/AIDS: Nigeria, Ethiopia, Russia, India, and China*, ICA 2002-04D, September 2002, <www.odci.gov/nic/pubs/index.htm> (21 November 2002).

15   UNAIDS, *AIDS Epidemic Update December 2002*, 13.

16   Ibid.

17   National Intelligence Council, *The Next Wave of HIV/AIDS: Nigeria, Ethiopia, Russia, India, and China.*

18   See UNAIDS and World Health Organization, *AIDS Epidemic Update December 2001.*

19   Ibid.

20   For a history of Russia's current health crisis, see Mark Field, David Kotz, and Gene Bukhman, "Neoliberal Economic Policy, 'State Desertion,' and the Russian Health Crisis" in *Dying for Growth: Global Inequality and the Health of the Poor*, 155-73.

21   UNAIDS, *AIDS Epidemic Update December 2002*, 7.

22   UNAIDS/WHO, *AIDS Epidemic Update December 2001*, 2.

23   UN Theme Group on HIV/AIDS in China, *HIV/AIDS: China's Titanic Peril* (Geneva: UN, 2002), <http://www.unaids.org/whatsnew/ newadds/index.html> (21 November 2002); National Intelligence Council, *The Next Wave of HIV/AIDS.*

24   World Health Organization, *HIV/AIDS in Asia and the Pacific Region* (Geneva: WHO, 2001), <http://www.wpro.who.int/pdf/sti/aid s2001/complete.pdf> (7 March 2002), 42.

25   Elisabeth Rosenthal, "With Ignorance as the Fuel, AIDS Speeds across China," *New York Times*, 30 December 2001.

26   UNAIDS and World Health Organization, *AIDS Epidemic Update, December 2001.*

27   Elisabeth Rosenthal, "AIDS Scourge in Rural China Leaves Villages of Orphans," *New York Times*, 25 August 2002; UN Theme Group on HIV/AIDS in China, *HIV/AIDS: China's Titanic Peril.*

28   Ibid.; National Intelligence Council, *The Next Wave of HIV/AIDS.*

29   UNAIDS, *Report on the Global HIV/AIDS Epidemic 2002*, 30.

30 S. Ramasundaram, "Can India Avoid Being Devastated by HIV?" *British Medical Journal* 324 (2002), <http://bmj.com/cgi/content/full/324/7331/182?maxtoshow=&HITS=10&hits=10&RESULTFOR MAT=&searchid=1037908716783_16738&stored_search=&FIRST INDEX=0&volume=324&firstpage=182&resourcetype=1,2,3,4,10 > (21 November 2002), 182–183.

31 World Health Organization, *HIV/AIDS in Asia and the Pacific Region*, 41.

32 Ibid., 40, fig. 8.

33 Patricio V. Marquez et al., *HIV/AIDS in the Caribbean: Issues and Options. A World Bank Country Study* (Washington, DC: 2001), <http://wbln0018.worldbank.org/LAC/lacinfoclient.nsf/d29684951174975 c85256735007fef12/0191899ca02a3f6885256905007be3d0/$FILE/HIVAIDSCaribbean.pdf> (7 March 2002), 9, 17.

34 Marquez et al., *HIV/AIDS in the Caribbean*, 8.

35 UNAIDS, *Report on the Global HIV/AIDS Epidemic July 2002*, 198.

36 Marquez et al., *HIV/AIDS in the Caribbean*.

37 For a thorough analysis of the relationship between Haiti's political economy and current infectious disease epidemics, see Paul Farmer, *The Uses of Haiti* (Monroe, ME: Common Courage Press, 1994); Paul Farmer, *AIDS and Accusation: Haiti and the Geography of Blame* (Berkeley: University of California Press, 1992); Farmer and Bertrand, "Hypocrisies of Development and the Health of the Haitian Poor," in *Dying for Growth: Global Inequality and the Health of the Poor*, 91-125.

38 UNAIDS, *Global HIV/AIDS and S.D. Surveillance, Cuba: Epidemiologica: Fact Sheet* (Geneva: UNAIDS, 2000), <http://www.unaids.org/hivaidsinfo/statistics/fact_shets/pdfs/Cuba_en.pdf> (7 March 2002), 3.

39 UNAIDS, *AIDS Epidemic Update December 2002*, 34. Nancy Scheper-Hughes, "AIDS, Public Health, and Human Rights in Cuba," *Lancet* 342, no. 8877 (1993): 965–967; Aviva Chomsky, "The Threat of a Good Example: Health and Revolution in Cuba," in *Dying for Growth: Global Inequality and the Health of the Poor*, 331–357. For in-depth analysis of Cuba's AIDS program, see *Paul Farmer, Pathologies of Power: Health, Human Rights, and the New War on the Poor* (Berkeley: University of California Press, 2003), 51-90.

40 UNAIDS, *AIDS Epidemic Update December 2002*, 22.

41 MAP, World Health Organization and Pan American Health Organization, *HIV and AIDS in the Americas: An Epidemic with Many Faces*, November 2000, <http://www.unaids.org/hiv

aidsinfo/statistics/june00/map/MAP_Stats_america.pdf> (7 March 2002), 10.

42	Detailed epidemiological data on Brazil are available from AGNATES at <http://www.unaids.org/hivaidsinfo/statistics/fact_sheets/pdfs/Brazil_en.pdf> (5 March 2002).

43	See Tina Rosenberg, "How to Solve the World's AIDS Crisis: Look at Brazil," *New York Times*, 28 January 2001, sec. 6, p. 26.

44	AGNATES, *Report on the Global HIV/AIDS Epidemic 2002*, 37. The Brazilian government's anti-AIDS efforts are discussed in greater detail in Myths 3 and 5.

45	Associated Press, "Officials Voice Alarm over Halt in AIDS Decline," *New York Times*, 14 August 2001, sec. A.

46	Ibid.

47	Ibid.

48	CDC, *No Turning Back: Addressing the HIV Crisis Among Men Who Have Sex With Men* (Atlanta, 2001), 13.

49	Associated Press, "Officials Voice Alarm over Halt in AIDS Decline."

50	CDC, *No Turning Back,* 13.

51	Ibid., 5.

52	CDC, "Estimated Incidence of AIDS and Deaths of AIDS Cases Attributed to Heterosexual Contact, 1985-1999, United States," 4 March 2002,<http://www.cdc.gov/hiv/graphics/images/L207/L207-3.htm> (13 March 2002).

53	Laurie Garrett and Richard Dalton, "The Changing Face of AIDS," *Newsday*, 29 May 2001.

54	Alicia Montgomery, "A Deadly Taboo," *Salon*, 22 June 2001, <www.salon.com/news/feature/2001/06/22/aids/print.html> (16 June 2002); AGNATES and World Health Organization, *AIDS Epidemic Update, December 2001*.

55	CDC, *No Turning Back, 4.*

56	CDC, "U.S. HIV and AIDS Cases Reported Through December 1999," *HIV/AIDS Surveillance Report* 11, no. 2 (1999), <http://www.cdc.gov/hiv/stat-trends.htm> (17 October 2002).

57	CDC, "Deaths Among Persons with AIDS through December 2000," *HIV/AIDS Surveillance Supplemental Report* 8, no. 1 (2002), <http://www.cdc.gov/hiv/stat-trends.htm> (17 October 2002).

58	Garrett and Dalton, "The Changing Face of AIDS."

59	Louise Frechette, "The UN and the Global Fight against HIV/AIDS: Myth and Reality," speech to the Carnegie Council on Ethics and International Affairs, New York, 20 September 2001, <http://www. carnegiecouncil.org/programs/frechette_transcript.html> (13 March 2002).

60 AGNATES and World Health Organization, *AIDS Epidemic Update December 2001*, 5. In 1990, less than 1 percent of South African women attending prenatal clinics tested positive for HIV. By the end of 2000, prevalence among pregnant women reached 24.5 percent.

MYTH TWO: Dangerous Behavior

1 See Paula A. Treichler, "AIDS, Homophobia, and Biomedical Discourse: An Epidemic of Signification," in *AIDS: Cultural Analysis, Cultural Activism*, ed. Douglas Crimp (Cambridge, MA: MIT Press, 1988), 31–37.

2 See Steven Epstein, *Impure Science: AIDS, Activism, and the Politics of Knowledge* (Berkeley: University of California Press, 1996), 45–78.

3 See Paul Farmer, *AIDS and Accusation: Haiti and the Geography of Blame* (Berkeley: University of California Press, 1992), introduction and chapter 20.

4 We put quotation marks around "promiscuous" to signal the problems associated with this term. In popular parlance, "promiscuity" and "promiscuous" inevitably carry negative connotations. Ostensibly scientific uses of these words are often based on implicit cultural norms, which vary widely among social and historical settings. On the uses and abuses of the concept of promiscuity in the AIDS-related medical and public health literature, see R. Bolton, "AIDS and Promiscuity: Muddles in the Models of HIV Prevention," *Medical Anthropology* 14, nos. 2-4 (1992): 145–223. The view of promiscuity as the primary cause of AIDS is by no means exclusively Western. In China, some health educators and government officials have maintained that AIDS is the punishment for promiscuity. Y. G. Wang, "AIDS, Policy and Bioethics: Ethical Dilemmas Facing China in HIV Prevention: A Report from China," *Bioethics* 11, nos. 3-4 (1997): 323–327. A study among residents of a Calcutta slum found that the majority of people with some awareness of AIDS believed only promiscuous people were at risk. A. K. Poddar, D. S. Poddar, and R. N. Mandal, "Perceptions About AIDS Among Residents of a Calcutta Slum," *Indian Journal of Public Health* 40, no. 1 (1996): 4–9.

5   In the health field, in particular, Americans have been exposed to a "virtual media and professional blitz for a particular model of health promotion: one that emphasizes lifestyle change and individual responsibility." This has led to an understanding of health primarily in terms of individual choices, "self-control," and "will power." Rob Crawford, "A Cultural Account of 'Health': Control, Release, and the Social Body," *Issues in the Political Economy of Health Care,* ed. John McKinlay (New York: Tavistock, 1984), 66, 75. Cited and discussed in Hans Baer, Merrill Singer, and Ida Susser, *Medical Anthropology and the World System: A Critical Perspective* (Westport, CT: Bergin and Garvey, 1997), 176.

6   For current global AIDS epidemiology, see Myth 1.

7   See AGNATES, "Gender and HIV. The Facts About Women and HIV/AIDS," <http://www.unaids.org/fact_sheets/files/GenderFS_en.pdf> (8 January 2002); Lori L. Heise and Christopher Elias, "Transforming AIDS Prevention to Meet Women's Needs: A Focus on Developing Countries," *Social Science and Medicine* 40, no. 7 (1995): 931–943.

8   Rhaki's situation was recorded by a Harvard Medical School student, Molly McNairy, in July and August 2001 in the course of a research study designed to create a protocol for the provision of comprehensive HIV prevention and care.

9   Constance Chay-Nemeth, "Demystifying AIDS in Thailand: A Dialectical Analysis of the Thai Sex Industry," *Journal of Health Communication* 3 (1998): 217–231.

10 AGNATES, "Gender and HIV."

11 J. W. McGrath et al., "Anthropology and AIDS: The Cultural Context of Sexual Risk Behavior Among Urban Baganda Women in Kampala, Uganda," *Social Science and Medicine* 36, no. 4 (1993): 429–439.

12 Paul Farmer, *Infections and Inequalities: The Modern Plagues* (Berkeley: University of California Press, 1999): 134–135.

13 Margaret Connors, "Sex, Drugs, and Structural Violence," *Women, Poverty, and AIDS* (Monroe: Common Courage Press, 1992): 120.

14 Roderick Wallace, "Urban Desertification, Public Health, and Public Order: 'Planned Shrinkage,' Violent Death, Substance Abuse, and AIDS in the Bronx," *Social Science and Medicine* 31 (1990), 801–813, cited and discussed in Baer, Singer, and Susser, *Medical Anthropology,* 172.

15 Ibid.

16 Donald McNeil Jr., "AIDS and Death Hold No Sting for Fatalistic

Men at African Bar," *New York Times,* 29 November 2001, A14, col. 1.

17 Philippe Bourgois, "In Search of Horatio Alger: Culture and Ideology in the Crack Economy," in *Crack in America: Demon Drugs and Social Justice,* Craig Reinarman and Harry Levine, eds., (Berkeley: University of California Press, 1997), 72.

18 Ibid., 62–63.

19 Ibid.

20 See Philippe Bourgois, *In Search of Respect: Selling Crack in El Barrio* (Cambridge: Cambridge University Press, 1995).

21 Carlos's story was collected in September 2002 by Kedar Mate, a medical student and volunteer research associate with the Prevention and Access to Care and Treatment (PACT) Project of Partners In Health and the Department of Social Medicine and Health Inequalities, Brigham and Women's Hospital, Boston. Carlos's name and certain details of his background have been changed to protect his identity.

22 See Bourgois, "In Search of Horatio Alger."

23 See AGNATES, UNICEF, and USAID, *Children on the Brink 2002: A Joint Report on Orphan Estimates and Program Strategies* (Washington, DC: TvT Associates/USAID, 2002).

24 The following two paragraphs are based on an investigative report by *New York Times* China correspondent Elisabeth Rosenthal. Elisabeth Rosenthal, "AIDS Scourge in Rural China Leaves Villages of Orphans," *New York Times,* 25 August 2002. See also The UN Theme Group on HIV/AIDS in China, *HIV/AIDS: China's Titanic Peril* (Geneva: AGNATES, 2002), <http://www.unaids.org/whatsnew/n ewadds/AIDSchina2001update.pdf> (7 December 2002).

25 Rosenthal, "AIDS Scourge in Rural China Leaves Villages of Orphans."

26 Bourgois, "In Search of Horatio Alger," 72–74. One reason historically subjugated minorities in the US are more vulnerable to HIV infection is that such groups are typically poorer than the majority population. The combination of racial discrimination and economic exclusion is precisely what Bourgois seeks to capture with his notion of "conjugated oppression."

27 Lisa Garbus, "United States," *HIV InSite,* January 2002, <http://hiv insite.ucsf.edu/InSite.jsp?page=cr07-us-00> (5 April 2002).

28 National Black Leadership Commission on AIDS, "Heed the Call! An HIV/AIDS State of Emergency Requires a New Chapter in the Civil Rights Movement," 8 June 2001, <http://www2.aftermeeting.com/

templates/blca.62001/index.asp?i=93> (20 November 2002).

29 Jonathan Lemire, "Harlem Parley on AIDS Crisis," *Daily News* (New York), 31 August 2001.

30 Claudia Garcia-Moreno and Charlotte Watts, "Violence Against Women: Its Importance for HIV/AIDS," *AIDS* 14, Suppl. 3 (2000): S253–265.

31 World Health Organization, *Violence against Women: A Priority Health Issue* (Geneva: WHO, 1997); World Health Organization, Database on Violence against Women (Geneva: WHO, 1999, cited in Garcia-Moreno and Watts, "Violence against Women: Its Importance for HIV/AIDS."

32 Ibid.

33 Ibid.

34 Namibian Network of AIDS Service Organizations, Sexual Knowledge, *Attitudes and Practices Among Namibian Youth: A Baseline Survey*, (Windhoek, Namibia: Social Impact Assessment and Policy Analysis Corporation Ltd.; 1995). Statistics cited in Garcia-Moreno and Watts, "Violence against Women: Its Importance for HIV/AIDS."

35   A. L. Coker and D. L. Richter, "Violence Against Women in Sierra Leone: Frequency and Correlates of Intimate Partner Violence and Forced Sexual Intercourse," *African Journal of Reproductive Health* 2 (1998): 61–72. Statistics cited in Garcia-Moreno and Watts, "Violence against Women: Its Importance for HIV/AIDS." J. Abma, A. Driscoll, and K. Moore, "Young Women's Degree of Control over First Intercourse and Exploratory Analysis. National Family Growth Survey 1995," *Family Planning Perspectives* 30 (1998): 12–18.

36 G. M. Wingood and R. J. DiClemente, "The Effects of an Abusive Primary Partner on the Condom Use and Sexual Negotiation Practices of African-American Women," *American Journal of Public Health* 87 (1997): 1016-1018.

37 Charlotte Watts et al., "Women, Violence and HIV/AIDS in Zimbabwe," *SAfAIDS News* 5 (1997): 2–6.

38 T. Luster and S. A. Small, "Sexual Abuse History and Number of Sex Partners Among Female Adolescents," *Family Planning Perspectives* 29 (1997): 204–211.

39 Garcia-Moreno and Watts, "Violence against Women: Its Importance for HIV/AIDS." Overall, average HIV incidence rates among African adolescent girls are over five times higher than those among boys in the same age group. See Lisa Garbus, "South Africa," *HIVInSite,*

April 2001, <http://hivinsite.ucsf.edu/InSite.jsp?page=cr-02-01&do
c=2098.410f#N> (5 April 2002).

40 McNeil, "AIDS and Death Hold No Sting for Fatalistic Men at African Bar": Garbus, "South Africa."

41 See Shula Marks and Richard Rathbone, eds., *Industrialisation and Social
Change in South Africa: African Class Formation, Culture, and Consciousness,
1870-1930* (London: Longman, 1982). For a study of the health effects
of the South African labor system focused on the instructive case of
tuberculosis, see Randall Packard, *White Plague, Black Labor: Tuberculosis
and the Political Economy of Health and Disease in South Africa* (Berkeley:
University of California Press, 1989).

42 See Frederick A. Johnstone, *Class, Race, and Gold: A Study of Class Rela-
tions and Racial Discrimination in South Africa* (London: Routledge, 1976);
Owen Crankshaw, *Race, Class, and the Changing Division of Labour Under
Apartheid* (London: Routledge, 1997).

43 Laurine Platzky and Cheryl Walker, *The Surplus People: Forced Removals
in South Africa* (Johannesburg: Ravan Press, 1985).

44 K. Jochelson, M. Mothibeli, and J. P. Leger, "Human Immunodeficiency Virus and Migrant Labor in South Africa," *International Journal of
Health Services* 21, no. 1 (1991): 157–173.

45 J. Decosas et al., "Migration and AIDS," *Lancet* 346, no. 8978 (1995):
826–828.

46 F. Kane, "Temporary Expatriation is Related to HIV-1 Infection in
Rural Senegal," *AIDS* 7, no. 9 (1993): 1261–1265.

47 Decosas et al., "Migration and AIDS."

48 Peter Piot, "The Global Impact of HIV/AIDS," *Nature* 410 (2001):
968–973.

49 A. J. Nunn et al., "HIV-1 Infection in a Ugandan Town on the
Trans-African Highway: Prevalence and Risk Factors," *International
Journal of Sexually Transmitted Diseases and AIDS* 7, no. 2 (1996):
123-130.

50 Michael Fleshman, "Drug Price Plunge Energizes AIDS Fight, AIDS
Prevention in the Ranks, UN Targets Peacekeepers, Combatants in
War against the Disease," *Africa Recovery* 15, no. 1-2 (2001),
<http://www.un.org/ecosocdev/geninfo/afrec/vol 15, no1/aidsmi
l.htm> (7 December 2002), 16.

51 Stefan Lovgren, "African Army Hastening HIV/AIDS Spread," re-
printed in *Jenda, A Journal of Culture and African Women Studies* 1 (2001),
<http://www.jendajournal.com/jenda/vol1.2/lovgren.html> (8 April

2002), 2. The incidence of STIs among military personnel tends to be higher than that of the general population. See AGNATES, "Experts Meet to Discuss AIDS and Security," 8 December 2000, <http://www.unaids.org/whatsnew/press/eng/pressarc00/stock1112.html> (8 April 2002).

52 See Jeanne Ward, *If Not Now, When? Addressing Gender-Based Violence in Refugee, Internally Displaced, and Post-conflict Settings* (New York: The Reproductive Health for Refugees Consortium, 2002).

53 UNICEF, *Women in Transition. The MONEE Project CEE/CIS/Baltics Regional Monitoring Report* No. 6 (Florence: United Nations Children's Fund International Child Development Centre; 1999), cited in Garcia-Moreno and Watts, "Violence against Women: Its Importance for HIV/AIDS."

54 J. E. Giller, P. J. Bracken, and S. Kabaganda, "Uganda: War, Women, and Rape," *Lancet* 337 (1991): 604.

55 S. Swiss, and J. E. Giller, "Rape as a Crime of War: A Medical Perspective," *The Journal of the American Medical Association* 270, no. 5 (1993): 612–615.

56 A pilot study of 35 women and girls raped in Uganda's Luwero Triangle area between 1982 and 1985 found an HIV seropositivity of 26 percent. Ages of study participants ranged from 11 to 45. Giller, Bracken, and Kabaganda, "Uganda: War, Women, and Rape."

57 Jeanne Ward, *If Not Now, When?*, 28.

58 Baer, Singer, and Susser, "AIDS: A Disease of the Global System."

59 See M. E. Beksinska et al., "Acceptability of the Female Condom in Different Groups of Women in South Africa-A Multicentred Study to Inform the National Female Condom Introductory Strategy," *South African Medical Journal* 91, no. 8 (2001): 672–678. Also Jivasak-Apimas et al., "Acceptability of the Female Condom Among Sex Workers in Thailand: Results from a Prospective Study;" and G. Raphan, S. Cohen, and A. M. Boyer, "The Female Condom, a Tool for Empowering Sexually Active Urban Adolescent Women," *Journal of Urban Health* 78, no. 4 (2001): 605–613.

60 Ideally, such agents could be produced in many forms, including gels, creams, or suppositories. World Health Organization, *Women and Microbicides* (Geneva: WHO, 2000), <http://www.who.int/inf-fs/en/fact246.html> (11 November 2002).

61 While there are presently more than 60 experimental microbicides in the pipeline, experts believe it will be several years, at best, before a

safe, effective product reaches the public. Increased funding would accelerate this process. See World Health Organization, *Women and Microbicides*. The Global Campaign for Microbicides was launched in 1999 as a broad-based international coalition aiming to build support among policymakers and the general public for increased private and public sector investment in microbicide research and development. For more information, see the organization's website, <www.global-campaign.org> (7 December 2002).

62   The importance of taking measures to strengthen women's empowerment was underscored in the Declaration of Commitment on HIV/AIDS, produced at the UN Special Session on HIV/AIDS held in New York from 25-27 June 2001. See United Nations Special Session on HIV/AIDS, "Declaration of Commitment on HIV/AIDS. 'Global Crisis - Global Action,'" 2 August 2001, <http://www.unaid s.org/whatsnew/others/un special/Declaration020801 en.htm> (11 November 2002), articles 58-64 on HIV/AIDS and human rights as well as vulnerability.

63   M. E. Beksinska et al., "Acceptability of the Female Condom in Different Groups of Women in South Africa—A Multicentred Study to Inform the National Female Condom Introductory Strategy;" Jivasak-Apimas et al., "Acceptability of the Female Condom among Sex Workers in Thailand: Results from a Prospective Study."

64   D. L. Roth, et al., "Sexual Practices of HIV Discordant and Concordant Couples in Rwanda: Effects of a Testing and Counselling Programme for Men," *International Journal of Sexually Transmitted Diseases and AIDS* 12, no. 3 (2001): 181–188. Another Rwandan study confirmed that "participation of the male partner is crucial for successful HIV risk reduction in couples." A. van der Straten et al., "Couple Communication, Sexual Coercion and HIV Risk Reduction in Kigali, Rwanda," *AIDS* 9, no. 8 (1995): 935–944.

MYTH THREE: Corruption

1   This definition of corruption is adapted from Jeremy Pope, *TI Source Book 2000: Confronting Corruption: The Elements of a National Integrity System* (Berlin: Transparency International, 2000), <http://www.trans parency.org/sourcebook/01.html> (3 November 2002), chap. 1.

2   According to Alec Irwin, the speaker was a member of the staff of Illinois congressman Henry Hyde, addressing a delegation of activists led by ACT UP and Health GAP at the Rayburn House Office Building,

Washington, DC, 10 April 2002. At a recent meeting in Washington between AIDS activists and lawmakers, a senior Congressional staffer said he was dubious about increasing AIDS funding to African countries, because the leaders of those countries would just take the money and "go buy themselves another Lear Jet."

3   See Transparency International, *Bribe Payers' Index 2002* (Berlin: Transparency International, 2002), <http://www.transparency.cpi/org/2002/bpi2002.en.html> (9 November 2002).

4   Enery Quinones, "Implementing the Anti-Bribery Convention: An Update from the OECD," in *Global Corruption Report 2000*, Transparency International, (Berlin: Transparency International and Medialis, 2001), <http://www.globalcorruptionreport.org/download/gi_oecd convention.pdf> (1 November 2002).

5   Peter Eigen, "Introducing the Global Corruption Report 2001," in *Global Corruption Report 2001*, Transparency International, 2.

6   Ibid.

7   See <http://www.transparency.org/> (10 November 2002).

8   Transparency International, *Global Corruption Report 2001*.

9   Gitau Warigi, "East and East-Central Africa," in *Global Corruption Report 2001*, Transparency International, <http://www.globalcorruptio nreport.org/download/rr_eec_africa.pdf> (10 November 2002), 79.

10   Philip P. Pan, "As China Faces Crisis, People with HIV Are Kept Largely Invisible," *Washington Post*, 20 November 2001.

11   On Angola, see Gavin Hayman, "Corruption Undermines Relief to Angola," Reuters, 1 November 2002, <http://www.alertnet.org/the facts/reliefresources/544536?version=1> (1 November 2002). On Kenya and Zimbabwe, see the respective chapters on Eastern and Southern Africa in Transparency International's *Global Corruption Report 2001*, <http://www.globalcorruptionreport.org/#download> (10 November 2002).

12   See the assessment of a recent European Union delegation to Tanzania, discussed in Warigi, "East and East-Central Africa," 69.

13   Africare, "Democratic Ideals from the Grassroots Up," 2000, <http://www.africare.org/at_work/democracy-ngo/> (5 March 2002). See also Thomas Carothers, "Democracy Without Illusions," *Foreign Affairs* 76, no. 1 (1997): 85–99. In large part, positive changes were catalyzed by civil society movements demanding political reform and greater accountability. See E. Gyimah-Boadi, "Civil Society in Africa," *Journal of Democracy* 7, no. 2 (1996): 118-132.

14 Penny Dale, "Southern Africa," in *Global Corruption Report 2001*, Transparency International, <http://www.globalcorruptionreport.org/download/rr_southern_africa.pdf> (10 November 2002).

15 Warigi, "East and East-Central Africa," 73.

16 Ibid., 75.

17 Organization of African Unity, "Abuja Declaration on HIV/AIDS, Tuberculosis, and Other Related Infectious Diseases," 27 April 2001, <http://www.uneca.org/adf2000/Abuja%20Declaration.htm> (7 January 2002).

18 World Health Organization, *Scaling up the Response to Infectious Diseases: A Way out of Poverty* (Geneva: WHO, 2002), <http://www.who.int/infectious-disease-report/2002/pdfversion/indexpdf.html> (15 October 2002), 93.

19 World Health Organization, *Scaling Up the Response*, 84-88.

20 The World Health Organization has recommended nevirapine for the prevention of mother-to-child transmission, and the pharmaceutical giant Boehringer Ingelheim has offered to donate the drug to South Africa for use in mother-to-child transmission prevention programs. Studies showed that if implemented throughout the country, mother-to-child transmission prevention with nevirapine could save tens of thousands of South African babies each year from contracting HIV during labor and delivery. Yet the South African government initially limited distribution of the drug to a handful of pilot sites, arguing that nevirapine was toxic, that its efficacy was unproven, and that in any case an inclusive national program would be too expensive to implement. In reality, the government's reluctance appeared ideologically motivated, prompted by sympathies with the views of AIDS skeptics who question the causal link between HIV and AIDS. In 2001, after exhausting other means of persuasion, TAC brought a lawsuit against the government, demanding that nevirapine immediately be made available to HIV-positive pregnant women in all state-run hospitals and clinics. A December 2001 court ruling in TAC's favor cleared the way for implementation, though the government pursued a series of appeals. See "HIV/AIDS: TAC vs. State," *Johannesburg Mail and Guardian,* 22 November 2001, <http://allafrica.com/stories/200111220258.html> (5 March 2002); Henri E. Cauvin, "South African Court Orders Medicine for HIV-Infected Mothers," *New York Times*, 15 December 2001, A9, col. 1.

21 See the South African Government, "Cabinet Statement on HIV/AIDS," 17 April 2002. <http://www.gov.za/speeches/cabinet aids02.htm> (14 June 2002).

22 "Government Gets Ultimatum on HIV/AIDS Drug," *Financial Gazette* (Harare), 13 June 2002, <http://allafrica.com/stories/20020613 0145.html> (16 June 2002).

23 See Pan-African HIV/AIDS Treatment Access Movement, "Declaration of Action," 24 August 2002, <http://www.tac.org.za/> (1 November 2002).

24 World Health Organization, *Scaling Up the Response*, 94.

25 Global Fund to Fight AIDS, Tuberculosis, and Malaria, "Private Sector Enlisted to Ensure AIDS, TB and Malaria Funds Are Effectively Spent: Global Fund Unveils New System to Improve Financial Accountability; Grant Negotiations Begin with Initial Countries," 6 October 2002, <http://www.globalfundatm.org/journalists/press% 20releases/pr061002.html> (4 November 2002).

26 Michael M. Phillips, "Disease-Fighting Fund Has Yet to Donate," *Wall Street Journal*, 5 August 2002.

27 "UNGASS Will Make Governments Accountable," *AIDS 2002 Conference News*, 25 July 2002, <http://www.aids2002.com/ViewArticle. asp?article=/T-CMS_Content/News/7252002023513PM.xml> (9 November 2002).

28 Transparency International, *Corruption Perceptions Index 2002* (Berlin: Transparency International, 2002), <http://www.transparency.org/ pressreleases_archive/2002/dnld/cpi2002.Epressrelease.en.pdf> (1 November 2002).

29 AIDS Education and Research Trust (AVERT), "AIDS in Thailand," 15 October 2001, <http://www.avert.org/aidsthai.htm> (7 January 2002); Wiput Phoolcharoen, "HIV/AIDS Prevention in Thailand: Success and Challenges," *Science* 280 (1998): 1873–1874.

30 UNAIDS and Thai Red Cross, "New Report Documents the Thai National Programme on Zidovudine Donation," 23 April 2001, <http://www.unaids.org/whatsnew/press/eng/pressarc01/MTCT 230401.html> (7 January 2002).

31 M. Ainsworth, C. Beyrer, and A. Soucat, "Success and New Challenges for AIDS Control in Thailand," *AIDScience* 1, no. 5 (2001), <http://aidscience.org/Articles/aidscience005.asp> (5 March 2002).

32 Phoolcharoen, "HIV/AIDS Prevention in Thailand."

33 Kenrad E. Nelson et al., "Changes in Sexual Behavior and a Decline in

HIV Infection Among Young Men in Thailand," *New England Journal of Medicine* 335, no. 5 (1996): 297–303; Jessica Berman, "Thailand Attacks AIDS with Two-Pronged Approach," *Lancet* 353 (1999): 1600.

34   World Health Organization, *HIV/AIDS in Asia and the Pacific Region* (Geneva: WHO, 2001), <http://www.wpro.who.int/pdf/sti/aids 2001/complete.pdf> (7 March 2002); David Celentano et al., "Decreasing Incidence of HIV and Sexually Transmitted Diseases in Young Thai Men: Evidence for Success of the HIV/AIDS Control and Prevention Program," *AIDS* 12 (1998): 29–36.

35   AIDS Education and Research Trust (AVERT), "AIDS in Thailand." Thailand's HIV/AIDS programs are now being successfully imitated by other countries in the region. Using a vigorous condom promotion strategy modeled on Thailand's "100 percent condom" campaign, Cambodia cut HIV infection rates among female sex workers under the age of 20 by almost half, from 40 percent to 23 percent, between 1998 and 2000. See World Health Organization, *Scaling up the Response to Infectious Diseases, 38.*

36   See International Gay and Lesbian Human Rights Commission, "Thailand: PLWHAs 1, BMS 0: Thai AIDS Activists Win First of Two Court Cases Against Bristol-Myers Squibb," 9 October 2002, <http://www.iglhrc.org/world/se_asia/Thailand2002Oct.html> (4 November 2002).

37   Transparency International, *Corruption Perceptions Index 2002.*

38   R. D. Mugerwa, L. H. Marum, and D. Serwadda, "Human Immunodeficiency Virus and AIDS in Uganda," *East African Medical Journal* 73, no. 1 (1996): 20–26.

39   Akin Jimoh, "Raise the Alarm Loudly': Africa Confronts the AIDS Pandemic," *Dollars and Sense,* no. 235 (2001): 17.

40   A. H. Kilian et al., "Reductions in Risk Behaviour Provide the Most Consistent Explanation for Declining HIV-1 Prevalence in Uganda," *AIDS* 13, no. 3 (1999): 391–398; G. Asiimwe-Okiror et al., "Change in Sexual Behaviour and Decline in HIV Infection Among Young Pregnant Women in Urban Uganda," *AIDS* 11 (1997): 1757–1763.

41   *HIV InSite,* "Uganda: Country Profile," 9 November 2001, <http://hivinsite.ucsf.edu/InSite.jsp?page=cr-02-01&doc=2098.41a6> (7 January 2002).

42 N. Kaleeba et al., "Participatory Evaluation of Counseling Medical and Social Services of the AIDS Support Organization (TASO) in Uganda," *AIDS Care* 9, no. 1 (1997): 13–26.

43 *HIV InSite*, "Uganda: Country Profile." See also International AIDS Vaccine Inititaive, "Innovative AIDS Vaccine on Fast Track to Developing Countries," 19 May 2000, <http://allafrica.com/stories/200005190114.html> (4 March 2002).

44 HIVInSite, "Uganda: Country Profile."

45 Tina Rosenberg, "How to Solve the World's AIDS Crisis: Look at Brazil," *New York Times Magazine*, 29 January 2002.

46 Sarna Avina, A Profile of the AIDS Epidemic in Brazil: The Impact of the New AIDS Drug Policy, 16 November 2000, <http://www.gwu.edu/~cih/Sarna.pdf> (29 March 2002).

47 The AIDS death rate dropped from 12.2 per 100,000 in 1995 to 6.3 per 100,000 in 1999. See Ministry of Health of Brazil, *National AIDS Drug Policy* (Brasilia: Ministry of Health of Brazil, 2001), 20.

48 Ibid.

49 Ibid., 3. See also proceedings from the conference "Lessons from the Brazilian AIDS Program," 13 October 2001, <http://www.pih.org/calendar/011013aids/011013aids_proceedings.pdf> (15 March 2002), 3.

50 As the number of patients receiving treatment rose, the Ministry of Health was obliged to spend an increasing percentage of its budget on drugs until 1999. See Ministry of Health of Brazil, *National AIDS Drug Policy: June 2001*, 12.

51 See the proceedings from the October 2001 conference "Lessons from the Brazilian AIDS Program," 10.

52 Brazil's per capita income is about $6,600 per year, while that of countries in sub-Saharan Africa is about $310. Professor Jeffrey Sachs, director of Columbia University's Earth Institute, estimates that the economic burden of AIDS treatment is roughly 800 times heavier for Africans than for Brazilians. See proceedings from "Lessons from the Brazilian AIDS Program," 10.

53 Ministry of Health of Brazil, Secretariat of Health Policies and National Programme for STD/AIDS, *HIV/AIDS Control: The Brazilian Experience 1994–1998* (Brasilia: Ministry of Health of Brazil, 1999).

54 In addition to TASO's work in Uganda, discussed above, a crucial example is the cooperation between international health NGO Médecins Sans Frontières (MSF) and South Africa's Treatment Action Campaign in delivering AIDS education, treatment, and support to patients in Khayeltisha, a poor township outside Cape Town. See Jean Nachega, "Antiretroviral Treatment in Developing Countries," *Hopkins HIV Report,* September 2002, <http://www.hopkins-aids. edu/publications/report/sept02_4.html> (4 November 2002).

55 World Health Organization, *Scaling up the Response to Infectious Diseases,"* 84.

MYTH FOUR: Prevention vs. Treatment?

1 Edward M. Connor et al., "Reduction of Maternal-Infant Transmission of Human Immunodeficiency Virus Type 1 with Zidovudine Treatment," *New England Journal of Medicine* 331, no. 18 (1994): 1173–1180.

2 Frank J. Palella et al., "Declining Morbidity and Mortality among Patients with Advanced Human Immunodeficiency Virus Infection. HIV Outpatient Study Investigators," *New England Journal of Medicine* 338, no. 13 (1998): 853–860; Caroline A. Sabin, "Assessing the Impact of Highly Active Antiretroviral Therapy on AIDS and Death," *AIDS* 13 (1999): 2165–2166.

3 More expensive and demonstrably efficacious forms of HIV prevention—including voluntary counseling and testing, treatment of STDs, and mother-to-child transmission prevention using nevirapine or AZT—are recommended by health officials as highly cost-effective, but have yet to be widely implemented in most poor countries. See Elliot Marseille, Paul B. Hofmann, and James G. Kahn, "HIV Prevention Before HAART in Sub-Saharan Africa," *Lancet* 359, no. 9320 (2002): 1851-1856; Andrew Creese et al., "Cost-Effectiveness of HIV/AIDS Interventions in Africa: A Systematic Review of the Evidence," *Lancet* 359, no. 9318 (2002): 1635–1642.

4 Marseille, Hofmann, and Kahn, "HIV Prevention before HAART." Questioned about his plan for tackling AIDS in Africa, Andrew Natsios, head of the United States Agency for International Development (USAID), affirmed: "Just keep talking about prevention, that's the strategy we're using." John Donnelly, "Prevention Urged in AIDS Fight," *Boston Globe,* 7 June 2001. Some of Mr. Natsios's recent interventions reflect a more flexible stance on the prevention vs. treatment issue.

5 Marseille, Hofmann, and Kahn, "HIV Prevention before HAART in sub-Saharan Africa;" Creese et al., "Cost-Effectiveness of HIV/AIDS Interventions in Africa: A Systematic Review of the Evidence." For an alternate view, see Peter Hale et al., "Success Hinges on Support for Treatment," *Nature* 412 (2001): 272.

6   Robert S. Hogg et al., "One World, One Hope: The Cost of Providing Antiretroviral Therapy to All Nations," *AIDS* 12 (1998): 2203–2209; Evan Wood et al., "Extent to Which Low-Level Use of Antiretroviral Treatment Could Curb the AIDS Epidemic in Sub-Saharan Africa," *Lancet* 355, no. 9221 (2000): 2095-2100; Individual Members of the Harvard Faculty, "Consensus Statement on Antiretroviral Treatment for AIDS in Poor Countries," *Topics in HIV Medicine* 9, no. 2 (2001).

7   Médecins Sans Frontières, "Campaign for Access to Essential Medicines," <http://www.accessmed-msf.org/campaign/hiv01.shtm> (11 April 2002).

8   Karen DeYoung, "Global AIDS Strategy May Prove Elusive; More Funds Available, but Consensus Lacking," *Washington Post*, 23 April 2001, A1.

9   Salih Booker and William Minter, "Global Apartheid," *Nation,* 9 July 2001, <http://www.thenation.com/doc.mhtml?i=20010709&s=booker> (11 April 2002).

10 Pat Sidley, "Fighting Inequalities in AIDS Treatment," *British Medical Journal* 324 (2002): 192.

11 Paul Farmer, "Prevention Without Treatment is Not Sustainable," *National AIDS Bulletin* 13, no. 6 (2000): 6–9.

12 Personal statements from participants in the MSF South Africa pilot antiretroviral treatment program, included in the exhibition *Positive Lives,* National Gallery, Cape Town, South Africa, February–May 2002.

13 Ibid.

14 Creese et al., "Cost-Effectiveness," 1640.

15 Ibid. Calculate $1100 per life-year gained for pilot ARV treatment programs in Senegal and Ivory Coast, $1800 per life-year for a treatment program in South Africa.

16 See Creese et al., "Cost-Effectiveness," 1639–1641.

17 Eric Goemaere, Nathan Ford, and Solomon Benatar, "Letter to the Editor," *Lancet* 360, no. 9326 (2002): 87. Dr. Goemaere is chief physician at the MSF/TAC clinic in Kayelitsha.

18 A. W. Logie, "Africa Revisited: A Distressing Experience," *British Medical Journal* 322, no. 59 (2001).

19 Peter Piot, "The Global Impact of HIV/AIDS," *Nature* 410 (2001): 968–973; C. Moses-Sagoe et al., "Risks to Health Care Workers in Developing Countries," *New England Journal of Medicine* 345, no. 7 (2001): 538–541; International Labour Office, *HIV/AIDS: A Threat to Decent Work, Productivity and Development* (Geneva; ILO, 2000), <http://www.ilo.

iorg/public/english/protection/trav/aids/pdf/aidse.pdf> (21 March 2002).

20   Martha Ainsworth and Waranya Teokul, "Breaking the Silence: Setting Realistic Priorities for AIDS Control in Less-Developed Countries," *Lancet* 356, no. 9223 (2000): 55–60.

21   Peter Piot, Debrework Zewdie, and Tomris Türmen, "HIV/AIDS Prevention and Treatment," *Lancet* 360, *no. 9326 (2002): 86.*

22   The Henry J. Kaiser Family Foundation, "Key Recommendations at the Leadership Forum on HIV Prevention," 22 June 2001, <http://www.kff.org/content/2001/20010627a/recommendations.pdf> (12 April 2002), 3.

23   Michael Sweat et al., "Cost-Effectiveness of Voluntary HIV-1 Counseling and Testing in Reducing Sexual Transmission of HIV-1 in Kenya and Tanzania," *Lancet* 356, no. 9224 (2000): 113–121; Elliot Marseille et al., "Cost Effectiveness of Single-Dose Nevirapine Regimen for Mothers and Babies to Decrease Vertical HIV-1 Transmission in Sub-Saharan Africa," *Lancet* 354, no. 1918 (1999): 803–809; S. Moses et al., "Controlling HIV in Africa: Effectiveness and Cost of an Intervention in a High-Frequency STD Transmitter Core Group," *AIDS* 5 (1991): 407–411; H. Grosskurth et al., "Impact of Improved Treatment of Sexually Transmitted Diseases on HIV Infection in Rural Tanzania: Randomised Controlled Trial," *Lancet* 346 (1995): 530–536; C. Luo, "Achievable Standard of Care in Low-Resource Settings," *Annals of the New York Academy of Sciences* 918 (2000): 179–187.

24   For a recent review of this literature, see Richard G. Parker, Delia Easton, and Charles H. Klein, "Structural Barriers and Facilitators in HIV Prevention: A Review of International Research," *AIDS* 14, Suppl. 1 (2000): S22–32.

25   A recent community-based HIV prevention project in the mining city of Carletonville, South Africa, illustrates the limits imposed on prevention efforts by poverty, gender inequality, and the heritage of institutionalized racism. See Catherine Campbell and Yodwa Mzaidume, "How Can HIV Be Prevented in South Africa? A Social Perspective," *British Medical Journal* 324 (2002): 229-232.

26   In Uganda, national adult HIV prevalence dropped from its 1995 peak of approximately 18 percent to a reported 5 percent at the end of 2001, according to estimates published by UNAIDS. UNAIDS, *Report on the Global HIV/AIDS Epidemic July 2002* (Geneva: UNAIDS, 2002),

<http://www.unaids.org/barcelona/presskit/report.html> (15 October 2002), 190.

27 Peter Hale et al, "Success Hinges on Support for Treatment," *Nature* 412 (2001): 271–272.

28 J. P. Bakari et al., "Rapid Voluntary Testing and Counseling for HIV. Acceptability and Feasibility in Zambian Antenatal Care Clinics," *Annals of the New York Academy of Sciences* 918 (2000): 64–76; D. L. Higgins et al., "Evidence for the Effects of HIV Antibody Counseling and Testing on Risk Behaviors," *Journal of the American Medical Association* 266, no. 17 (1991): 2419–2429; The Voluntary HIV-1 Counseling and Testing Efficacy Study Group, "Efficacy of Voluntary HIV-1 Counselling and Testing in Individuals and Couples in Kenya, Tanzania, and Trinidad: A Randomised Trial," *Lancet* 356, no. 9224 (2000): 103–112.

29 Noerine Kaleeba et al., "Participatory Evaluation of Counselling Medical and Social Services of The AIDS Support Organization (TASO) in Uganda," *AIDS Care* 9, no. 1 (1997): 13–26.

30 R. S. Janssen et al., "The Serostatus Approach to Fighting the HIV Epidemic: Prevention Strategies for Infected Individuals," *American Journal of Public Health* 91, no. 7 (2001): 1019–1024.

31 Higgins et al., "Efficacy of Voluntary HIV-1 Counselling and Testing in Individuals and Couples in Kenya, Tanzania, and Trinidad: A Randomised Trial"; "The Voluntary HIV-1 Counseling and Testing in Individuals and Couples in Kenya, Tanzania, and Trinidad: A Randomised Trial"; Sweat et al., "Cost-effectiveness of Voluntary HIV-1 Counseling and Testing."

32 Kevin M. De Cock et al., "Prevention of Mother-to-Child HIV Transmission in Resource-Poor Countries: Translating Research into Policy and Practice," *Journal of the American Medical Association* 283, no. 9 (2000): 1175; Peter Piot and A. Coll-Seck, "Preventing Mother-to-Child Transmission of HIV in Africa," *Bulletin of the World Health Organization* 77, no. 11 (1999): 869–870.

33 Knut Fylkesnes et al., "HIV Counselling and Testing: Overemphasizing High Acceptance Rates. A Threat to Confidentiality and the Right Not to Know," *AIDS* 13, no. 17 (1999): 2469–2474.

34 Yacouba Nebie et al., "Sexual and Reproductive Life of Women Informed of Their HIV Seropositivity: A Prospective Cohort Study in Burkina Faso," *Journal of Acquired Immune Deficiency Syndromes* 28, 4 (2001): 367–372; J. Ladner et al., "A Cohort Study of Factors Associated with Failure to Return for HIV Post-Test Counselling in Preg-

nant Women: Kigali, Rwanda, 1992–1993," *AIDS* 10, no. 1 (1996): 69–75; M. Temmerman et al., "The Right Not to Know HIV-Test Results," *Lancet* 345, no. 8955 (1995): 969–970.

35 Rachel Baggaley et al., "HIV Counselling and Testing in Zambia: The Kara Counselling Experience," *Southern Africa AIDS Information Dissemination Service* 6, no. 2 (1998): 2–9.

36 Rachel Baggaley et al., "HIV Counsellors' Knowledge, Attitudes and Vulnerabilities to HIV in Lusaka, Zambia, 1994," *AIDS Care* 8, no. 2 (1996): 15–166.

37 C. N. Brouwer et al., "Psychosocial and Economic Aspects of HIV/AIDS and Counselling of Caretakers of HIV-Infected Children in Uganda," *AIDS Care* 12, no. 5 (2000): 535–540.

38 Peter R. Lamptey, "Reducing Heterosexual Transmission of HIV in Poor Countries," *British Medical Journal* 324, no. 7331 (2002): 207–211; Joan M. MacNeil and Sandra Anderson, "Beyond the Dichotomy: Linking HIV Prevention with Care," *AIDS* 12, Suppl. 2 (1998): S19–26.

39 Kevin M. De Cock, "From Receptionalism to Normalisation: A Reappraisal of Attitudes and Practice around HIV Testing," *British Medical Journal* 316, no. 7127 (1998): 290–293.

40 Tina Rosenberg, "How to Solve the World's AIDS Crisis: Look at Brazil"; Paul Farmer et al., "Community-Based Treatment of Advanced HIV Disease: Introducing DOT-HAART (Directly Observed Therapy with Highly Active Antiretroviral Therapy)," *Bulletin of the World Health Organization* 79, no. 12 (2001):1145–1151.

41 X. P. Wei et al., "Viral Dynamics in Human Immunodeficiency Virus Type I Infection," *Nature* 373 (1995): 117–122; D. D. Ho et al., "Rapid Turnover of Plasma Virions and CD4 Lymphocytes in HIV Infection," *Nature* 373 (1995): 123–126; S. M. Hammer et al., "A Controlled Trial of Two Nucleoside Analogues Plus Indinavir in Persons with Human Immunodeficiency Virus Infection and CD4 Cell Counts of 200 per Cubic Millimeter or Less," *New England Journal of Medicine* 337, no. 11 (1997): 725–733; R. M. Gulick et al., "Treatment with Indinavir, Zidovudine, and Lamivudine in Adults with Human Immunodeficiency Virus Infection and Prior Antiretroviral Therapy," *New England Journal of Medicine* 337, no. 11 (1997): 734–739; Stephan Taylor et al., "Dynamics of Seminal Plasma HIV-1 Decline after Antiretroviral Treatment," *AIDS* 15, no. 3 (2001): 424–426.

42 Tzong H. Lee et al., "Correlation of HIV-1 RNA Levels in Plasma and Heterosexual Transmission of HIV-1 from Infected Transfusion Recipients," *Journal of Acquired Immune Deficiency Syndromes and Human Retrovirology* 12, no. 4 (1996): 427–428; Margaret V. Ragni, Hawazin Faruki, and Lawrence A. Kingsley, "Heterosexual HIV-1 Transmission and Viral Load in Hemophilic Patients," *Journal of Acquired Immune Deficiency Syndromes and Human Retrovirology* 17, no. 1 (1998): 42–45; E. A. Operskalski et al., "Role of Viral Load in Heterosexual Transmission of Human Immunodeficiency Virus Type 1 by Blood Transfusion Recipients," *American Journal of Epidemiology* 146, no. 8 (1997): 655–661; Maria A. Pedraza et al., "Heterosexual Transmission of HIV-1 is Associated with High Plasma Viral Load Levels and a Positive Viral Isolation in the Infected Partner," *Journal of Acquired Immune Deficiency Syndromes & Human Retrovirology* 21, no. 2 (1999): 120–125; Patricia M. Garcia et al., "Maternal Levels of Plasma Human Immunodeficiency Virus Type 1 RNA and the Risk of Perinatal Transmission," *New England Journal of Medicine* 341, no. 6 (1999): 394-402; Thomas C. Quinn et al., "Viral Load and Heterosexual Transmission of Human Immunodeficiency Virus Type 1," *New England Journal of Medicine* 342, no. 13 (2000): 921–929.

43 In the presence of antiretroviral drugs, cell-associated HIV is still retained in the form of proviral DNA, a quiescent stage ready to reactivate upon termination of suppressive therapy or in response to missed doses of medications. This cell-associated virus remains a potential source of infection.

44 Mitchell H. Katz et al., "Impact of Highly Active Antiretroviral Treatment on HIV Seroincidence Among Men Who Have Sex with Men: San Francisco," *American Journal of Public Health* 92, no. 3 (2002): 388-394.

45 Marseille, Hofmann, and Kahn, "HIV Prevention before HAART," 1855.

46 See the preface by Zackie Achmat in this volume.

47 Peter Piot, "Letter to the Editor," *Lancet* 360, no. 9326 (2002): 86.

48 U.K. NGO AIDS Consortium Working Group on Access to Treatment for HIV in Developing Countries, "Access to Treatment for HIV in Developing Countries; Statement from International Seminar on Access to Treatment for HIV in Developing Countries, London, June 5 and 6, 1998," *Lancet* 352, no. 9137 (1998): 1379–1380; David Wilson et al., "Global Trade and Access to Medicines: AIDS Treatments in Thailand," *Lancet* 354, no. 9193 (1999): 1893–1895.

MYTH FIVE: Obstacles to AIDS Treatment in Poor Countries

1 International HIV Treatment Access Coalition, *A Commitment to Action for Expanded Access to HIV/AIDS Treatment* (Geneva: WHO, 2002), 1.

2 Paul Farmer, *Infections and Inequalities,* 264.

3 Paul Farmer, Fernet Léandre et al., "Community-based treatment of advanced HIV disease: introducing DOT-HAART," *Bulletin of the World Health Organization* 79, no. 12 (2001): 1148.

4 See documentation at <http://www.accessmed-msf.org/index.asp> (October 17, 2002).

5 By comparison, when Cipla's $350 per year proposal was announced in February 2001, health officials in Senegal were paying between $1,008 and $1,821 per year for brand name combination therapy purchased through a UN-brokered program. Reuters, "Indian Firm Offers AIDS Cocktail for $1 a Day," February 9, 2001,<http://www.accessmedmsf.org/prod/publicaions.asp?scntid=3082001126503&contenttype=PARA&> (18 April 2002).

6 See Médecins Sans Frontières, *Untangling the Web of Price Reductions: A Pricing Guide for the Purchase of ARVs for Developing Countries* (Geneva: MSF, 2002). <http://www.accessmed-msf.org/upload/Reports and Publications/1872002161586/Purpledoc.pdf> (October 17, 2002).

7 See United Nations, "Joint Communiqué from Secretary-General and Seven Leading Research-Based Pharmaceutical Companies on Access to HIV/AIDS Care and Treatment," 4 October 2001. <http://www.un.org/News/Press/docs/2001/sgsm7982.doc.htm> (16 April 2002).

8 Anders Nordstrom, "The Global Fund: Raising the Stakes," Electronic Response, *British Medical Journal* (11 February 2002) <http://bmj.com/cgi/eletters/324/7331/181> (22 April 2002) and Gavin Yamey and William W Rankin, "AIDS and Global Justice," *British Medical Journal* (2002):181–182.

9 See Donald McNeil, Jr., "U.N. Disease Fund Opens Way to Generics," *New York Times,* 16 October 2002. National ministries of health are also reaching out to form novel strategic alliances. Brazil's health ministry has collaborated with local pharmaceutical manufacturers to produce generic AIDS drugs. The government of Botswana is partnering with the Bill & Melinda Gates Foundation and Merck Pharmaceuticals to fund a $100 million program promising Bot-

swana's citizens universal access to AIDS treatment. See Harvard AIDS Institute, "Antiretroviral Therapy Course Offered to Nurses and Pharmacy Technicians in Botswana," <http://www.aids.harvard.edu/overview/news_events/news/press_releases/art_course.html> (19 April 2002). Middle-income countries with demonstrated success in AIDS control, such as Brazil and Thailand, are now donating technical assistance to poor countries to scale up their prevention and treatment efforts. See e.g., World Health Organization, "Mekong Countries Join Hands In Preventing HIV Transmission to Children" (2002) <http://www.who.int/inf-new/mate2.htm> (19 April 2002); and Ministry of Health of Brazil, *National AIDS Drug Policy* (Brasilia: Ministry of Health of Brazil, 2001), 24. Also see "Thailand to Assist Zimbabwe in Production of Generic AIDS Drugs," *Kaiser Daily HIV/AIDS Report*, January 29, 2002, <http://lists.essential.org/pipermail/ip-health/2002-January/0026222.html> (April 26, 2002).

10   Ministry of Health of Brazil, *National AIDS Drug Policy*, 29.

11   International HIV Treatment Access Coalition, *A Commitment to Action for Expanded Access to HIV/AIDS Treatment* (Geneva: WHO, 2002), 1.

12   Panos Institute, "Beyond our means? The cost of treating HIV/AIDS in the developing world," < http://www.panos.org.uk/aids/BeyondOurMeans.pdf> (15 April 2002).

13   For a discussion about the health consequences of the debt crisis and the structural adjustment policies imposed on indebted countries by the IMF and World Bank, see Myth 1.

14   K. Hanson et al., "Constraints to Scaling Up Health Interventions: A Conceptual Framework and Empirical Analysis," May 2001, <http://www.cmhealth.org/docs/wg5_paper14.pdf> (15 April 2002).

15   Meredith Turshen, *Privatizing Health Services in Africa* (Trenton, NJ: Rutgers University Press, 1999). Also see Gerald A. Arbuckle, *Healthcare Ministry: Refounding the Mission in Tumultuous Times.* (Collegeville, MN: Liturgical Press, 2000).

16   World Health Organization, "Scaling Up Antiretroviral Therapy in Resource-Limited Settings: Guidelines for a Public Health Approach" June 2002 < http://www.who.int/hiv/topics/arv/ISBN9241545674.pdf> (21 January 2003); S.M. Hammer, T. Turmen, B. Vareldzis, J Terriens, "Antiretroviral guidelines for resource-limited settings: The WHO's public health approach," *Nature Medicine* 8, no. 7 (2002): 649-650. World Health Organization, *Scaling Up the Response to Infectious*

Diseases: A Way Out of Poverty (Geneva: WHO, 2002), <http:://www.who.int/infectious-disease-report/> (15 April 2002).

17 See Anne-Christine d'Adesky, "Poor Countries Need Faster, Cheaper, Better HIV Monitoring," (January 2002)<http://www.aegis.com/pubs/amfar/2002/AM020101.html> (22 January 2003); presentations at Project Inform website, <http://www.projinf.org/presentations/bethesda.html>

18 Please see the resource guide at the end of the book to contact Physicians for Human Rights and Partners In Health about "Pragmatic Partnerships to Combat the AIDS Pandemic: A Guide for Health Professionals."

19 Pfizer, "African and Western Alliance to Build First Large-Scale AIDS Medical Training Facility in Africa," press release, June 2001, <http://www.pfizer.com/are/news_releases/mn_2001_0611.html> (22 January 2003); Infectious Disease Society of America, *AIDS Training Program*, <www.idsociety.org/ATP/Background.htm> (22 January 2003); Foundation University of Medicine and Dentistry of New Jersey "UMDNJ-New Jersey Medical School Leads World-Wide Alliance to Fight HIV/AIDS in Africa,"<http://www.umdnj.edu/foundweb/news/news_aids.htm> (22 January 2003).

20 Pfizer, "African and Western Alliance."

21 The collaborative programs of the Harvard AIDS Institute, founded in 1988, offer one example. See <http://www.aids.harvard.edu/index.html>.

22 Paul Farmer, "Introducing ARVs in Resource-Poor Settings: Expected and Unexpected Challenges and Consequences" (plenary address at the XIV International AIDS Conference, Barcelona, 11 July 2002), 5.

23 Ibid, 5-7.

24 Farmer, Léandre, et al., "Community-Based Treatment," 1145–51. See also Paul E. Farmer, "DOTS and DOTS-Plus, Not the Only Answer," *Annals of the New York Academy of Sciences* 953 (December 2001):165–184.

25 Paul Farmer et al., "Community-Based Approaches to HIV Treatment in Resource-Poor Settings," *Lancet* 358 (2001):404–409.

26 Farmer, Léandre et al., "Community-Based Treatment," 1147.

27   Jennifer Singler and Paul Farmer, "Treating HIV in Resource-Poor Settings," *Medical Student Journal of the American Medical Association,* 288 (2002): 13.

28   Farmer, "Introducing ARVs in Resource-Poor Settings," 5.

29   Farmer, "Introducing ARVs in Resource-Poor Settings," 13.

30   Médecins Sans Frontières, "Equitable Access: Scaling Up HIV/AIDS Treatment in Developing Countries (World AIDS Day 2002 Briefing Paper)," 27 November 2002; "Scaling Up HIV/AIDS Treatment Jeopardized by WTO Negotiations" 1 December 2002, <http://www.accessmed-msf.org/index.asp>.

31   Examples of successful AIDS treatment in resource-poor settings also include a pilot program initiated in Uganda in 1998. See P.J. Weidle et al, "Assessment of a Pilot Antiretroviral Drug Therapy Programme in Uganda: Patient's Response, Survival, and Drug Resistance," *Lancet* 360 (2002): 34–40.

32   World Health Organization, "3 Million HIV/AIDS Sufferers Could Receive Anti-Retroviral Therapy by 2005," 9 July 2002, <http://www.who.int/inf/en/pr-2002-58.html>.

33   Jon Cohen, "Confronting the Limits of Success" *Science* 5577 (2002): 2320–2324, <http://aidscience.org/Science/2320.html>.

34   World Health Organization, "Scaling Up Antiretroviral Therapy."

35   Jon Cohen, "Confronting the Limits of Success," *Science* 296(5577):2320–2324, 28 June 2002, <http://www. aidscience.org/Science/2320.html>.

36   World Health Organization, "Scaling Up Antiretroviral Therapy."

37   Richard Horton, "African AIDS beyond Mbeki: Tripping into anarchy" *Lancet* 356 (2000):1541–42.

38   N.Z. Noisome et al., "Antiretroviral (ARV) Drug Utilization in Harare," *Central African Journal of Medicine* 46, no. 4 (2000): 89–93.

39   As quoted in Richard Horton, "African AIDS Beyond Mbeki."

40   Horton, "African AIDS Beyond Mbeki"; A.D. Harries, D.S. Nyangulu, N.J. Hargreaves, O. Kaluwa, F.M. Salaniponi, "Preventing antiretroviral anarchy in sub-Saharan Africa," *Lancet* 358 (2001):410–14; G.P. Garnett, L. Bartley, N.C. Grassly, R.M. Anderson, "Antiretroviral Therapy to Treat and Prevent HIV/AIDS in Resource-Poor Settings," *Nature Medicine* 8, no. 7 (2002): 651–52.

41   David L. Paterson et al., "Adherence to Protease Inhibitor Therapy and Outcomes in Patients with HIV Infection," *Annals of Internal Medicine* 133, no. 1 (2000): 21–30; D.R. Bangsberg et al., "Adherence to Protease Inhibitors, HIV-1 Viral Load, and Development of Drug Resistance in an Indigent Population," *AIDS* 14 (2000): 357–66.

42 Johanna Daily, Department of Internal Medicine, Harvard Medical School, personal communication.

43 Médecins Sans Frontières, "MSF and HIV/AIDS," *The Campaign: Target Diseases: HIV/AIDS* <http://www.accessmed-msf.org/campaign/hiv01.shtm> (22 January 2003).

44 C. Orrell, L. G. Bekker and R. Wood. "Adherence to Antiretroviral Therapy–Achievable in the South African Context?" *South African Medical Journal.* 91 (2001): 4 83–484 and C. Orrell and R. Wood, Abstract no. 696 (presented at the 1st International AIDS Society Conference on HIV Pathogenesis and Treatment, Buenos Aires, 2001).

45 C. Laurent et al. "The Senegalese government's highly active antiretroviral therapy initiative: an 18-month follow-up study" *AIDS* 16 (2002): 1363–70.

46 See J.A. Bartlett, "Addressing the Challenges of Adherence," *Journal of Acquired Immune Deficiency Syndrome* 29 (2002): Suppl. 1:S2-10; P.A. Frick et al, "Antiretroviral medication commonplace in patients with AIDS," *AIDS Patient Care STDS* 12 (1998): 463-70; C.E. Golin, "A prospective study of predictors of adherence to combination antiretroviral medication," *Journal of General Internal Medicine* 17 (2002):756-65.

47 Anthony Harries et al., "Preventing Antiretroviral Anarchy in sub-Saharan Africa," *Lancet* 358 (2001): 410-14.

48 Ibid.

49 See e.g., "Consensus Statement on Antiretroviral Treatment for AIDS in Poor Countries by Individual Members of the Faculty of Harvard University," *Topics in HIV Medicine* 9 (2001): 14–26.

50 Harries et al., "Preventing antiretroviral anarchy."

51 International HIV Treatment Access Coalition, *A Commitment to Action for Expanded Access to HIV/AIDS Treatment* (Geneva: World Health Organization, 2002), 6.

52 Paul Farmer, "Introducing ARVs."

MYTH SIX: Vaccines

1 Steve Sternberg, "Closer to AIDS Vaccine? 20 Prototypes Are in Trials; Researchers Feel They'll Beat the Virus," *USA Today*, 5 September 2001, sec 1D, <http://www.usatoday.com/usatonline/20010905/3602694s.htm> (6 September 2001).

2   Daniel DeNoon, "Optimism at AIDS Vaccine Meeting—Behind the Scenes, Science Leaps Forward," *WebMD Medical News,* 2002, <http://my.webmd.com/content/article/1624.51030> (9 November 2002).

3   Dennis Blakeslee, "HIV Vaccines: Are They Possible?" *Journal of the American Medical Association* HIV/AIDS Information Center, 3 February 1999, <www.ama-assn.org/special/hiv/newsline/special/jamadb/vacjan99.htm> (6 September 2001).

4   Sternberg, "Closer to AIDS Vaccine?"

5   Brian Vastag, "HIV Vaccine Efforts Inch Forward," *Journal of the American Medical Association* 286, no. 15 (2001), <http://jama.ama-assn.org/issues/v286n15/ffull/jmn1017-2.html> (25 October 2002).

6   World Health Organization, Regional Office for Africa, "Accelerating HIV Vaccine Development for Africa," 18 June 2002, <http://www.afro.who.int/note_press/2002/pr20020618.html> (9 November 2002); Emily Bass, "Africa AIDS Vaccine Programme Arrives on the Global Stage," *AVI Report,* March/April 2002, <www.iavi.org/reports/282/AAVP.htm> (9 November 2002); Medical Research Council of South Africa, "The Nairobi Declaration: An African Appeal for an AIDS Vaccine," *MRC News* 31, no. 6 (2000), <http://www.mrc.ac.za/mrcnews/dec2000/nairobi.htm> (9 November 2002).

7   Michelle R. Galloway, "South African Aids Vaccine Initiative: Working, Not Waiting," SA HealthInfo, 1999, <www.sahealthinfo.org/hivaids/working.htm> (9 November 2002); Galloway, "South African AIDS Vaccine Initiative Funds First Projects," *SA HealthInfo,* 1999, <www.sahealthinfo.org/hivaids/firstvaccine.htm> (9 November 2002); Marthali Nicodemus, Hakima Sbai, and Anne S. De Groot, "Urgency and Optimism at the AIDS Vaccine 2001 Conference," *AIDScience* 1, no. 11 (2001), <http://aidscience.org/Articles/aidscience009.asp> (25 October 2002).

8   International AIDS Vaccine Initiative, "AVI Outlines New, Intensive R&D Agenda to Fast-Track Promising AIDS Vaccine Candidates to Final-Stage Human Testing," 9 July 2002, <http://www.iavi.org/press/74/n20020709b.asp> (9 November 2002). See also link on this page to Scientific Blueprint 2000, <http://www.iavi.org/pdf/sblueprint2000.pdf> (9 November 2002).

9   International AIDS Vaccine Initiative, "AVI-Sponsored AIDS Vaccine Approaches in Development and Testing," 2002, <http://www.

iavi.org/vaccinedev/pipeline.htm> (9 November 2002).

10   Malegapuru W. Makgoba, Nandipha Solomon, and Timothy J. P. Tucker, "The Search for an HIV Vaccine," *British Medical Journal* 324 (2002), <http://bmj.com/cgi/reprint/324/7331/211.pdf> (25 October 2002), 211-213. For industry's perspective, see Amie Batson and Martha Ainsworth, "Private Investment in AIDS Vaccine Development: Obstacles and Solutions," *Bulletin of the World Health Organization* 79, no. 8 (2001): 721–727 <http://www.who.int/bulletin/pdf/2001/issue8/vol79.no.8.721-727.pdf> (9 November 2002).

11   Aids Vaccine Advocacy Coalition, *6 Years and Counting: Can a Shifting Landscape Accelerate an AIDS Vaccine?* (New York: AVAC, 2001), <http://www.avac.org/pdf/reports/6years.pdf> (25 October 2002), 4.

12   Merck, "Merck Presents First Human Data on HIV-1 Vaccine Candidates," 28 February 2002, <www.merck.com/newsroom/press_releases/022802.html> (9 November 2002).

13   John W. Shiver et al., "Replication-Incompetent Adenoviral Vaccine Elicits Effective Anti-Immunodeficiency-Virus Immunity," *Nature* 415, no. 6869 (2002): 331–335. It should be pointed out that a vaccine used to slow disease progression does not act to protect people from being infected. This type of vaccine could be used as a therapeutic in already infected individuals or as a partially preventive vaccine to interrupt transmission, as discussed later in the chapter. For more information about debates on animal studies, see Jon Cohen, "Monkey Puzzles," *Science* 296, no. 5577 (2002): 2325–2326; M. B. Feinberg and J. P. Moore, "AIDS Vaccine Models: Challenging Challenge Viruses," *Nature Medicine* 8, no. 3 (2002): 207–210.

14   NIAID, "NIAID and Merck to Collaborate on HIV Vaccine Development," 20 December 2001, <www.nih.gov/news/pr/dec2001/niaid-20.htm> (9 November 2002). For a good discussion on this and other current vaccine strategies, see also Carol Ezzell, "Hope in a Vial? Will There Be an AIDS Vaccine Anytime Soon?" *Scientific American*, 13 May 2002.

15   Glaxo Smith Kline, "Start of First Clinical Trial with Glaxo Smith Kline Biologicals' Novel HIV Vaccine," 31 January 2002, <http://www.gsk.com/media/archive.htm> (25 October 2002).

16   For a good review in nontechnical language, see Bill Snow, "Vaccine Basics," in *HIV Vaccine Handbook*, ed. Bill Snow (New York: AVAC, 1999), <http://www.avac.org/pdf/primer/basics.pdf> (9 November 2002).

17 Bette Korber et al., "Evolutionary and Immunological Implications of Contemporary HIV-1 Variation," *British Medical Bulletin* 58 (2001): 19–42; Robin A. Weiss, "Gulliver's Travels in HIVland," *Nature* 410, no. 6831 (2001): 963–967.

18 John P. Moore, Paul W. Parren, and Dennis R. Burton, "Genetic Subtypes, Humoral Immunity, and Human Immunodeficiency Virus Type 1 Vaccine Development," *Journal of Virology* 75 (2001): 5721–5729.

19 Jaap Goudsmit, "Do HIV Clades Really Matter?" *AVI Report*, 1 October 1999, <http://www.iavi.org/reports/73/sep-oct-1999-4.html >(9 November 2002); Gary Nabel, William Makgoba, and Jose Esparza, "HIV-1 Diversity and Vaccine Development," *Science* 296, no. 5577 (2002): 2335, <www.aidscience.org/Science/2335.html> (9 November 2002). Jose Esparza and Natth Bhamarapravati, "Accelerating the Development and Future Availability of HIV-1 Vaccines: Why, When, Where, and How?" *Lancet* 355, no. 9220 (2000): 2061–2066.

20 NIAID, "Challenges in Designing HIV Vaccines," *NIAID Factsheet,* May 2001, <www.niaid.nih.gov/factsheets/challvacc.htm> (9 November 2002); Gary J. Nabel, "Challenges and Opportunities for Development of an AIDS Vaccine," *Nature* 410, no. 6831 (2001): 1002–1007.

21 The Johns Hopkins AIDS Vaccine Evaluation Unit, "Background Information," 2 April 1999, <http://www.jhsph.edu/cir/aveg/jhubac k.htm> (20 March 2002).

22 Jose Esparza, "An HIV Vaccine: How and When?" *Bulletin of the World Health Organization* 79, no. 12 (2001), <http://www.who.int/bulletin/ pdf/2001/issue12/79(12)1133-1137.pdf> (25 October 2002).

23 Food and Drug Administration, "Vaccine Product Approval Process," 27 July 2001, <www.fda.gov/cber/vaccine/vacappr.htm> (25 October 2002); Isadora B. Stehlin, "How FDA Works to Ensure Vaccine Safety," *FDA Consumer Magazine* 29, no. 10 (1995), <www.fda.gov/fdac/features/095 vacc.html> (25 October 2002).

24 Ibid.

25 Batson and Ainsworth, "Private Investment."

26 Makgoba, Solomon, and Tucker, "The Search for an HIV Vaccine," Roy D. Mugerwa et al., "First Trial of the HIV-1 Vaccine in Africa: Ugandan Experience," *British Medical Journal* 324 (2002): 226–229; Paul Farmer, "New Malaise: Medical Ethics and Social Rights in the

Global Era," *Pathologies of Power: Health, Human Rights, and the New War on the Poor* (Berkeley: University of California Press, 2003) 196-212.

27 Gary Nabel, "HIV Vaccine Strategies," *Vaccine* 20, no. 15 (2002): 1945–1947; NIAID Division of AIDS, *HIV Vaccine Development Status Report,* May 2000, <www.niaid.nih.gov/daids/vaccine/whsummaryst atus.htm> (9 November 2002).

28 Margaret I. Johnston and Jorge Flores, "Progress in HIV Vaccine Development," *Current Opinion in Pharmacology* 1 (2001): 504–510; Emily Bass and Richard Jefferys, "Warming Trends at Keystone Vaccine Conference," *AVI Report*, March/April 2002, <www.iavi.org/reports /282/keystone.htm> (9 November 2002); International AIDS Vaccine Initiative, "New Vaccines in the Pipeline," *AVI Report*, July–September 2002, <www.iavi.org/iavireport/0902/HTML/new vax0902.htm> (9 November 2002).

29 International AIDS Vaccine Initiative, "Preventive AIDS Vaccine Approaches Currently in Human Testing," 2002, <www.iavi.org/sci ence/trials.htm> (9 November 2002); Jose Esparza, "An HIV Vaccine: How and When?"

30 NIAID Division of AIDS, "NIAID: Interim Analysis of Vaxgen's Phase III AIDSVAX Trial: Questions and Answers," 29 October 2001, <http://www.niaid.nih.gov/daids/vaccine/studies/vaxgenq& a.htm> (9 November 2002).

31 International AIDS Vaccine Initiative, "Preventive AIDS Vaccine Approaches Currently in Human Testing."

32 Michael Balter, "AIDS Research: Impending AIDS Vaccine Trial Opens Old Wounds," *Science* 279, no. 5351 (1998): 650; International AIDS Vaccine Initiative, "One Trial, Many Opinions," *AVI Report*, October–December 1998, <www.iavi.org/reports/132/One_Trial_ Many_Opinions.htm> (9 November 2002); Ezzell, "Hope in a Vial?"

33 For information on this trial, see Jon Cohen "Debate Begins over New Vaccine Trials," *Science* 293, no. 5537 (2001): 1973; "Disappointing Data Scuttle Plans for Large-Scale AIDS Vaccine Trial," *Science* 295, no. 5560 (2002): 1616–1617.

34 Jon Cohen, *Shots in the Dark: The Wayward Search for an AIDS Vaccine* (New York: W. W. Norton & Company, 2001); John P. Moore, "On the Trail of Two Trails. Development of an AIDS Vaccine Will Not be Helped by Duplicative Trials," *Nature* 24, no. 415 (2002): 364–365.

35 AIDS Vaccine Advocacy Coalition, *6 Years and Counting,* 4.

36 Ibid., 11.

37 Heinz Köhler, Sybille Müller, and Veljko Veljkovic, "No Hope for an AIDS Vaccine Soon," *AIDScience* 2, no. 5 (2002); Harold Varmus and Neal Nathanson, "Science and the Control of AIDS," *Science* 280, no. 5371 (1999): 1815.

38 Vaxgen, "Our Vaccine Candidates: Determination of Efficacy," <http://www.vaxgen.com/products/index.html> (9 November 2002). A 30 percent vaccine efficacy means that there were 30 percent fewer HIV infections in people who were vaccinated than in those who were not.

39 Nicodemus, Sbai, and De Groot, "Urgency and Optimism"; Emily Bass, "Barcelona Sessions Spark Full Discussion of Partially Effective Vaccines," *AVI Report,* July-September 2002, <http://www.iavi.org/iavireport/0902/HTML/parteffect0902.htm> (9 November 2002).

40 Susan Scheer et al., "Effect of Highly Active Antiretroviral Therapy on Diagnosis of Sexually Transmitted Diseases in People with AIDS," *Lancet* 357, no. 9254 (2001): 432–435; N. H. Dukers et al., "Sexual Risk Behaviour Relates to the Virological and Immunological Improvements During Highly Active Antiretroviral Therapy in HIV-1 Infection," *AIDS* 15, no. 3 (2001): 369–378; Christopher Heredia, "Study Shows Gay Men in SF Less Afraid of HIV: Attitude May be Leading to More Infections," *San Francisco Chronicle,* 22 October 2001.

41 Esparza, "An HIV Vaccine: How and When?"

42 Makgoba, Solomon, and Tucker, "The Search for an HIV Vaccine."

43 International AIDS Vaccine Initiative, "AIDS Vaccines for the World: Preparing Now to Assure Access," *AVI Access Blueprint,* <http://www.iavi.org/access/blueprint.htm> (9 November 2002); Hans Binswanger, "Follow the Money: The Economics of AIDS Vaccine Development. An Interview with the World Bank's Hans Binswanger," interview by Joe Wright <http://www.avac.org/lib/libOACW6a.htm> (9 November 2002).

44 Makgoba, Solomon, and Tucker, "The Search for an HIV Vaccine."

45 AIDS Vaccine Advocacy Coalition, *6 Years and Counting,* 5.

46 Ibid., 6.

47 AVI, "AVI Releases Scientific Blueprint; Bill Gates, UK Government Provide Support," *AVI Report,* July–September 1998, <http://www.iavi.org/reports/139/IAVI_Releases_Blueprint.htm> (13 December 2002).

48 On testing of the new drug known as "T-20," see Andrew Pollack, "AIDS Drug Fares Well in Big Trial," *New York Times,* 19 April 2002, p. C6.

49 Mugerwa et al., "First Trial."

50 Esparza and Bhamarapravati, "Accelerating the Development."

MYTH SEVEN: Drug Company Profits vs. Poor People's Health

1 See Pharmaceutical Research and Manufacturers of America, *The Value of Medicines* (Washington, DC: PhRMA, 2001).

2 See Tufts Center for the Study of Drug Development, "Tufts Center for the Study of Drug Development Pegs Cost of a New Prescription Medicine at $802 Million," 30 November 2001, <http://csdd.tufts.ed u/NewsEvents/RecentNews.asp?newsid=6> (9 November 2002). Public Citizen has argued that average drug development costs are actually much lower, probably about $240 million for each new product. See Public Citizen, "Tufts Drug Study Sample Is Skewed; True Figure of R&D Costs Likely is 75 Percent Lower," 4 December 2001, <http://www.citizen.org/pressroom/release.cfm?ID=954> (9 November 2002).

3 Public Citizen's Congress Watch, "Pharmaceuticals Rank as Most Profitable Industry, Again," 17 April 2002, <http://www.citizen.org/ documents/fortune500_2002erport.PDF> (9 November 2002).

4 Panos Institute, *Patents, Pills and Public Health:: Can TRIPS Deliver?* (London: Panos, 2002), 10.

5 Ibid, 9.

6 Ibid, 9.

7 The absence of price controls on pharmaceuticals in the most lucrative markets, such as the US, is another important factor contributing to the industry's profitability and power.

8 Z. Griliches and I. Cockburn, "Generics and New Goods in Pharmaceutical Price Indexes," *American Economic Review* 84, no. 5 (1994): 1213–1232.

9 Ivette Madrid, Germán Velázquez, and Enrique Ferer, *Pharmaceuticals and Health Sector Reform in the Americas: An Economic Perspective* (Washington, DC: WHO/PAHO, 1998), 59.

10 Commission on Intellectual Property Rights, *Integrating Intellectual Property Rights and Development Policy* (London: Commission on Intellectual Property Rights, 2002), 29-31.

11 Ibid., 33.

12 Robert Weissman, "AIDS and Developing Countries: Facilitating Access to Essential Medicines," *Foreign Policy in Focus* 6, no. 6 (2001),

<http://fpif.org/briefs/vol6/v6n06aids_body.html> (9 November 2002).

13 Tina Rosenberg, "How to Solve the World's AIDS Crisis: Look at Brazil."

14 Médecins Sans Frontières, *Untangling the Web of Price Reductions: A Pricing Guide for the Purchase of ARVs for Developing Countries* (Geneva: MSF, 2002).

15 See John Barton, "Differentiated Pricing of Patented Products," Working Paper No. WG4:2 (Geneva) 10–11.

16 Weissman, "AIDS and Developing Countries."

17 Commission on Intellectual Property Rights, *Integrating Intellectual Property Rights and Development Policy*, 42.

18 H. E. Cauvin, "Zimbabwe Acts to Obtain AIDS Drugs at Low Prices," *New York Times*, 1 June 2002.

19 US Public Law 105-277 (105th Congress, 1999) blocked certain types of foreign aid funding for the South African government pending "repeal, suspension, or termination" of offending passages in South Africa's Medicines and Related Substances Control Amendment Act. See Carlos Correa, *Implications of the Doha Declaration on the TRIPS Agreement and Public Health* (Geneva: WHO, 2002), 1–2.

20 Gavin Yamey, "US Trade Action Threatens Brazilian AIDS Programme," *British Medical Journal* 322 (2001): 383.

21 Benjamin Shepard and Ronald Hayduk, eds., *From Act Up to the WTO: Urban Protest and Community Building in the Era of Globalization* (New York: Verso Books, 2001).

22 Sam H. Verhovek, "Talks and Turmoils: The Hosts; Seattle is Stung, Angry and Chagrined as Opportunity Turns to Chaos," *New York Times*, 2 December 1999.

23 D. Montgomery, "Protests End with Voluntary Arrests; Police, Demonstrators Say They Met Goals," *Washington Post*, 18 April 2000.

24 J. Burgess, "Africa Gets AIDS Drug Exception; Clinton Order May Lower Prices," *Washington Post*, 11 May 2000.

25 D. Brown, "AIDS Drug Discounts Offered to 3rd World," *Washington Post*, 12 May 2000.

26 While the launch of the Accelerating Access Initiative constituted a symbolically important first step toward lowering prices of AIDS drugs in developing countries, many analysts consider the Initiative deeply flawed. Some have denounced it as a strategic concession on the part of the research-based drug companies, the real purpose of which was to

undermine the legitimacy of activists' campaigns for compulsory licensing of AIDS medications in poor countries. See letter from Ralph Nader to Dr. Gro Harlem Brundtland, director-general of the World Health Organization, 23 July 2001, <http://www.cptech.org/ip/health/nadebrun07232001.html> (12 October 2002).

27 B. Gellman, "A Conflict of Health and Profit; Gore at Center of Trade Policy Reversal on AIDS Drugs to S. Africa," *Washington Post*, May 2000.

28 ACT UP New York, "AIDS Activists Take over Glaxo Smith Kline Investor Relations Office," 20 February 2001, <http://www.actupny.org/reports/gsk2-20-01.html> (16 April 2002).

29 Treatment Action Campaign, "Why TAC Is Joining the Court Case Against the PMA," 1 February 2001, <www.globaltreatmentaccess.org>, Press Center, Year 2001 (9 November 2002).

30 Kavaljit Singh, "Patents vs. Patients: AIDS, TNCs and Drug Price Wars," <http://www.twnside.org.sg/title/twr131c.htm> (9 November 2002).

31 World Trade Organization, Ministerial Conference, "Declaration on the TRIPS Agreement and Public Health," 14 November 2001, <http://www.wto.org/english/thewto_e/minist_e/min01_e/mindecltrips_e.htm> (9 November 2002), paragraph 4.

32 Correa, *Implications of the Doha Declaration*, vii.

33 Geoff Winestock and Helene Cooper, "Health Deal Will Allow Poor Nations to Ignore Patents to Meet Public-Health Needs," *Wall Street Journal*, 14 November 2001.

34 Ibid.

35 See Correa, *Implications of the Doha Declaration,* 19.

36 World Trade Organization, Ministerial Conference, "Declaration on the TRIPS Agreement and Public Health," paragraph 6.

37 Bebe Loff, "No agreement reached in talks on access to cheap drugs," *Lancet* 360 (14 December 2002): 1950.

38 Elements of such a plan can be found in the 2001 report of the Commission on Macroeconomics and Health and in some of the background papers written for that report, as well as in the materials developed by MSF in connection with its Access to Essential Medicines campaign. See Commission on Macroeconomics and Health, *Macroeconomics and Health: Investing in Health for Economic Development* (Geneva: WHO, 2001); Médecins Sans Frontières, Access to Essential

Medicines literature at <http://www.accessmed-msf.org/index.asp> (9 November 2002).

39   M. Kremer, "Public Policies to Stimulate the Development of Vaccines and Drugs for the Neglected Diseases," (Geneva: World Health Organization, 2001).

40   See World Health Organization and World Trade Organization, "Report of the Workshop on Differential Pricing and Financing of Essential Drugs" (Geneva: World Health Organization and World Trade Organization, 2001). The landmark 2001 report of the World Health Organization's Commission on Macroeconomics and Health also endorsed the idea of tiered pricing. Commission on Macroeconomics and Health, *Macroeconomics and Health: Investing in Health for Economic Development.*

41   Barton, "Differentiated Pricing," Hans P. Binswanger, "Public Health: AIDS Treatment for Millions," *Science* 292, no 5515 (2001): 221–223; P. Danzon, "Differential Pricing for Pharmaceuticals: Reconciling Access, R & D, and Patents," Working Paper No. WG2:10 (Geneva: 2001.)

42   *Macroeconomics and Health: Investing in Health for Economic Development*, 88–89.

43   Gavin Yamey, "The World's Most Neglected Diseases," *British Medical Journal* 325 (27 July 2002): 176-177.

44   D. Perlman, "Drug Firms Seek Cures over Cash: S.F. Non-Profit Wants to Help Poor Nations," *Christian Science Monitor*, 19 August 2002.

45   See Commission on Intellectual Property Rights, *Integrating Intellectual Property Rights and Development Policy.*

MYTH EIGHT: Limited Resources

1   World Health Organization, "Tuberculosis," April 2000, <http://www..who.int/inf-fs/en/fact104.html> (May 12, 2002) and "Malaria at a Glance," March 2001, <http://mosquito.who.int/cmc_upload/0/000/014/813/Malaria_at_a_glance1.htm> (May 12, 2002).

2   For a popular presentation of these views, see Michael Specter, "India's Plague," *The New Yorker*, 17 December 2001. For a more technical analysis of HIV/AIDS control strategies informed by the logic of cost-effectiveness analysis and an awareness of the developing world's

many health challenges, see World Bank, *Confronting AIDS: Public Priorities in a Global Epidemic* (Washington, DC: World Bank, 1996). For critiques of HAART's cost-effectiveness in comparison with HIV prevention in sub-Saharan Africa, see: A. Creese et al., "Cost-effectiveness of HIV/AIDS interventions in Africa: a systematic review of the evidence," *Lancet* 359 (May 11, 2002) 1635–42; E. Marseille et al., "HIV Prevention Before HAART in sub-Saharan Africa," *The Lancet,* vol. 359 (May 25, 2002), pp. 1851–56.

3   On the logic and methods of cost-effectiveness analysis in the health field, see L.B. Russell, M.R. Gold, J.E. Siegel, N. Daniels, and M.C. Weinstein, "The role of cost-effectiveness analysis in health and medicine," *Journal of the American Medical Association,* 276 (1996): 1172-79.

4   Because the benefits of prevention have been widely discussed by analysts and advocates, we focus our discussion on treatment to illustrate the range of positive social and public health effects a wide deployment of HAART in poor, high-burden countries will bring. Earlier (in Myth 4) we showed why prevention and treatment must be implemented together, rather than viewed as mutually exclusive alternatives. Effective prevention protects the future, but treatment is needed now, to stem an overwhelming tide of sickness, premature death, and socioeconomic disintegration in heavily affected regions.

5   World Bank, *Confronting AIDS* (Washington, DC: World Bank, 1995) <http://www.worldbank.org/aids-econ/confront/confrontfull> (April 12, 2002).

6   Karen Stanecki, "The AIDS Pandemic in the 21st Century: The Demographic Impact in Developing Countries" (paper presented at the XIIIth International AIDS Conference, Durban, South Africa, July 2000), 3.

7   Ibid.

8   Ibid.

9   Commission on Macroeconomics and Health, *Macroeconomics and Health: Investing in Health for Economic Development* (Geneva: World Health Organization, 2001), 24-25.

10   Ichiro Kawachi and Bruce P. Kennedy, *The Health of Nations: Why Inequality is Harmful to Your Health* (New York: New Press, 2002); Jim Kim, Joyce Millen, Alec Irwin, and John Gershman, eds., *Dying for Growth: Global Inequality and the Health of the Poor* (Monroe, ME: Com-

mon Courage Press, 2000); David A. Leon and Gill Walt, eds., *Poverty, Inequality, and Health: An International Perspective* (New York: Oxford University Press, 2001).

11 UNAIDS, *Report on the Global HIV/AIDS Epidemic June 2000* <http://www.unaids.org/epidemic%5Fupdate/report/Epi_report_chap_devastation.htm> (22 April 2002), 32.

12 Food and Agriculture Organization of the United Nations, *The State of Food and Agriculture 2001,* <http://www.fao.org/docrep/003/x9800e/x9800e00.htm> (23 April 2002).

13 Lisa Garbus, "Sub-Saharan Africa," *HIV InSite* regional profile, December 2001, <http://hivinsite.ucsf.edu/ InSite.jsp?page=cr-02-01> (15 March 2002). See also International Labour Office, "HIV/AIDS: A Threat to Decent Work, Productivity and Development," 2000, <http://www.ilo.org/public/english/protection/trav/aids/pdf/aidse.pdf> (21 March 2002).

14 UNAIDS, *Report on the Global HIV/AIDS Epidemic, June 2000.*

15 Sumalee Pitayanon, Sukhontha Kongsin, and Wattana S. Janjareon, "The Economic Impact of HIV/AIDS Mortality on Households in Thailand," <http://www.iaen.org/impact/thai/thai.pdf> (23 April 2002).

16 Lisa Garbus, "Sub-Saharan Africa," *HIV InSite,* December 2001, <http://hivinsite.ucsf.edu/ InSite.jsp?page=cr-02-01> (15 March 2002). See also International Labour Office, "HIV/AIDS: A threat ."

17 Peter Piot et al., "The global impact of HIV/AIDS," *Nature* 410 (2001): 968–973.

18 Daphne Topouzis, "The Impact of HIV on Agriculture and Rural Development: Implications for Training Institutions," in Human Resources in Agriculture and Rural Development (FAO, 2000), <http://www.fao.org/DOCREP/003/X7925M/X7925M10.htm> (23 April 2002).

19 Ibid. Original Source: P. Kwaramba, "The Socio-Economic Impact of HIV/AIDS on Communal Agricultural Production Systems in Zimbabwe," Working Paper 19, Economic Advisory Project (1999) Harare, Zimbabwe Farmers' Union and Friederich Ebert Stiftung, <http://www.unaids.org/epidemic%5Fupdate/report/Epi_report_chap_devastation.htm.>

20 Ranjan Roy, "Southern Africa Food Crisis Exacerbated by HIV/AIDS Pandemic, U.N. Officials Say," Associated Press, 26 September 2002. Available at <http:www.aegis.com > (September 27, 2002).

21 "Tuberculosis: Strategy and Operations: TB/HIV," <http: www.who.int/gtb/po9licyrd/TBHIV.htm>. Abhik Kumar Chanda and Emmanuel Goujon, "African AIDS Summit to Kick Off with UN Chief's Action Plan," 26 April 2001, <http://www.stoptb.org/material/news/press/AFP.010426.htm> (22 April 2002) and UNAIDS, *Report on the Global HIV/AIDS Epidemic, June 2000,* <http://www.unaids.org/epidemic%5Fupdate/report/Epi_report_chap_devastation.htm> (22 April 2002), 31. Among people with HIV infection, TB is now the leading cause of death, accounting for one-third of AIDS-associated deaths worldwide. See Centers for Disease Control, "The Deadly Intersection Between TB and HIV," November 1999, <http://www.cdc.gov/hiv/pubs/facts/hivtb.pdf> (22 April 2002).

22 "Stop TB Partnership," *The Global Plan to Stop Tuberculosis* (Geneva: World Health Organization, 2002), 53.

23 World Health Organization, "Tuberculosis," April 2000, <http://www.who.int/inf-fs/en/fact104.html> (May 12, 2002).

24 World Bank, *Confronting AIDS,* <http://www.worldbank.org/aids-econ/confront/confrontfull/chapter1/chp1sub2.html#6>. Cf. UN-AIDS, *Report on the Global HIV/AIDS Epidemic,* June 2000 <http://www.unaids.org/epidemic%5Fupdate/report/Epi_report_chap_devastation.htm>.

25 Indeed, co-infection with HIV has been found to be the most potent risk factor for conversion of latent into active TB. See Stop TB Partnership, *Global Plan,* 52.

26 Even as HIV/AIDS accelerates the spread of TB, it also makes diagnosing TB more difficult. In patients with HIV co-infection, results of TB diagnostic tests often appear atypical and may be difficult to interpret, particularly if the HIV status of the patient is unknown. J.L. Johnson et al., "Impact of Human Immunodeficiency Virus Type-q Infection on the Initial Bacteriologic and Radiographic Manifestations of Pulmonary Tuberculosis in Uganda, Makerere University-Case Western Reserve University Research Collaboration," *International Journal of Tuberculosis and Lung Disease* 2, no.5 (May 1998): 397–404.

27 Motasim Badri, Douglas Wilson, and Robin Wood, "Effect of Highly Active Antiretroviral Therapy on Incidence of Tuberculosis in South Africa: a Cohort Study," *Lancet* 359 (2002), pp. 2059–2064.

28 Paul Farmer, Fernet Léandre, et al., "Community-based treatment of advanced HIV disease: introducing DOT-HAART," *Bulletin of the World Health Organization*, 2001, 79(12), pp. 1147-48.

29 Stop TB Partnership, *Global Plan*, 64-71. See also Paul Farmer, "Introducing ARVs in Resource-Poor Settings: Expected and Unexpected Challenges and Consequences" (paper presented at the XIV International AIDS Conference, Barcelona, 11 July 2002) 7-9.

30 Badri et. al, "Effect of Highly Active Antiretroviral Therapy," 2059–2064.

31 World Bank, *Confronting AIDS*, <http://www.worldbank.org/aids-econ /confront/confrontfull/chapter1/chp1sub2.html>.

32 UNAIDS, "Botswana: Epidemiological Fact Sheet," 2000. <http://www.unaids.org/hivaidsinfo/statistics/fact_sheets/pdfs/ Botswana_en.pdf> (25 April 2002), 3.

33 Botswana Institute for Development Policy Analysis, *Macroeconomic Impacts of the HIV/AIDS Epidemic in Botswana* (Botswana: BIDPA, 2000), quoted in UNDP, "Botswana Human Development Report: Towards an AIDS-Free Generation," <http://www.bw.undp.org/ docs/undp_bhdp.pdf> (25 April 2002).

34 Botswana Institute for Development Policy Analysis, *Macroeconomic Impacts*.

35 UNAIDS, *AIDS Epidemic Update, December 2001*. <http://www.unai ds.org/epidemic_update/report_dec01/> (23 April 2002), 7.

36 Sumalee Pitayanon, Sukhontha Kongsin, and Wattana S. Janjareon, "The Economic Impact of HIV/AIDS Mortality on Households in Thailand," <http://www.iaen.org/impact/thai/thai.pdf> (23 April 2002).

37 Pitayanon et. al. "Economic Impact."

38 UNAIDS, *Report on the Global HIV/AIDS Epidemic, June 2000*.

39 Amid these discussions of the oblique—though often no less lethal—effects of parental AIDS on children, we should not forget that the disease kills children by more direct means as well. Almost three million of the 40 million people living with HIV/AIDS are under the age of 15. See UNAIDS, UNICEF, and USAID, *Children on the Brink 2002: A Joint Report on Orphan Estimates and Program Strategies* (Washington, DC: TvT Associcates/USAID, 2002), p. 3. In 26 sub-Saharan African countries, child mortality rates are higher than they would be. In Zimbabwe, 70 percent of all deaths among children under 5 are due to AIDS. In South Africa, the figure is 45 percent. See Stanecki, "The AIDS Pandemic," 5.

40 UNAIDS, *AIDS Epidemic Update, December 2001*, 8.

41 Geoff Foster and John Williamson, "A Review of Current Literature

of the Impact of HIV/AIDS on Children in sub-Saharan Africa," *AIDS* 14, suppl. 3 (2000): S275-284.

42 Ibid.

43 UNAIDS, *Children on the Brink*, p. 10.

44 J. Sengendo and J. Nambi, "The Psychological Effect of Orphanhood: a Study of Orphans in Rakai District," *Health Transition Review*, Suppl. 7 (1999):105–124.

45 UNAIDS/UNICEF/USAID, *Children on the Brink*, p. 10.

46 Foster and Williamson, "A Review of Current Literature on the Impact of HIV/AIDS," as cited in U. Sharpe et al., "Orphans' sexual behaviour in Masaka Diocese, Uganda" (paper presented at IXth International Conference on AIDS, Berlin, July 1993, abstract WS-D26-5).

47 HIV-infected patients tend to have higher treatment costs and to require longer hospitalizations than patients without HIV. See, e.g., K. Hansen et al., "The Costs of HIV/AIDS Care at Government Hospitals in Zimbabwe," *Health Policy and Planning* 15, no. 4 (2000): 432–440.

48 UNAIDS, *Report on the Global HIV/AIDS Epidemic, June 2000*, 31, and Robert C. Davidson, "The Modern Plague," *American Medical Association Ethics Resource Center Virtual Mentor* 3, no. 7 (2001), <htp://www.ama-assn.org/ama/pub/printcat/5334.html> (23 April 2002).

49 Similarly, a study in Zimbabwe found that 50 percent of inpatients in hospital wards surveyed were HIV-infected. See UNAIDS, *Report on the Global HIV/AIDS Epidemic 2002*, 51. Alan Whiteside, head of the Health Economics and HIV/AIDS Research Division of the University of Natal in South Africa, estimated in 2000 that patients with AIDS occupied up to 50 percent of the beds in regional hospitals in South Africa. Whiteside's estimates were cited by P. Wehrwein, "AIDS leaves Africa's economic future in doubt," CNN Analysis <http://europe.cnn.com/SPECIALS/2000/aids/stories/economic.impact/> (April 27, 2002)

50 UNAIDS, *Report on the Global HIV/AIDS Epidemic, June 2000*, 31.

51 A 1988 study of 2,002 adult employees in a hospital in Kinshasa, Zaire (now Democratic Republic of Congo), showed an alarming prevalence of HIV infection among physicians (5.9 percent), laboratory workers (2.9 percent), clerical workers (7.9 percent), female nurses (11.4 percent), and manual workers (11.8 percent). B. N'Galy et al., "Human Immunodeficiency Virus Infection Among Employees in an African Hospital," *New England Journal of Medicine* 319, no. 17 (1988):

1123–1127. In 2000, a study in South Africa found that 20 percent of the country's student nurses were HIV-positive. L. Altenroxel, "AIDS Taking a Toll on Student Nurses," *Star* (Johannesburg), 4 September 2000, cited in S. Dixon, S. McDonald, and J. Roberts, "The Impact of HIV and AIDS on Africa's Economic Development," *British Medical Journal* 324 (2002): 232–234. Malawi and Zambia are currently experiencing fivefold to sixfold increases in health-worker illness and death rates (UNAIDS, *Report on the Global HIV/AIDS Epidemic 2002,* p. 51). Increased workloads and stress due to the AIDS crisis may also prompt health workers to emigrate from high-prevalence countries, further exacerbating the shortage of qualified personnel. Health workers' distress at not being able to provide patients with adequate treatment may be contributing to the burnout phenomenon.

52 Ibid.

53 Ministry of Health of Brazil, *National AIDS Drug Policy* (Brasilia: Ministry of Health of Brazil 2001), p. 29.

54 Ibid.

55 Jane Galvão, "Access to Antiretroviral Drugs in Brazil," *Lancet* 360 (2002): 1862–65.

56 Commission on Macroeconomics and Health (CMH), *Macroeconomics and Health.*

57 The CMH report estimates that antiretroviral therapy, including drugs and medical services, will cost between $500 and $1,000 per patient per year in sub-Saharan Africa. This roughly equals the average annual income of prime-age workers in the region. Meanwhile, the economic gain from a year of productive life saved through medical intervention should be reckoned at considerably more than the patient's annual income—perhaps as much as three times annual income (ibid, 31–32). When one considers the full range of social and economic benefits associated with treatment (e.g., reduction in the number of orphans), ARV treatment clearly emerges as cost-effective (ibid, 49–51). Note that falling prices on ARVs may continue to reduce drug costs below the levels assumed in these calculations.

58 Commission on Macroeconomics and Health, "Investment in Global Health Will Save 8 Million Lives a Year and Generate at Least a $360 Billion Annual Gain Within 15 Years, Says a New Report Presented to WHO," 20 December 2001, <http://www3.who.int/whosis/cmh

/cmh_press/e/who_hq_20Dec2001.pdf?path=cmh,cmh_press,cmh_press02&language=english>.

59 See e.g., Marseille et al., "HIV Prevention."

MYTH NINE: Nothing to Gain

1 Commission on Macroeconomics and Health, *Macroeconomics and Health: Investing in Health for Economic Development* (Geneva: WHO, 2001), <http://www3.who.int/whosis/cmh/cmh_report/report.cfm?path=cmh,cmh_report&language=english> (15 October 2002), 76.

2 Stop TB Partnership, *The Global Plan to Stop Tuberculosis* (Geneva: WHO, 2002), <http://www.stoptb.org/GPSTB/default.asp> (15 October 2002), 74–75.

3 Giovanni Berlinguer, "Health and Equity as a Primary Global Goal," *Development* 42, no. 4 (1999): 17–21, quoted in T. Sandler and D. Arce, "A Conceptual Framework for Understanding Global and Transnational Goods for Health" (working paper, Commission on Macroeconomics and Health Working Paper Series, 2000), <http://www.cmhealth.org/docs/wg2_paper1.pdf> (18March 2002), 2.

4 Stop TB Partnership, *The Global Plan to Stop Tuberculosis*, 52–53.

5 Joshua Lederberg, "Infection Emergent," *Journal of the American Medical Association* 275, no. 3 (1996), 244.

6 World Health Organization, *Scaling up the Response to Infectious Diseases: A Way out of Poverty* (Geneva: WHO, 2002), <http://www.who.int/infectious-disease-report/2002/pdfversion/indexpdf.html> (15 October 2002), 97.

7 Ibid.

8 Commission on Macroeconomics and Health, *Macroeconomics and Health:*, 77.

9 See Lederberg, "Infection Emergent," 243–245; "Infectious Disease: A Threat to Global Health and Security," *Journal of the American Medical Association* 276, no. 5 (1996), 417–419; National Science and Technology Council, Committee on International Science, Engineering, and Technology Working Group on Emerging and Re-emerging Infectious Diseases, *Infectious Disease: A Global Health Threat* (Washington, DC: National Science and Technology Council, 1995); Mary E. Wilson, Richard Levins, and Andrew Spielman, eds., "Disease in Evolution: Global Changes and Emergence of Infectious Diseases," *Annals of the New York Academy of Sciences* 740 (1994), 1-503.

10 Mark Schoofs, "Holbrooke Enlists Multinational Firms to Battle AIDS Among Their Workers," *Wall Street Journal*, 30 November 2001.

11 Commission on Macroeconomics and Health, *Macroeconomics and Health*, 39.

12 Steve Sternberg, "AIDS' Toll Damaging Africa Socially, Economically," *USA Today*, 25 June 2002, <http://www.usatoday.com/news/healthscience/health/aids/2002-06-25-effects.htm> (28 June 2002).

13 World Economic Forum, "World Economic Forum CEOs Call for Greater Corporate Engagement against HIV/AIDS, TB and Malaria," 2002, <http://www.weforum.org/site/homepublic.nsf/Content/World+Economic+Forum+CEOs+Call+for+Greater+Corporate+rEngagement+Against+HIV%2FAIDS%2C+TB+and+Malaria> (26 April 2002).

14 United Nations General Assembly Special Session on HIV/AIDS, "Socioeconomic Impact of the Epidemic and the Strengthening of National Capacities to Combat HIV/AIDS," 2001, <http://www.unaids.org/ungass/index.html> (26 April 2002), Round-table 3.

15 Tony De Coito, Stori Ralepeli, and Richard Steen, "Forging Multisectoral Partnerships to Prevent HIV and Other STIs in South Africa's Mining Communities," *Impact on HIV* 2, no. 1 (2000), <http://www.fhi.org/en/aids/impact/iohiv/ioh21/ioh216.html> (26 April 2002).

16 Richard Holbrooke, interview by Willow Bay, *Business Unusual*, CNN, 3 February 2002, <http://www.cnn.com/TRANSCRIPTS/0202/03/bun.00.html> (26 April 2002).

17 UNAIDS, *Report on the Global HIV/AIDS Epidemic 2002* (Geneva: UNAIDS, 2002), <http://www.unaids.org/barcelona/presskit/report.html> (6 July 2002), 56.

18 International Labour Office, *HIV/AIDS: A Threat to Decent Work, Productivity and Development,* (Geneva: ILO, 2000), <http://www.ilo.org/public/english/protection/trav/aids/pdf/aidse.pdf> (21 March 2002).

19 UNAIDS, *Report on the Global HIV/AIDS Epidemic July 2002*, 57.

20 Steve Sternberg, "AIDS' Toll Damaging Africa Socially, Economically," *USA Today*, 25 June 2002.

21 Commission on Macroeconomics and Health, *Macroeconomics and Health: Investing in Health for Economic Development*, 31–32.

22 UNAIDS, *Report on the Global HIV/AIDS Epidemic 2002*, 57.

23 Commission on Macroeconomics and Health, *Macroeconomics and Health:*, 11.

24　Ernest G. Green, opening remarks at African Development Foundation Workshop at the National Summit on Africa, Washington, DC, 17 February 2000, <http://www.adf.gov/nationalsummit/greensummit.html> (16 March 2002), paragraph 15.

25　See G8 Africa Action Plan, June 27, 2002 <http://www.g8.gc.ca/kananaskis/afraction-en.asp>. See also Sarah Coleman, "Crumbs from the Table," *World Press Review* online, July 1, 2002 <http://www.worldpress.org/article_model.cfm?article_id=730&don't=yes>.

26　Reacting to the fears stirred by September 11, some have gone so far as to suggest that AIDS and the misery and social disintegration provoked by the pandemic could provide a breeding ground for terrorism. In a period when security issues and the "war on terror" dominate US lawmakers' agendas, one can understand the appeal of this claim for some advocates struggling to get a hearing for global AIDS. However, the suggestion of an AIDS-poverty-terrorism link will enmesh activists in serious problems. For one thing, this notion reinscribes racist stereotypes of Africans and other Third World people as irrational. Moreover, while AIDS is unquestionably aggravating poverty, a strong body of social science literature challenges the notion of a causal connection between poverty and terrorism.

27　United Nations Security Council, "Security Council Holds Debate on Impact of AIDS on Peace and Security in Africa," 10 January 2000, <http://www.unis.unvienna.org/en/news/2000/pressrels/sc1173e.htm> (8 February 2002), paragraph 2.

28　UNAIDS, "UNAIDS Releases New Data Highlighting the Devastating Impact of AIDS in Africa," 25 June 2002, <http://www.unaids.org/whatsnew/press/eng/pressarc02/G8_250602.html> (1 July 2002).

29　UNAIDS, *Report on the Global HIV/AIDS Epidemic 2002*, 58.

30　Ibid., 58–59.

31　The other two predictors of state failure are lack of democracy and lack of open economy. See State Failure Task Force, "State Failure Task Force Report: Phase II Findings," *Environmental Change and Security Project Report* 5 (1999): 49–72, cited in Commission on Macroeconomics and Health, *Macroeconomics and Health: Investing in Health for Economic Development*, 126.

32　State Failure Task Force, "State Failure Task Force Report."

33　National Intelligence Council, *The Global Infectious Disease Threat and its Implications for the United States*, (Washington, DC: National Intelligence Council, 2000), <http://www.cia.gov/nic/graphics/infectiousdiseas

es.pdf> (17 January 2002), 5.

34   Samuel Berger, "National Security Threat," interview by Jim Lehrer, *News Hour with Jim Lehrer*, 2 May 2000, <http://www.pbs.org/news hour/bb/health/jan-june00/aids_threat_5-2.html> (13 January 2002), paragraph 12.

35   For a controversial application of the idea of moral pluralism to the context of bioethics, see H. Tristram Engelhardt, *The Foundations of Bioethics* (New York: Oxford, 1996).

36   Commission on Macroeconomics and Health, *Macroeconomics and Health*;, Global Fund to Fight AIDS, Tuberculosis, and Malaria, "The Global Fund to Fight AIDS, Tuberculosis and Malaria Says: 'Additional $2 Billion Needed Next Year to Fund AIDS, TB and Malaria Programs,'" 11 October 2002, <http://www.globalfundatm.org/jour nalists/journalists_pr.html#top> (16 October 2002).

37   See UNAIDS, *Report on the Global HIV/AIDS Epidemic 2002*, 62–69.

38   United Nations, International Covenant on Economic, Social, and Cultural Rights, (Geneva: United Nations, 1966), <http://www.hr web.org/legal/escr.html> (16 October 2002); United Nations, Convention on the Rights of the Child (Geneva: United Nations: 1989) <http://www.hrweb.org/legal/child.html> (16 October 2002).

39   World Health Organization, *Constitution*, cited in Jonathan Mann et al., eds., *Health and Human Rights: A Reader* (New York: Routledge, 1999), 8.

40   Ibid., 7–20.

41   UNAIDS, *Report on the Global HIV/AIDS Epidemic July 2002*, 64–65.

42   Ibid., 65.

MYTH TEN: Nothing We Can Do

1   See Steven Epstein, *Impure Science: AIDS, Activism, and the Politics of Knowledge* (Berkeley: University of California Press, 1996), 225-226.

2   See the famous declaration drafted in 1983 by the Advisory Committee of the group People with AIDS and known as the "Denver Principles." <http://www.actupny.org/documents/Denver.html>.

3   See Epstein, 225-226.

4   Ibid.

5   Personal communication with Alec Irwin, March 2002.

6   ACT UP, "Treatment for All...Now!" July 2000, <http://www.actup ny.org/reports/durban-access.html>(3 May 2002).

7   "An Explanation of the Medicines Act and the Implications of the

Court Victory," 24 April 2001, <http://www.globaltreatmentaccess. org/content/press releases/sa med act.htm> (22 March 2002).

8   Daryl Lindsey, "Amy and Goliath," *Salon.com*, 1May, 2001.

9   Ibid.

10   See <http://www.peacecorps.org/assignments/focusareas.cfm > (3 May 2002).

11   Personal communication with Alec Irwin, March 2002.

12   *HIV Vaccines Explained: Making HIV Vaccines a Reality* (Washington, DC: National Institutes of Health, 2001), p. 6. NIAID's Vaccine Research Center can be contacted at <http://www.vrc.nih.org>, or by phone at 866-833-LIFE.

13   See Deputy Secretary-General Louise Fréchette, "The UN and the Global Fight Against HIV/AIDS: Myth and Reality." 20 September 2001 <http://www.carnegiecouncil.org/programs/frechette transc ript.html>.

14   See the Student Global AIDS Campaign (SGAC) website: <http://www.fightglobalaids.org.> (31 January 2003).

15   See GAA's website, <http://www.globalaidsalliance.org/cd Action. html> (22 January 2003).

16   See Physicians for Human Rights website <http://www.phrusa.org/ campaigns/aids/call.php> (22 January 2003).

17   See ACT UP website, "Protestors Take AIDS Message to White House," <http://www.actupny.org/reports/WAD02.html> (22 January 2003).

18   Stephen Lewis, interview with *PlusNews*, 3 December 2001 <http://www.irinnews.org.>

INDEX

About the Contributors

Alexander Irwin is research associate at the Institute for Health and Social Justice and the Program in Infectious Disease and Social Change, Harvard Medical School. He is an editor and author of *Dying for Growth: Global Inequality and the Health of the Poor* (Common Courage Press, 2000), and author of *Saints of the Impossible: Bataille, Weil and the Politics of the Sacred* (University of Minnesota Press, 2002). He has taught religion at Amherst College and Harvard University.

Joyce Millen is director of the Institute for Health and Social Justice and a research associate in the Department of Social Medicine at Harvard Medical School. She is a medical anthropologist with degrees in public health and international relations. She worked for several years in West Africa where she conducted extensive ethnomedical and epidemiological research. She is an editor and author of *Dying for Growth: Global Inequality and the Health of the Poor*, and is preparing a book entitled *The Evolution of Vulnerability: Ethnomedicine and Social Change in the Context of HIV/AIDS in Southwestern Senegal.*

Dorothy Fallows is a molecular biologist with research interests in infectious diseases and international health. She has her PhD from Columbia University, where she studied mechanisms of reverse transcription in retroviruses and human hepatitis B virus. She also has a degree in control of infectious diseases from the London School of Hygiene & Tropical Medicine.

Paul Farmer is a founder of Partners In Health and the Institute for Health and Social Justice. He is an infectious disease physician and medical anthropologist whose work draws primarily on active clinical practice and focuses on diseases disproportionately afflicting the poor. He is the author of *Pathologies of Power: Health, Human Rights, and the New War on the Poor* (University of California Press, 2003); *Infections and Inequalities: The Modern Plagues* (University of California Press, 2001); *Women, Poverty and AIDS: Sex, Drugs, and Structural Violence* (Common Courage Press, 1997).

Zackie Achmat is a former anti-apartheid activist and the founder and chairperson of the Treatment Action Campaign (TAC), a powerful AIDS activist organization in South Africa. Under Achmat's leadership, TAC has used civil protest and the legal system to successfully challenge pharmaceutical industry practices and government policies harmful to people living with HIV/AIDS. A gay man of color living with HIV, Achmat is internationally recognized as a leader in the fight for global equity in HIV/AIDS treatment.

The Institute for Health and Social Justice is the research, education, and advocacy wing of the larger international health organization Partners In Health (PIH). The Institute's mission is to bring a critical perspective—grounded in political economy, anthropology, epidemiology, medicine and bioethics—to bear on the chief health problems afflicting poor and disadvantaged populations. The Institute sponsors fellowship and internship programs, teaches public health and medical students, organizes conferences and seminars, and produces scholarly articles and books.

Treatment Action Campaign was launched on December 10, 1998, International Human Rights Day. Its main objective is to campaign for greater access to treatment for all South Africans, by raising public awareness and understanding about issues surrounding the availability, affordability and use of HIV treatments.

About South End Press

South End Press is a nonprofit, collectively run book publisher with more than 200 titles in print. Since our founding in 1977, we have tried to meet the needs of readers who are exploring, or are already committed to, the politics of radical social change. Our goal is to publish books that encourage critical thinking and constructive action on the key political, cultural, social, economic, and ecological issues shaping life in the United States and in the world. In this way, we hope to give expression to a wide diversity of democratic social movements and to provide an alternative to the products of corporate publishing.

Through the Institute for Social and Cultural Change, South End Press works with other political media projects—Alternative Radio; Speakout, a speakers' bureau; and *Z Magazine*—to expand access to information and critical analysis. movements and to provide an alternative to the products of corporate publishing.

Write or e-mail southend@southendpress.org for a free catalog, or visit our web site at www.southendpress.org.

Related Titles from South End Press

Women, AIDS, and Activism
The ACT UP/New York Women and AIDS Book Group
0-89608-393-4 paper $9

Abortion Without Apology:
A Radical History for the 1990s
Ninia Baehr
0-89608-384-5 paper $6

Policing Public Sex:
Queer Politics and the Future of AIDS Activism
Dangerous Bedfellows Collective, editors
0-89608-549-X paper $20

Women Under Attack:
Victories, Backlash, and the Fight for Reproductive Freedom
Susan E. Davis, editor
0-89608-356-X paper $5

From Abortion to Reproductive Freedom:
Transforming a Movement
Marlene Gerber Fried, editor
0-89608-387-X paper $18

Haiti:
Dangerous Crossroads
North American Congress on Latin America (NACLA), editors
0-89608-505-8 paper $15

Dangerous Intersections:
Feminist Perspectives on Population, Environment, and Development
Jael Silliman and Ynestra King, editor
0-89608-597-X paper $20

Policing the National Body:
Race, Gender, and Criminalization
Jael Silliman and Anannya Bhattacharjee, editors
0-89608-660-7 paper $18

To order books, please send a check or money order to: South End Press, 7 Brookline Street, #1, Cambridge, MA 02139-4146. To order by credit card, call 1-800-533-8478. Please include $3.50 for postage and handling for the first book and 75 cents for each additional book.